CAMBRIDGE G

M000201339

TACITUS

DIALOGVS DE ORATORIBVS

EDITED BY

ROLAND MAYER

Professor of Classics, University of London

PUBLISHED BY THE PRESS SYNDICATE OF THE UNIVERSITY OF CAMBRIDGE
The Pitt Building, Trumpington Street, Cambridge, United Kingdom

CAMBRIDGE UNIVERSITY PRESS
The Edinburgh Building, Cambridge CB2 2RU, UK
40 West 20th Street, New York NY 10011-4211, USA
10 Stamford Road, Oakleigh, VIC 3166, Australia
Ruiz de Alarcón 13, 28014 Madrid, Spain
Dock House, The Waterfront, Cape Town 8001, South Africa

http://www.cambridge.org

First published 2001

Printed in the United Kingdom at the University Press, Cambridge

Typeset in Baskerville and New Hellenic Greek [AO]

A catalogue record for this book is available from the British Library

Library of Congress Cataloguing in Publication data
Tacitus, Cornelius.
Dialogus de oratoribus / Tacitus ; edited by Roland Mayer.
p.   cm. — (Cambridge Greek and Latin classics)
Includes bibliographical references (p.   ) and indexes.
ISBN 0 521 47040-4 (hardback)   ISBN 0 521 46996 1 (paperback)
1. Dialogues, Latin. 2. Oratory, Ancient.   I. Mayer, Roland, 1947–
II. Title. III. Series.
PA6706.D5 T34 2001
808.5'1'0937—dc21   00-062142

ISBN 0 521 47040 4 hardback
ISBN 0 521 46996 1 paperback

CONTENTS

PREFACE

Old Sippy's one-time headmaster, Mr Waterbury, 'author of "Some Little-Known Aspects of Tacitus" and muck like that', would have been among the first to welcome a new English-language commentary on the *Dialogus de oratoribus* (see 'Inferiority complex of old Sippy', in P. G. Wodehouse, *Very good, Jeeves* (London 1930) 49). Indeed a century is a long time to leave a work of such interest and flair unequipped with the sort of introduction and notes an anglophone undergraduate might want. University teachers too are constantly in need of manageable prose works for their classes and seminars (poetry will always be well served), and it is surprising that the *Dialogus*, a brilliant work by a classic author in a reasonably familiar style, has not attracted a commentator in English since the final decade of the nineteenth century, when to be sure there was something of a glut.

The present work has benefited greatly both from a visit to the Fondation Hardt at Vandoeuvres (made possible by the British Academy and the Fonds National pour la Recherche Scientifique), and from the assistance and advice of eminent colleagues: Professor R. H. Martin of the University of Leeds, and Professor M. Winterbottom of Oxford University were unfailingly helpful in their notes upon the commentary, and the reader owes them as much as does the editor himself for improvements in clarity and precision. As usual the Series Editor, Professor E. J. Kenney, read and advised upon the whole work, and, also as usual, he is owed my warmest thanks for his support. I should also like to thank Pauline Hire and Susan Moore for their help and interest.

ABBREVIATIONS AND REFERENCES

CAH	(eds.) A. K. Bowman et al., *The Cambridge ancient history*, x: *The Augustan empire 43 BC – AD 69*. (2nd edn) Cambridge 1995.
CHCL	(eds.) E. J. Kenney and W. V. Clausen, *The Cambridge history of classical literature*, II: *Latin literature*. Cambridge 1982.
DNP	(eds.) H. Cancik and H. Schneider, *Der neue Pauly*. Stuttgart and Weimar 1996– .
EAA	*Enciclopedia dell'arte antica, classica e orientale*. Rome 1958–66.
G–G	A. Gerber and A. Greef, *Lexicon Taciteum*. Leipzig 1903.
G–L	B. L. Gildersleeve and G. Lodge, *Latin grammar*. London 1895.
HRL	M. von Albrecht, *A history of Roman literature from Livius Andronicus to Boethius with special regard to its influence on world literature*. 2 vols. Leiden, etc. 1997.
H–S	J. B. Hofmann and A. Szantyr, *Lateinische Syntax und Stilistik*. Munich 1965.
ILS	(ed.) H. Dessau, *Inscriptiones Latinae selectae*. 5 vols. Berlin 1892–1916.
K–S	R. Kühner and C. Stegmann, *Ausführliche Grammatik der lateinischen Sprache*. 4th edn rev. A. Thierfelder. 2 vols. Munich 1962.
LS	S. A. Handford, *The Latin subjunctive*. London 1947.
N–H	R. G. M. Nisbet and M. Hubbard, *A commentary on Horace: Odes Book I* 1970; *Book II* 1978. Oxford.
NLS	E. C. Woodcock, *A new Latin syntax.*. London 1959, repr. 1985.
OCD	(eds.) S. Hornblower and A. Spawforth, *The Oxford classical dictionary*. 3rd edn. Oxford 1996.
OLD	(ed.) P. G. W. Glare, *Oxford Latin dictionary*. Oxford 1968–82.
Otto	A. Otto, *Die Sprichwörter und sprichwörtlichen Redensarten der Römer*. Leipzig 1890, repr. 1962.

PIR	*Prosopographia Imperii Romani saec. I, II, III.* 2nd edn. Berlin 1933– .
RAC	(ed.) T. Klauser, *Reallexikon für Antike und Christentum: Sachwörterbuch zur Auseinandersetzung des Christentums mit der antiken Welt.* Stuttgart 1950– .
RE	(eds.) A. Pauly, G. Wissowa and W. Kroll, *Real-Encyclopädie der classischen Altertumswissenschaft.* Stuttgart 1894–1972.
Roby	H. J. Roby, *A grammar of the Latin language from Plautus to Suetonius.* Part II *Syntax.* London 1889.
Schanz–Hosius	M. Schanz and C. Hosius, *Geschichte der römischen Literatur bis zum Gesetzgebungswerk des Kaisers Justinian* (Handbuch der Altertumswissenschaft, VIII.1,2.). 4th edn. Munich 1927, 1935.
TLL	*Thesaurus linguae Latinae.* Munich 1900– .

Except where there might be ambiguity, the name of Tacitus is omitted from references to his other works.

See also the list of *Works cited by author and date*, below pp. 217–21.

> = 'is the source of' or 'leads to'.
< = 'is derived from'.

INTRODUCTION

1. THE BACKGROUND

When Domitian was assassinated on 18 September 96, the senatorial class heaved a sigh of relief. In particular, aspirants to literary renown within that élite looked for release from a prolonged (if self-imposed) silence. To be fair to Domitian, he had encouraged poetry and rhetoric: Martial, Statius, and Quintilian all attest his interest and patronage.[1] But neither Martial nor Statius were public figures in the socio-political élite; they had not felt the need to bridle their tongues, or risk the fates of Helvidius Priscus, of Junius Arulenus Rusticus and Herennius Senecio: all were senators (the first two consular), and all died for their imprudent literary productions.[2] But everything changed at the accession of Nerva, and even though his reign was short, his successor in 98, Trajan, did nothing that checked the 'revival' of letters. Pliny is our best contemporary witness of this renaissance, which he hailed in his first book of letters, most of which seem to date from 97.[3] In April of that year he drew attention to the number of recitations of new works (*Ep.* 1.13), and he was clearly eager to start publishing some of his own speeches.[4] It is not so surprising then that another noted senatorial orator should at last take up his pen with a view to writing for publication.

In 97, the year of his suffect consulship, Tacitus too embarked

---

1 For Domitian's patronage of poetry generally, and his motivation, see A. Hardie, *Statius and the Silvae. Poets, patrons and epideixis in the Graeco-Roman world* (ARCA Classical and Medieval Texts, Papers and Monographs 9; Liverpool 1983) 45-7.

2 For the former see note on *offendisse* 2.1 below, for the latter Suet. *Dom.* 10.3-4 and Sherwin-White on Plin. *Ep.* 1.5.3. For Domitian's relations with the Senate, and his victims see Brian W. Jones, *Domitian* (London 1992) 180-92.

3 The actual date and the form of their publication (as opposed to their public recitation), whether by individual book, or groups of books, or of the nine books as a whole, remain matter for debate (see esp. Murgia (1985)).

4 See *Ep.* 1.2, and Sherwin-White's n. on 1.2.6.

upon a programme of writing, which issued in due course in the publication of the *Agricola*, a biography of his father-in-law, the *Germania*, an ethnography perhaps designed to demonstrate the hollowness of Domitian's claim to conquest of that nation, the *Histories*, and the *Dialogus*.[5]

   The *Agricola* and the *Dialogus* are reckoned to form a kind of diptych,[6] which reveals their author's disillusion with the careers open to a Roman in public life.[7] They may be regarded as his attempt to come to terms with and describe for others the emptiness that he himself found at the end of the traditional paths to glory and prestige in Rome, paths which he and his father-in-law had so successfully trodden in their different ways. The *Dialogus* is, to be sure, one of the most brilliant literary performances to have come down to us from antiquity. What makes it poignant, however, is that it betrays the disillusion of a man successful in society's terms, who had awakened at length to a reality at odds with convention. We may detect in the *Dialogus* Tacitus' sense of thwarted effort, when he reflected upon the obsolescence of the skill to which he had successfully, but as he had come to believe, pointlessly, devoted his youth and early manhood. It was an expense of spirit – for Tacitus, his oratorical talent – in a waste of shame (above all, the silence of the Senate when its own good men were hauled to punishment, *Agr.* 3.2). A silent orator is a contradiction in terms. With the death of Domitian, however, some men in public life, like Pliny, began to hope for a revival of oratory (cf. *Ep.* 6.11). Quintilian, for instance, Pliny's teacher (*Ep.* 2.14.9) and the author of a twelve-book treatise on the training appropriate to an orator (it was published in 96), clearly did not think he was wasting his time in recalling men to a Ciceronian ideal of education for public life. Tacitus none the less decided upon reflection that such hopes were delusory, however well-disposed the

5 The ascription of *D.* to Tacitus will be discussed below, §7 Authenticity.

6 For *D.* as the companion piece to *Agr.* (words~deeds) see Syme (1958) 109 n. 5.

7 We have recently been warned to restrict use of the word 'career' in a Roman context (see *OCD* s.v.), but unfortunately no better term is on offer.

new emperors might prove, and in the *Dialogus* he aimed to give his grounds for pessimism.[8]

Three spheres of public activity (the only activity that mattered) – warfare, statecraft, and the law – were deemed appropriate for a Roman who aspired to realize his potential as a citizen. (Antonius, in Cicero's *De orat.* 1.209–12, rehearses the three with exemplary figures.) Success in any of them, or any combination of them, led to prestige and renown, as well as conferring certain material benefits. Statecraft, however, came to be associated particularly with the power to persuade one's fellow-citizens in the Senate or at a public assembly *(contio)* or in court to adopt one's own point of view, and so for Cicero at any rate eloquence as a general term typified the paramount skill of the statesman.[9] This is exemplified in such lists as we find in the *Dialogus* itself at 28.6, in Cicero's *De orat.* 2.226, 3.136, in Ovid's *Amores* 1.15.4–6 *praemia militiae ... leges ediscere ... uocem prostituisse foro*, or in Livy's description of the elder Cato, 39.40.5: *ad summos honores alios scientia iuris, alios eloquentia, alios gloria militaris prouexit* (cf. the elder Pliny, *NH* 7.100 *Cato ... tres summas in homine res praestitisse existimatur, ut esset optimus orator, optimus imperator, optimus senator*). Livy used similar terms in his description of Licinius, 30.1.5 *facundissimus habebatur, seu causa oranda, seu in senatu et apud populum suadendi ac dissuadendi locus esset; iuris pontificii peritissimus ... bellicae ... laudis compotem.*[10] Under the monarchy of the Caesars these traditional

8 Such is the assessment of Syme (1958) 115: 'The *Dialogus* confutes and supersedes Quintilian. There was no cure or remedy, since eloquence itself was obsolete. Tacitus furnishes a political and historical diagnosis'; at (1958) 333 he speaks of *D.* as the epitaph on Roman oratory. Crook (1995) 167–71 is also important.

9 See Douglas's introduction to the *Brutus* pp. xli–xlii for Cicero's ideal. It is worth noting that Douglas reckons we may 'assume' that Cicero would have agreed with Quintilian that the orator must be a good man; in fact, the issue had not crystallized in those terms just yet.

10 It is interesting to note however that the prestige of *iuris prudentia* declined in favour of advocacy (cf. Cic. *Mur.* 30 *duae sunt artes quae possunt locare homines in amplissimo gradu dignitatis, una imperatoris, altera oratoris boni*); Crook (1995) 143 refers also to Quint. *Inst.* 12.3.9 *quod si plerique desperata facultate agendi ad discendum ius declinauerunt, quam id scire facile est oratori quod discunt qui sua quoque confessione oratores esse non possunt.*

occupations were still needed and rewarded; as Syme (1958) 607 put it: 'Two paths lie open to the highest honours. The one is law and oratory, with diplomatic arts that manage the Senate for the Princeps, with loyal talent to defend Caesar's friends and destroy his enemies in the high court of justice. The other is the administrative or military career.'[11] The roles of both oratory and warfare were, however, becoming reduced in scope; as Syme's formulation makes clear, all men now served the Princeps personally.

Deliberative oratory in the Senate took its cue from the emperor (or his mouthpiece), and did not question his policies; even the loyal Pliny has cause to complain of the Senate's ineffectuality.[12]

Forensic oratory too underwent considerable change in the early principate. The *quaestiones perpetuae*, in which the orators of the Ciceronian age had made their reputations, were largely superseded as jurisdiction came increasingly under direct imperial scrutiny. The business left to *iudices* in the centumviral court seemed trivial, whilst the more politically significant trials were morally compromised by the rise of the *delatores*.[13] On the other hand, it was still the case that a member of the élite might have to rely solely upon himself for his legal protection: witness the dismay of C. Silanus, proconsul of Asia, charged with extortion, bereft of support, having to mount his own defence – *solus et orandi nescius* – against the most eloquent of Asia's orators and before a hostile Princeps (*A.* 3.66–7); or that of Publius

11 See too his essay 'Ministers of the Caesars' in (1991) 521–40, esp. 523–35. These two paths virtually replicate those mentioned to Achilles by Phoenix at *Il.* 9.440–1.

12 See Sherwin-White's nn. on *Ep.* 3.20.10 *haec tibi scripsi ... ut non nunquam de re publica loquerer, cuius materiae nobis quanto rarior quam ueteribus occasio tanto minus omittenda est* and 12 *sunt quidem cuncta sub unius arbitrio* (cf. *D.* 41.4), with references to 4.25, 2.11.1, 4.12.3, 5.4.1. For a brisk overview of deliberative oratory at this time see Kennedy (1972) 430–4, and for the dreariness of senatorial oratory Syme (1958) 224, 230, 285 n. 4, 330.

13 For changes in jurisdiction see H. Galsterer in *CAH* x 408–9, 412–13; for forensic oratory see Kennedy (1972) 437–42; for *delatores* see *OCD* s.v. maiestas. The still widespread need for skilled verbal presentation of a case (sometimes in the form of written pleadings) is fascinatingly charted by Crook (1995).

Celer, to whom *neque animus in periculis neque oratio suppeditauit* (*H.* 4.40.3).[14] But in the main trials were not as politically interesting as they had been before Augustus, a point made in the *Dialogus* (37.4–8). Tacitus pondered the changes in the character of the traditional Roman careers, and saw that they entailed a reorientation of *uirtus*, that Roman concept which incorporated a large ideal of excellence and publicly recognized achievement.[15] That in turn brought into question the foundations of enduring fame: how was a man to acquire a reputation with posterity, once the means of achieving it were so circumscribed? The sorts of activities that secured *uirtus* and *gloria* in the days of the free *respublica* were no longer possible under an autocrat, especially if he turned out a bad man. How, he clearly asked himself, was one to be a good senator or general in the reign of a Domitian and leave a name to be remembered for all ages?

Tacitus attempted an answer to this basic question in two of his early monographs, *Dialogus* and *Agricola*; in them he set out to show his sense of the altered conditions of a traditional career. In the former he aimed to demonstrate not so much the decline of forensic oratory (though he makes it clear that he is aware of a sort of decline both in the importance of the cases and in the conditions of trials), as its now restricted scope. In the latter, the treacherous rewards of military success and administrative skill are realized in the life of his father-in-law, Julius Agricola. Before turning to them, a partial account of Tacitus' own public life will set the stage.

14 Defendants on a charge of *maiestas*, like Libo at *A.* 2.39.1 or Piso at *A.* 3.11.2, had considerable difficulty in securing the support of others to speak on their behalf. But any man might plead his own case: cf. Plin. *Epp.* 4.22.2 [Trebonius Rufus] *egit ipse causam non minus feliciter quam diserte*, 6.22.2 *egit uterque pro se.*

15 It is possible that this question had been posed as long ago as the early 40s BC by M. Junius Brutus in his treatise *De uirtute*, which was dedicated to Cicero. Douglas, for instance, follows Hendrickson in speculating that the dialogue *Brutus* is Cicero's reply to the supposed quietism of Brutus' argument (Intro. p. xi), but this has now been questioned. Tacitus at any rate makes clear his view at *Agr.* 1.4: *tam saeua et infesta uirtutibus tempora.*

2. TACITUS' CAREER

Tacitus was a new man, *nouus homo*. His family had never advanced
far in the political life of the city (assuming that any of them had
even sought *honores*); his father was presumably equestrian, and may
have been an imperial agent, *procurator*,[16] so the son was well placed
to move up the social scale if he chose to. He did so choose, and
what enabled Tacitus to rise was his eloquence. He was the most
celebrated pleader of his day – Pliny refers to his speaking *eloquentissime*, and says that the remarkable quality of his style was its mag-
nificence (*Ep.* 2.11.17).[17] It was that which opened up to him a path to
political advancement. But there is a curious fact about his activity
as an advocate that suggests a certain disenchantment early on: he
never published any of his speeches. That was a common enough
practice in his day; Pliny refers frequently to several speeches he is
preparing for publication, as usual after elaborate rewriting.[18] Tacitus' refusal to publish could be attributed to any number of motives,
but it may here be suggested that what most weighed with him was a
sense of the ephemeral quality of contemporary oratorical effort. It
simply did not matter how well you spoke in public, the issues were
too trivial to justify their preservation in a published speech. Or,
worse yet, one's efforts might go for nothing. An instance of such
frustration was arguably the trial of Marius Priscus, of which more
below.

Of Tacitus' political (as distinct from oratorical) progress he tells
us himself in the opening paragraph of the *Histories*. The unspecific

16 The article s.v. in the *OCD* should be consulted for more information
on the status and function of the imperial *procuratores*. For a fuller discussion
of Tacitus' career see Martin (1981) 26–38 and Anthony R. Birley, 'The life
and death of Cornelius Tacitus', *Historia* 49 (2000) 230–47.

17 Pliny used the adverb σεμνῶς, a by then well-established descriptive
term for a grand style; see Hermogenes, *Id.* 1.6 (pp. 242–54 Rabe). Pliny also
calls Tacitus a *laudator eloquentissimus* at *Ep.* 2.1.6, describing the public funeral
of Verginius Rufus, at which Tacitus pronounced the eulogy.

18 For a handy list of them – Pliny mentioned about half a dozen being
readied for publication in his letters – see Sherwin-White's n. to *Ep.* 5.8.6. It
is worth noting that Quintilian, on the other hand, only ever published one
speech (*Inst.* 7.2.24).

reference there to a steady advance through the *cursus honorum* under three emperors omits notice of election to socially impressive priesthoods.[19] Later still he secured the proconsulate of Asia, the crown of any senatorial career. All in all, Tacitus had every reason to be as complacent as his junior friend, the only slightly less successful Pliny. Now Pliny was happy with everything he got and never repined, though he could complain about the distraction from his literary work that business entailed (*Epp.* 1.9 and 2.8). But Tacitus for his part reflected upon the diverse paths he and his father-in-law had followed and shook his head over their wasted effort. Why was he so disenchanted with contemporary oratory?

Tacitus had made his reputation as an advocate (and presumably for speaking in the Senate too); that had carried him up the *cursus honorum*. But he could not but see that his own success was exactly mirrored in the careers of men like Eprius Marcellus or M. Aquilius Regulus, scoundrels who battened on the unfortunate: they were two of the most infamous of the *delatores*, self-appointed prosecutors, who hauled the men they denounced as Caesar's enemies before the courts.[20] Like the imperial *procuratores* they were a new breed of men, engendered to meet the unprecedented demands of imperial government. Marcellus and Regulus had effectively persuasive skills at their command, and were acknowledged masters of forensic oratory, but unlike Tacitus or Pliny, they used their talent discreditably and yet prospered greatly. On the other hand, Tacitus had come to see that superb oratory in a good cause availed little. It was arguably the trial of Marius Priscus (to which allusion has already been made) that set the seal upon his own disenchantment.[21]

Priscus had been governor of Africa, and in January of 100 was tried for extortion.[22] Pliny assisted Tacitus in the trial, which he describes enthusiastically in one of his letters. They were successful

19 Tacitus may even have been a *quaestor Augusti*; see G. Alföldi in *MDAI(R)* 102 (1995) 251 on *CIL* vi 1574 (this reference is owed to Professor R. H. Martin).

20 Tacitus provides a thumbnail sketch of the type at *A.* 1.74.1–2.

21 This was certainly the belief of Syme (1958) 465: 'so little gained for all the expense of time and talent'; cf. pp. 66, 70, 191.

22 For Marius Priscus see *PIR* M 315.

up to a point, in that they secured Priscus' conviction; the usually
buoyant Pliny reckoned it was a triumph, worthy to be remembered
for ever (*Ep.* 2.11.1 *rei magnitudine aeternum*), and he seems to have had
every intention of publishing his speech for the prosecution (so
Sherwin-White on *Ep.* 2.19). But what actually happened to Priscus?
Not much; his lenient punishment became a byword and was mock-
ingly referred to by the satirist Juvenal (1.47–8 *damnatus inani | iudicio*,
and cf. 8.119–20). If therefore oratorical power was wasted on true
criminals and yet successful against the harmless, the morality of its
use became questionable (an issue that goes back to Plato's *Gorgias*).
Tacitus came thus to reflect upon the application of the skill that
had made him the man he was, and he found it either morally compromised or a sham. Oratory was moreover now flashy in style and
politically dead. Better to abandon it, and give fresh scope to talent
in other forms of *eloquentia*.

   Rather than keep his disillusion to himself, however, he expressed
it in literary productions, two short works, deliberately (it may be)
designed to be complementary to one another, since they each focus
on one of the major avenues of *uirtus* and *gloria*. The first, to be considered briefly, is the encomiastic biography of his father-in-law Cn.
Iulius Agricola.

3. THE *AGRICOLA*

Agricola, a *uir militaris*, was, like Tacitus' own father, essentially an
imperial administrator, a profession newly developed since the days
of the free *respublica*, and necessary to the running of an empire. His
career had been smooth and respectable, especially his military
commands in Britain. But darkness settled over him in the reign of
Domitian, who grew jealous of his successes as a general (§39);
charges were laid against Agricola (§41), only to be dropped without
explanation. He was later obliged to beg for release from a proposed
proconsulship. He perceived that under such an emperor promi-
nence was perilous, and he preferred to pass his life in peace and
quiet. The moral Tacitus draws is clear (§42): there can be great men
under bad rulers; accommodation or compliance, *obsequium*, and self-
restraint, *moderatio*, coupled with hard work, were more useful to Rome
as now governed than were the posturings of self-immolated martyrs.

All this was true and realistic, but it points up a gulf now separating the aspirant to traditional honours from his republican predecessors. Tacitus exposed the uselessness in the contemporary world of an old-fashioned realization of *uirtus* in the military sphere. The splendour had gone out of the life of the successful general. He describes the award to Agricola of the insignia of a triumph, the honorific statue, the many distinguished words, but all of this was 'instead of a triumph' (*pro triumpho*, 40.1). By that time triumphs were reserved for members of the imperial family. So we are left with the sense of a job well done for little reward yet at considerable personal risk. And there is the underlying problem of fame. Tacitus was clearly worried that for all Agricola's efforts his reputation might die with him: hence the need for the biography, stressed in the opening paragraph.[23] His sense of the fragility of renown is repeated in the concluding sentence of the work, and Richmond in his commentary rightly drew attention to the fact that but for Tacitus' encomium we should now know very little, and that confused, about his father-in-law.[24] (By writing the biography Tacitus also ensures that he too will be known about, a point he draws attention to with the word *narratus* at 46.4; Boswell had the like motivation in writing of Dr Johnson, to commend himself as well as his theme to posterity.) Tacitus would go on to deal with similar issues in his analysis of the current state of the still distinguished art of public speaking. This is dramatically analysed in the *Dialogus*, but before discussing that work it will be useful to consider in more detail two issues: one, the problem of fame, the other, the first-century debate about the state of contemporary oratory.

4. FAME

Cicero had repeatedly expressed what must have been a commonplace among the élite, that *uirtus* could expect to be attended both in this life and after death by fame (*gloria*); fame might not be so desir-

---

23 Biography was indeed becoming a popular literary form at this time (see Sherwin-White on Plin. *Ep.* 3.10.1).

24 Of course, Agricola may well have figured in contemporary histories now lost.

able in itself, but still it shadows *uirtus*.[25] A successful Roman expected renown, but the principate threw this along with so many other traditional concepts into confusion.[26] We have seen how Tacitus was concerned for the reputation of his father-in-law, but the most eloquent contemporary voice raised on this issue is Pliny's, and his anxious wooing of literary fame deserves more careful consideration (and perhaps more sympathy) than it usually receives.[27] He makes no secret of his yearning for what he calls the *praemium aeternitatis* (*Ep.* 9.3.1), and, since he is no *uir militaris*, and the opportunity for doing great deeds lies *in aliena manu* (i.e. that of the Princeps, *Ep.* 3.7.14), he can only hope to achieve lasting renown through his writings. Now Pliny is often felt nowadays to be complacent, but in this regard he displays extreme anxiety, and we can observe him desperately searching for means to secure literary immortality. Mark how he encourages Caninius Rufus to compose something, and Octavius to publish or at least recite his verses (*Epp.* 1.3.4, 2.10), or note his anguish that C. Fannius has died without publishing his monograph on Nero's victims, *pulcherrimum opus* (*Ep.* 5.5.7–8). He is determined to leave something to testify that he had lived (*Ep.* 3.7.14), but what? The publication of deliberative oratory was, as we have already noted from his own witness, out of the question; the themes were too trivial (see n. 12).[28] Of course, his forensic speeches, suitably revised, might do the trick, but here we meet with a complete lack of self-confidence. To be sure, he works away at preparing them for publication (see n. 4), but in that letter about Fannius he expresses his misgivings and terror: *occursant animo mea mortalitas, mea scripta. nec dubito te quoque eadem cogitatione terreri* (*Ep.* 5.5.7). He cannot be sure that his speeches will deserve the notice of posterity, probably even in his heart of hearts knows they do not (*Ep.* 5.8.6 *egi magnas et graues causas.*

25 So *Tusc.* 1.109; for some other representative passages see *Arch.* 28, *Mil.* 97, *Font.* 49 *tum enim uitae socia uirtus, mortis comes gloria fuisset.*

26 We catch a pre-echo of the issue in Cicero's *Brutus*, where he deplores the fact that the young Brutus' chances of securing the rewards of his *uirtus* have been blasted by political developments (§§331–2).

27 Very good so far as it goes on this matter is A.-M. Guillemin, *Pline et la vie littéraire de son temps* (Paris 1929) 13–22 'Conception de la gloire'.

28 In point of fact, however, deliberative oratory had never been much published.

has, etiamsi mihi tenuis ex iis spes, destino retractare).[29] Even the publication of his *Panegyricus*, of which he was so proud, cannot have reassured him all that much, for he will have known enough of the
history of oratory in Rome to appreciate that *laudationes* were its
least esteemed branch (cf. Cic. *De orat.* 2.341). For these reasons he
took out insurance policies, and tried his hand at other kinds of
composition, poems for instance. But these too he mistrusts, for he is
no poet. Should he perhaps take his friends' advice and write history
(*Ep.* 5.8)? That would extend his own renown along with his subject
(a consideration for Tacitus too in composing the *Agricola*), but would
distract him from work in hand. Yet none of his initiatives really
convinced him that he would be remembered.

It is important to appreciate that Pliny's lack of confidence is not
entirely self-generated; he knows that he can write well enough, it
is just that there is nothing to write about: *postquam desîmus facere
laudanda, laudari quoque ineptum putamus* (*Ep.* 3.21.3). Hence some dissatisfaction even with his letters. He was pleased at their success in
far-off Lyons (*Ep.* 9.11), but he again shows misgivings: the themes
that enliven the letters of Cicero no longer exist (*Ep.* 9.2.1–3), a
complaint we meet in Tacitus too, who finds the themes of his own
histories inferior to the great past (*A.* 4.32.1).[30] Indeed, so little confidence had Pliny in the products of his own pen, that he enlisted
Martial (*Ep.* 3.21, cf. *Epig.* 10.19) and Tacitus (*Ep.* 7.33.1) to eternize
his name.[31] His problem was that he could not be content with what
he called *gloria lata* (*Ep.* 4.12.7), the sort of widespread fame that
Aper will describe in the *Dialogus*; Pliny craved the fame that endures

29 Sherwin-White was right to point out that Pliny had no illusions about
the value of his cherished speeches (*Ep.* 5.8.3–4n.). Can we be so sure when
he refers to them as *oratiunculae* (e.g. at *Epp.* 5.12.1, 9.10.3) that the diminutive
is entirely owed to an author's expected modesty? (But he may be no more
than imitating Cicero's use of the same word to Atticus at *Att.* 2.1.3, 11.)

30 Good on this general sense of inferiority is S. Döpp, '*Nec omnia apud
priores meliora*: Autoren des frühen Principats über die eigene Zeit', *RM* 132
(1989) 73–101, esp. 93–4; at 81–2 he rightly sees this as part of a general sense
of an inability to realize *uirtus*.

31 In Martial's case misgivings again clearly arose: Pliny really was not sure
that his poems would survive, and that presumably is why he quoted some of
the epigram in his letter, which might: more insurance against oblivion.

(*magna*), and for that one needed not just literary skills but something to talk about. The tragedy of the age for men like him was that there seemed to be no theme that might make a claim on posterity's attention (compared with the age of Cicero), and Tacitus felt it as much as Pliny (cf. *Ep.* 9.14). The usual literary paths to enduring renown seemed barred. Forensic oratory was under the same cloud, as Tacitus aimed to demonstrate.

5. THE STATE OF ORATORY

We may now turn to earlier and contemporary discussions of the condition of oratory and rhetoric.[32] Ever since Aristophanes in the *Clouds* had raised the question of the morality of a training in verbal persuasion, the issue of rhetoric and of oratory at large remained matter for lively discussion in antiquity. Plato, as already noted, had addressed himself to the problem most aggressively in the *Gorgias*, whilst his contemporary Isocrates had tried to make of rhetorical training a universal education (in this he largely succeeded). But whatever the abundance and importance of the Greek tradition, for a Roman there was only one figure that mattered: Cicero.[33] He had created an impressive and deeply Roman body of theory on oratory and the orator in three treatises, the *De oratore* (composed in 55 BC), the *Brutus*, and the *Orator* (both composed in 46 BC).

These dialogues (*De orat.* and above all *Brut.*) are set in the context of political strife, and the role of oratory within the Roman state is always the issue. In *Brut.* the fate of oratory is seen to hang in the balance: despotism has once again silenced the forum.[34] For Tacitus'

32 Heldmann (1982) is the most important recent study.

33 See 40.2n. Syme (1958) 116 n. 7 referred to some earlier studies, of which E. Köstermann's 'Der taciteische *Dialogus* und Ciceros Schrift *De re publica*', *Hermes* 65 (1930) 396–421 is particularly important. Useful too are S. Döpp, 'Die nachwirkung von Ciceros rhetorische Schriften bei Quintilian und in Tacitus *Dialogus*. Eine typologische Skizze', in P. Neukam, ed., *Reflexionen antiker Kulturen* (Dialog Schule-Wissenschaft. Klassische Sprachen und Litteraturen 20; Munich 1986) 7–26; S. Rutledge, 'The literary, cultural, and historical background of Tacitus' *Dialogus de oratoribus*' (diss. Brown University 1996), esp. Chapter 2.

34 Here the question of style appropriate to such a situation arises: see Douglas's Intro. p. xv. In a somewhat later work, Cicero foretells the decline of oratory: *senescat, breuique tempore ad nihilum uentura uideatur* (*Tusc.* 2.5).

purpose, the *Brutus* was crucial, because in it Cicero adopted an historical view of the development of Roman eloquence.[35] In consequence of this, he had noted, albeit without making much of the fact, that the institution of the *quaestiones perpetuae* had given a boost to forensic pleading (*Brut.* 106, a section in which he also observed that there was an increased need for the activities of the *patronus*, i.e. people felt less able to stand on their own feet in court). He reckoned that there had been fewer notable orators in the generation in which he grew up because there were fewer trials, nor had the practice of securing more than one *patronus* yet taken root (*Brut.* 207). He thus showed an awareness of the influence of the legal system upon the rise of forensic oratory. In a very real way then the *Dialogus* picks up this thread first spun out in the *Brutus*, and shows that despotism has carried the day, and oratory as Cicero and Hortensius knew it no longer has a place in the newly reconstituted Roman state.

The historical framework of that dialogue provides too a foundation for some of the argumentative strategies found within the *Dialogus*. For instance, *Brutus* indulges in some chronological reckonings (§§41, 49, 60, 69, 74; see Douglas's Introduction pp. lii–liv), and frequently appeals to what passed muster *illis temporibus*. All this is reflected in the second speech of Aper, who accepts that oratory had not reached its acme in Rome until late. He too makes a complicated, and not entirely superficial calculation, and draws attention to the need for style to accommodate itself to an audience's expectations.

Another aspect of the historical point of view of the *Brutus* needs to be brought out. Since Cicero is not, as in the earlier *De oratore*, concerned with an abstract ideal, but with the actual representatives of Roman eloquence, he is far more alive in this dialogue than he was in the earlier one to the claims of renown: he often draws attention to how few make a secure name as orators (§§137, 244, 270, 299, 333), and he focuses (as we shall note again below) upon the written memorials of past speeches. This leads him to refer frequently to the renown that survives the orator: §§23, 25, 32, 63 (Lysias), 92 (those who do not aim to acquire *memoriam in posterum ingeni sui*). At §324 he says that he and Hortensius have left in their speeches an indication

35 See also S. Borzsák, 'Le "Dialogue" de Tacite et le "Brutus" de Cicéron', *BAGB* (1985) 289–98.

to posterity of what their styles were like. Hortensius secured *dicendi gloria*, and to it Cicero aspired as a youth (§§301, 314). (But he will note in the subsequent *Orator* 132 that Hortensius was not as good at writing as he was at speaking.)

After Cicero there is a considerable gap in our record concerning views on the state of oratory (if we leave to one side Virgil's oblique criticism at *Aen.* 6.849 *orabunt* [sc. *alii*] *causas melius*). But when our record resumes, in the reign of Tiberius, in the work of Velleius Paterculus and of the elder Seneca, we encounter a clear sense that oratory is not what it once was.[36] To their voices we may add those of Petronius, Longinus, Juvenal, among others.[37] The causes of decline are usually felt to be moral: the young are lazy nowadays. But there are often too references to a deterioration in style; a certain effeminacy was alleged to have sapped the strength of the oratory of old. This points up one problem which is going to be faced in the *Dialogus*. Those with a strong sense of the past (fed on the reading of published speeches) developed the conviction that contemporary oratory was, stylistically considered, not as good as that of the Ciceronian age (and perhaps down into the reign of Augustus).

And yet for all these complaints, Crook (1995) has demonstrated the buoyancy of advocacy at this time, though that was not the sort of oratory our critics were interested in. Moreover, men like the younger Seneca, Pliny, Tacitus, and Quintilian owed their prominent positions chiefly to their oratorical skill. We can draw attention as well to Salvius Liberalis, or to Junius Otho, who rose from the status of elementary school master to the praetorship (with Sejanus' help).[38]

36 See Vell. Pat. 1.16–18, and for Seneca Rhetor J. Fairweather, *Seneca the elder* (Cambridge 1981) 132–48; more general discussions are offered by H. Caplan in A. King and H. North, eds., *On eloquence* (Ithaca 1970) 160–95, Williams (1978) 6–51, Kennedy (1972) 446–64, Fantham (1978) 111–16, and Heldmann (1982).

37 See Petr. *Sat.* 1–2, 88; Long. *Subl.* 44, and Juv. 7.105–49; but Courtney in his commentary p. 348 notes the weakness of Juvenal's rhetorical method of 'proof' by *exempla*, and Crook (1995) 183 observes: 'Juvenal ... may be disallowed as evidence for his age on the ground that so many of the horses he flogs are dead.' See too Luce (1993) 13 for a collection of malcontents, and 16 n. 18 for two popular accounts of decline ignored in *D*.

38 For them see Sherwin-White on Plin. *Ep.* pp. 171, 237, and Furneaux on *A.* 3.66.4.

L. Fulcinius Trio, a famous *delator*, leapt to arraign Cn. Calpurnius
Piso before the Senate for the death of Germanicus on his return to
Rome from Syria; he reached the consulship (but committed suicide
as a consequence of the fall of Sejanus).[39] Despite a statement to the
contrary by the elder Seneca, the rewards of eloquence were still
very large and attainable.

So it was undeniable that oratorical skill remained an avenue to
wealth, influence, and prestige. There were other grounds too for
confidence in its continued value: Domitian, though an indifferent
orator himself, had supported oratory, by including a contest in
Greek and in Latin oratory in the Capitoline games (Suet. *Dom.* 4.4;
20). The rising status of rhetors is evidenced in the fact that there
are biographies of them by Suetonius. They had a respected role to
play in ensuring the quality of oratory in the principate. Even Pliny,
despite what was said above about his misgivings in respect of the
long-term merits of his own speeches, clearly believed contemporary
oratory to be in fairly good order, though there were signs of re-
cidivism.[40] Indeed, such a view was hardly unjustified, given the pre-
eminence of Tacitus at the time (and of Pliny himself, cf. *Ep.* 9.23.2–
3). Pliny could moreover point to some aspiring orators who took
him as a model (*Ep.* 6.11.2): all further proof that oratory was likely
to endure and prosper.

Quintilian provides far and away the most optimistic view of the
oratorical situation. He had composed a now lost work on the causes
of decline in contemporary oratory, but presumably he did not regard the situation as beyond remedy.[41] In his own educational treatise he draws attention to those who will serve as models for the
future (in effect, they were to become classics of the literature). So at
Inst. 2.5.25 (in a section on authors to be read by the schoolboy orator) he mentions *quosdam uero etiam, quos totos imitari oporteat, et fuisse
nuper* [e.g. Domitius Afer and Julius Secundus] *et nunc esse, quidni
libenter non concesserim modo, uerum etiam contenderim?* In his list of authors to be read for the acquisition of stylistic mastery he again notes
that there are contemporaries (whom by traditional courtesy he may

39 For him see Furneaux on *A.* 2.28.3, and cf. *A.* 3.10.1.
40 Syme (1958) 103.
41 See Brink (1989).

not name) whose works will last: his pupil, Pliny, and Tacitus are surely meant (*Inst.* 10.1.122). His most idealistic statement comes at *Inst.* 12.1.21, where he expresses the belief that a new Cicero might arise at any time.

Tacitus decided to join this lively debate about the condition of oratory. He raises his voice along with those complaining of decline, a position taken for granted at the outset of the *Dialogus*. But he had a fresh 'take' on the issue, and used the dialogue form in which to expound it.

6. THE *DIALOGUS*

We may now turn directly to the companion piece of the *Agricola*, in which Tacitus presents the case for and against forensic oratory. (A more detailed account of the layout and argument will be given below in §10.) There are three principal speakers: Aper, an enthusiastic barrister, Messalla, a young aristocrat with no time for contemporary standards of education or oratory, and Maternus, a barrister and senator, who is turning from active public life to the composition of tragedies. He writes a special kind of tragedy, called the *praetexta*, its argument founded upon Roman history. This sort of writing could prove risky, since all tragedies, but especially those on the Roman past, might be interpreted as having a contemporary political slant.[42] That has proved to be the case on this occasion, in 75, the sixth year after Vespasian became emperor.[43] Maternus' recent work, entitled *Cato*, has given offence in high places, and some of his friends, including Aper, are worried for his safety. They come (accompanied by Tacitus, but he is far too young to open his mouth), and urge moderation. Maternus is adamant that he will go

---

42 Indeed it was probably in the nature of the genre that the plots chosen and their treatment had a political colour. Ennius' *Ambracia* is reckoned to have been propaganda in favour of his patron, M. Fulvius Nobilior (A. Gratwick in *CHCL* II 128), and the anonymous *Octavia* was arguably welcomed for its hostility to Nero by Vespasian (L. Herrmann, *Octavie, tragédie prétexte* (Paris 1924) 96).

43 The dramatic date of 75 depends upon the interpretation of 17.3 *sextam iam felicis huius principatus stationem qua Vespasianus rem publicam fouet*, for which see Syme (1958) 670–1 and (1970) 117.

on composing. This riles his friend Aper, who minds terribly that Maternus has given up a public career for poetry. Maternus is unfazed, just because this is Aper's usual line of attack. But he sees in their present visit, which includes Secundus, the chance to debate the issue in the presence of one who might serve as an arbiter. Their discussion comprises a trio of paired speeches. Each of the three interlocutors speaks twice. The set speeches, six in all, have single themes, and are adversarial in form, since the dialogue parodies a trial. In each of the three pairs, the second is the shorter.

In the opening pair Aper rehearses the merits of oratory (5.3–10), while Maternus pleads for poetry (11–14), and both denigrate the other's 'client'. When they have done, a new figure, Messalla, appears and a fresh topic is introduced: is modern oratory inferior to ancient? This opens up the problematical issue of forensic oratory as a literary form.[44] Aper of course argues that modern oratory is not inferior (16.4–23), Messalla that it patently is so (25–6). The groundwork has now been laid, Aper moves into the background, and Maternus and Messalla get to grips with the main issue, why oratory has declined (both are in no doubt that it has, any more than Tacitus was at the outset). Messalla gives his reason first, and describes a slide in educational standards from the time of Cicero (28–35); he does not, in what is left of the text at this point, urge reform. Maternus then offers his opinion, and highly original it is; in it we are bound to detect the hand of Tacitus himself, the budding historian. The grounds for decline, Maternus urges, are to be seen in political change (36–41). He does not fault what Messalla has said, but decrying the slippage of standards in morality, art, and education is somewhat threadbare. Maternus offers instead an historically determined view. He reckons that what made the oratory of the past great was the political turmoil which fostered it. That has been suppressed by the sole government of a Princeps. It follows that the issues for public debate are reduced. Maternus therefore concludes that contemporary oratory is a dead end. We must now recall that the debate with which Aper and Maternus opened the dialogue was left unresolved. Clearly from what Maternus says at the end of the discussion, oratory, which can still make a man's career, must become reconciled to its reduced status. Aper (and Pliny and Tacitus) must not hope to challenge Cicero. So what is an ambitious man – ambitious for lasting fame – to do with his life?

The answer remains implicit in the work. A man can still be of use to his fellow citizens through the correct use of his skills, in this case verbal. Not oratory now, but poetry, and not exclusively fictional poetry (e.g. the myths of Greece, such as we find in Seneca's tragedies), but a poetry founded upon Roman historical experience. That validates Maternus' change of vocation. He is still in the thick of public affairs (the unusual setting of the dialogue is here to be remarked, see 2.1n.), but now he comments by implication through the imaginative re-creation of the tragic past. This sounds not unlike what Tacitus himself is to do as an historian.[45] Moreover, the relation between poetry and history was from the time of Aristotle recognized. Quintilian said that historiography was *proxima poetis et quodam modo carmen solutum* (*Inst.* 10.1.31). But what must be stressed in assessing the place of the *Dialogus* in the work of Tacitus, is that the figure of Maternus, the tragic poet whose subject matter is drawn from the Roman past, is clearly a type for the historian. Tacitus used the rejection of contemporary oratory which he put in Maternus' mouth to justify his own defection from the ranks of the active pleaders.

In what has just been said about the *Dialogus* certain assumptions have been made, concerning chiefly the authenticity and dating of the work. It is now time to turn in more detail to those matters, and to open up certain other related issues of literary interest.

7. AUTHENTICITY

No author in antiquity ever mentioned the existence of any of Tacitus' minor writings; he passed into the literary consciousness solely

---

45 Barnes (1986) goes further and speculates that Tacitus may even have contemplated a career as a poet at the time of writing the *D.* (which he follows Murgia in believing to be the earliest of the three *opera minora*, 232–3).

as an historian.[46] This is important because when Poggio Bracciolini was first informed in 1425 that there was a MS in the abbey at Hersfeld containing works by Tacitus, he made the point that all three – *Agricola, Germania*, and the *Dialogus* – were 'nobis ignota'.[47] The only reason he had for believing them to have been written by the historian was the express ascription of two of them, *Agricola* and *Germania*, to Tacitus in the MS itself, an ascription confirmed when the MS finally came into humanist hands. Some later scholars, however, Rhenanus and most importantly Lipsius (the chief of Tacitus' editors to date), doubted that the *Dialogus* was by Tacitus, and for about two centuries this doubt was widespread. Then in the early nineteenth century A. G. Lange detected an allusion to the phrase at 9.6, *in nemora et lucos*, apparently recalled by design in a letter from Pliny to Tacitus himself: *itaque poemata quiescunt, quae tu inter nemora et lucos commodissime perfici putas*.[48] This turned the tide and the work's authorship has been little questioned since, though even the great Madvig refused to believe it belonged to Tacitus, and recently another authoritative voice has been raised to query his authorship.[49] A brief account therefore of the *status quaestionis* is offered here,[50] since resolution of the issue also involves reflection upon the work's composition and style.

The first point to make about the author would command general assent: he is obviously not trying to appear to be Tacitus. That is to say, the work is not a forgery or a parody (unlike the pseudo-Sallustian invective against Cicero, which will be noticed below). If it was composed by someone other than Tacitus its author meant it to be acknowledged as his own work, and it would be unfortunate that through some accident of transmission his name has been lost, and with it his claim to one of the most remarkable pieces of Latin prose to have survived antiquity. If he were trying to appear

46 He is simply described as *scriptorem historiae Augustae* at *SHA* 27.10.3.

47 This will be discussed in §12 The transmission of the text.

48 See A. G. Lange, *Vermischte Schriften und Reden* (Leipzig 1832) 1–14; Luce (1993) 14 n. 16 crisply disposes of doubt on the issue.

49 Crook (1995) 10, 174, 184 'assumed to be by Tacitus'.

50 There is a short discussion by Heubner *apud* Güngerich (1980) 191–2, and by Merklin (1991) 2259–61.

Tacitean he would presumably have adopted some of the manner-
isms found in the historical works, in order to bamboozle the unsus-
pecting reader. Yet had he lifted stylistic peculiarities from them, he
would have spoiled the literary character appropriate to a conversation about oratory: the style suitable to such a work is an important
factor. This was overlooked by the author of the letters to Caesar
De re publica, composed in the manner of Sallust; he strove to replicate the style of an historian, but failed to see that it was inappropriate to political pamphlets. It is that (among other things) which
unmasks the fraud.[51] The author of the *Dialogus*, on the other hand,
knew that he must write in the character traditionally established for
discussion of oratory in Rome. That is why it is as it is, Ciceronian,
a matter to be further illustrated.[52] The issue then is simple: either
the *Dialogus* is by an unknown master who had no thought of per-
petrating a fraud, or it is by Tacitus himself, who for the occasion
has adopted a style different from what he was to use (or was already
using) in his historical works.

But style is not the whole of the story, so far as the use of language is concerned. All writers have peculiar usages, or turns of
phrase, which may be called 'style-free', in that they can crop up
anywhere. They just happen to appeal to the writer, who may reproduce them quite unconsciously (a pitfall for the intertextualist).
We do in fact find some peculiarly Tacitean phraseology in the *Dialogus*,[53] e.g. the pairing of *indefensus* and *inauditus* at 16.4, the plural
form *educationes* at 28.5,[54] the expressions *Forum ingressuri* at 33.2,[55]

51 See E. Fraenkel, *Kleine Beiträge zur klassischen Philologie* (Rome 1964) II 132,
136–7, a reference owed to Dr Michael Coffey.

52 See E. Löfstedt, 'The style of Tacitus', in *Roman literary portraits* (Oxford
1958; tr. P. M. Fraser) 162: 'Similarly in the *Dialogus de oratoribus* Tacitus em-
ploys a quite different, more Ciceronian, more classic style than in the historical writings – quite naturally, since according to the then current view the
Ciceronian style was prescribed once for all as the style for a literary theme.'

53 There is an important list in John (1899) 11–15, cf. Bennett (1894) viii–
ix.

54 The plural is found also at *A.* 3.25.1, and then not before Apuleius.

55 '*Forum ingredi* seems a Tacitean variant on the more normal *in Forum de-
duci*' (Woodman and Martin on *A.* 3.29.3).

principem in ciuitate locum at 34.1 (= *A.* 3.75.1), and *famam circumdederunt* at 37.6.[56] Such expressions, it should be stressed, are not especially unusual, but all appear in other works indubitably by Tacitus. It would have then to be supposed that either the author of the *Dialogus* had all of Tacitus' works at his fingers' ends (in other words that he wrote after publication of the *Annals*), or that Tacitus had memorized the text of the *Dialogus*, and picked up from it some peculiar, but not striking, expressions to recycle in his own writings. These are uneconomical assumptions. The linguistic evidence points to a single author.

Leaving linguistic quirks to one side, we notice too a shared historical ethos between the authors. There is, for example, a remarkable agreement in the starting-point adopted by the author(s) for the rule of Augustus. Many different attempts to pinpoint the start of his reign were made; Dio at 61.30.5 chose the Battle of Actium in 31 BC, and so came up with a total of just under forty-four years, while Suetonius counted fifty-six years, starting from the second triumvirate in November of 43 BC (*Aug.* 8.3). It might be coincidence, but exactly the same computation, fifty-six years (counting from Octavian's first consulship, which began on 19 August 43 BC, to his death on 19 August AD 14), is found only at *D.* 17.3 and at *A.* 1.9.1. Additionally, even Crook (1995) 184–5 observed that the view in the *Dialogus* that the biggest oratorical show available to contemporary pleaders was the centumviral court resembles Tacitus' own attitude to history at *A.* 4.32, where he complained that he had nothing grand to narrate. 'Both' authors sensed a diminution of the scope of their topics, oratory and history.

Similarities of linguistic usage have already been glanced at, but another issue that can usefully be addressed in this context is the difference in style between the *Dialogus* and Tacitus' other works. As has been mentioned, that difference is owed in the first place to the genre and theme, a conversation about oratory; it does not point necessarily to different writers. Individual writers in antiquity

---

56 Found also at *Agr.* 20.1, *H.* 4.11.2, and, NB, nowhere else; cf. *TLL* III 1133.49–70.

cultivated a variety of styles, appropriate to different genres or
occasions.[57] We may consider, for example, the flexible variety of
Pompeius Saturninus. His speeches in real life were impassioned,
and embellished with frequent aphorisms; his historical composition
was stylistically different: concise, radiant, even sublime in narration,
but the speeches were more compressed than his actual forensic
style.[58] Pliny himself attempted such virtuosity (see *Ep.* 1.2). A test
case is provided by Apuleius in the second century. We think of his
characteristic style as that of the narrative *Metamorphoses* (and perhaps the *Florida*), but we also find in his *Apologia*, the reworking of
a speech composed in his own defence, a style much soberer,
more Ciceronian.[59] No one however doubts that it is by the author
of the *Golden Ass*. Stylistic versatility was an accomplishment that
many practised. Who can doubt that Tacitus too was capable of
such virtuosity?

8. DATE OF COMPOSITION

It has been assumed up to now that the *Dialogus* was not written or
presented at a recitation to the Roman public until after Domitian's
death. This would be generally agreed nowadays, but attempts at
greater precision of dating have proved inconclusive.[60] Unlike the
other short works, the *Dialogus* provides no chronological references
which help to establish more precisely the time of its composition.[61]
Shared phraseology in all of the 'minor' works suggests, however,
a measure of contemporaneous composition. Brink (1994) conveniently reviews some nine proposed dates of composition. He, like
most nowadays, automatically dismissed the notion that the work
could have been composed under Vespasian (who died in 79) or

57 See Syme (1958) 672.

58 See Plin. *Ep.* 1.16, with Sherwin-White's notes, esp. that on p. 123:
'These paragraphs might be a description of Tacitus.'

59 For the Ciceronian colour see R. Helm's ed. of the *Florida* (Leipzig
1910) xxii–xxviii.

60 See Syme, 'The dating of the *Dialogus*' (1958) 670–3, Murgia (1980),
Heubner *apud* Güngerich (1980) 195–7, Brink (1994).

61 Contrast *Agr.* 3, and *Germ.* 37.2.

under Domitian.[62] He also demonstrated the weaknesses in the arguments of Murgia (1980), who had both plumped for a date in the reign of Nerva, and urged that the *Dialogus* was Tacitus' first published work.

That the *Dialogus* must be subsequent to Quintilian's *Institutio* is nowadays admitted,[63] and that dating has a crucial bearing on how we read Messalla's attack upon the poor standard of training given the contemporary student of oratory: this was the sort of thing Quintilian aimed to reform. There is also agreement that Pliny's *Panegyricus* betrays a knowledge of the *Dialogus*,[64] which was available in some form to Pliny whilst he was composing, or perhaps more precisely, revising for publication, the *Panegyricus* (but it must be stressed that the actual date of the publication of the revised and lengthened *Panegyricus* remains itself matter for debate).[65] Publication in first- and second-century Rome deserves some brief discussion here, especially in the light of the substantial essays by Murgia (1980) and Brink (1994), neither of whom quite did justice to this issue.

62 He rules out the earlier date because of the expression *iuuenis admodum* at 1.2: Tacitus, born in 55/6, was *c.* 19 (for the expression *H.* 4.5.1); this works against the view that *D.* is an early work (cf. Syme (1970) 117), as does the fact that Fabius Justus too would have been about 16/17, far too young to serve as dedicatee. The later date falls to the case made against it by Kappelmacher (1932); he emphasized that Quintilian had refused to name Eprius Marcellus in the *Institutio* so as not to offend Domitian, Vespasian's son, a point which suggested that *D.*, in which Eprius is mentioned frequently, could not be of Domitianic date (cf. also his article in *RE* vi 264.51–4).

63 R. Güngerich, 'Der *Dialogus* des Tacitus und Quintilians *Institutio oratoria*', *CP* 46 (1951) 159–64 (= Wege der Forschung 97 (Darmstadt 1969) 349–60), demonstrated the dependence of some passages in *D.* upon Quintilian's *Inst.*, which appeared in 96.

64 See R. T. Bruère, 'Tacitus and Pliny's *Panegyricus*', *CP* 49 (1954) esp. 164–8. His arguments are accepted and developed by R. Güngerich, 'Tacitus' *Dialogus* und der *Panegyricus* des Plinius', in *Festschrift Bruno Snell* (Munich 1956) 145–52, and by Brink (1994) 265–9.

65 The *Panegyricus* was actually delivered in a shorter form on 1 Sept. of 100; Pliny set about revising it, and delivered it again over three days at recitations (*Ep.* 3.13 and 18). Barnes (1986) 230 discusses possible publication dates, as does Brink (1994) 265. But Brink (1994) 269 did not explain why he thought it unlikely that the influence of *D.* on the *Panegyricus* had to be restricted to that later, published version.

When a writer was working on a piece, he might hand it round among trusted friends for their criticism. Once finished, a work was commonly presented to an invited audience at a *recitatio*. After revision, it might then be handed round again to close friends for their opinion, and yet further *recitationes* might be held.[66] There could thus be some considerable gap between the recitation and final publication in written form. Thus even if the *Dialogus* was being composed at the same time as the *Agricola, Germania*, and Pliny's *Panegyricus*, there is no way of knowing that it appeared either before or contemporaneously with them; even the arguments advanced by Murgia (1985) on the links between Pliny's letters, especially those in the early books, and the *Dialogus* do not enhance certainty, since Pliny's own letters underwent frequent revision, and their time and manner of publication are still shrouded in uncertainty (see n. 3 above). It should be borne in mind that the letters were probably treated in the same way as the epigrams of Martial, that is to say, they were recited to an audience before being gathered into books for publication. At the recitation only excerpts need have been given; the finished product will have contained matter that need never have been recited, or that was recited on quite different occasions.[67]

Murgia (1985) 192 suggested that the first four books of Pliny's letters might have been recited and distributed before the death of the *delator* Regulus in around 106, but that the letters insulting to him cannot have been included before then. (The same argument applies to the letters supposedly indebted to the *Dialogus*: they could as easily as the Regulus letters have been inserted at a much later date.) Murgia (1985) 205–6 therefore concluded that Pliny might have heard the *Dialogus* recited in the spring or summer of 97; it should in that case be recalled that Pliny was perfectly capable of memorizing what he heard at a recitation and of reproducing it later before the author himself 'published' the revised text.[68] Pliny might even have been sent a written version, in whole or in part. But that

66 For these three stages see Plin. *Ep.* 7.17.7, *D.* 9.3–4 (*recitatio*), and again *Ep.* 5.12.

67 See the important essay by Peter White, 'The presentation and dedication of the *Silvae* and the *Epigrams*', *JRS* 64 (1974) 40–50, esp. 44–5.

68 See *Ep.* 4.27 for an example.

would not prove publication to a wider audience, for Tacitus might have sent it to him only for critical comment; and it should be borne in mind that what was sent to friends for criticism need not be a whole work.[69] Murgia does not assert that the *Dialogus* was more widely available in that year (97), even assuming that Tacitus had completed it. We are thus not much further ahead, for all the sifting of Pliny's letters and his *Panegyricus* for clues, about the time at which Tacitus actually published his *Dialogus*.

A clue to the publication date has been sought in the date, 102, of the suffect consulship of the dedicatee, Fabius Justus (and he would have been consul-designate in the previous year).[70] If this date could be proved, it would guarantee the supposition offered above, that the pyrrhic victory in the trial of Marius Priscus was decisive in turning Tacitus against forensic oratory. But Brink (1994) 269–71 rightly concluded that the consular hypothesis, though not unreasonable, lacks cogent evidence.

The still common view, that the *Dialogus* was published at some time early in the first decade of the second century must remain the best we can manage. But the date of the *Dialogus* relative to its seeming companion pieces, the *Agricola* and *Germania*, still deserves a word. Murgia (1980) believed that it was the first of Tacitus' publications, and fairly argued that in the preface to *Agricola* there is no explicit statement that it is itself the first work to break the author's self-imposed silence. Against this Brink (1994) 268–9 invoked the tone of the works, a matter neglected by Murgia, and admittedly difficult to ascertain. Brink followed Friedrich Klingner,[71] in feeling that the opening of the *Agricola* sounded a note of elation at the end of oppression. He finds the *Dialogus*, in comparison, unemotional, sceptical, a work of maturer judgement. This is fair so far as it goes, but further support for the priority of the *Agricola* can be secured from consideration of how the three *opera minora* are introduced to their readership.

Germania has no introduction at all; it simply begins with a turn of

69 Again see Plin. *Ep.* 2.5.1–2 for a speech of which he sent only parts to a friend for comment.

70 So Kappelmacher (1932), followed hesitantly by Syme (1970) 117–18.

71 'Tacitus' in *Römische Geisteswelt* (Munich 1961) 506–7.

phrase, *Germania omnis*, which identifies the literary genre as ethno-
graphic. The *Dialogus* is a little more informative, in that it accounts
for the choice of topic and the occasion of publication (a friend's in-
sistence). Of the three only the *Agricola* offers a fairly spacious justification for its publication. It alone refers to antecedent silence, now
broken (though not explicitly for the first time). This introduction
sounds like a début, in which the author introduces himself to his
audience. If he had already appeared before the public as a writer,
the introduction to the *Agricola* would read a little preposterously.
What is more, at *Agr.* 3.3 Tacitus refers to his intention to compose
a history of his own times, and insists that for lack of practice in
composition (*per silentium*) it will be written *incondita ac rudi uoce*.
Could he really have had the nerve to use such a commonplace self-
depreciation if his audience had already the dazzling *Dialogus* in its
hands? That reference to clumsy style could only pass muster in a
literary novice, one whose very first published work is now before us.
The *Dialogus* and *Germania* ought by rights to be later publications
than *Agricola*, just because they make no bows.

In the context of discussing the date of the work, it is appropriate
to notice the old, but now thoroughly discredited, view that the work
was written before Domitian's reign. The justification for this opinion was the Ciceronian style, which, it was thought, the writer
adopted before he had found his own characteristic voice. It was
Friedrich Leo (1960) II 285–93 who argued that a Ciceronian style
was no proof of early composition; as was stressed above, such a
style was entirely due to the genre and theme.[72] We may glance
again at Apuleius: his *Apologia* used to be considered an early work,
partly because of the sobriety of its style compared with the supposedly more characteristic *Metamorphoses*.[73] Once style is seen to be
determined up to a point by genre, however, we must accept that a
'Ciceronian' style has more to do with the kind of work composed

72 This is his review of Gudeman's 1894 edition; his view was endorsed by
Norden (1909) I 322–6.

73 See the edition of H. E. Butler and A. S. Owen (Oxford 1914) xlv, and
for the now established date *CHCL* II 933; cf. above under the question of
authenticity. The *Met.* on the other hand may be earlier or contemporary, see
E. J. Kenney, *Apuleius, The Golden Ass* (Harmondsworth 1998) xxviii–xxix.

than with the supposedly as-yet-unformed stylistic character of the writer.

If the work was composed, or at least finished off, under the shadow of the trial of Marius Priscus, then Tacitus ironically put himself in the position of having no grounds for complaint about the waste of his talent and effort: he supposedly had had his warning whilst he was yet *iuuenis admodum*, and it was administered by Maternus. As he pretends, he was presented at a formative stage in his career with arguments for and against the course of action he was embarked upon. He implicitly condemns himself for not having followed Maternus' example and admonition.

9. THE STYLE OF THE WORK

Frequent reference has been made to the Ciceronian character of the style of the *Dialogus* and it is time to give closer attention to that issue.[74] It should be made clear at the outset that Tacitus is no ape of his model. Many of his words or expressions (e.g. *inuicem* for the older *inter se, me nolente* for *me inuito, in quantum* for the simple *quantum*) and syntactical constructions (e.g. *habeo* + gerund(ive), 8.2n.) were quite unknown in Cicero's day;[75] Tacitus is not slavishly reproducing his manner, but rather evoking it, without abandoning the linguistic resources of his own day.

A further difference from the model is that the style Tacitus adopts here is not as markedly conversational as we find in Cicero's

74 Discussions will be found in Peterson (1893) xliii–lxii, Gudeman (1894) 20–9, G. Sörbom, *Variatio sermonis Tacitei aliaeque apud eundem quaestiones selectae* (Uppsala 1935), H. Bardon, 'De nouveau sur Tacite et le Dialogue des orateurs. Les critères grammaticaux et stylistiques', *Latomus* 12 (1953) 485–94, J. Perret, 'La formation du style de Tacite', *REA* 56 (1954) 90–120, H. Gugel, *Zu Stil und Aufbau von Tacitus, Dialogus de oratoribus* (diss. Graz 1964), 'Die Urbanität im Rednerdialog des Tacitus', *SO* 42 (1967) 127–40, and (1969).

75 A number of the older commentaries go to considerable lengths to point out what was regarded as 'non-classical', i.e. unCiceronian, language or usage. So far as this was done with a view to establishing the difference of Tacitus' practice, and the development of the language, well and good. But one often has the sense that the old-style prose composition is really at the back of the commentator's mind, and the reader is being warned against certain usages.

own dialogues. For instance, there is a surprising lack of the colloquial (and often *ad hoc*) compounds formed from *per-* or *sub-*, which
are prominent in Ciceronian dialogues, e.g., in *De orat.*, *perfacilem ...
perpugnacem* (1.93), *pertenuem* (1.107), *pergrata ... perque iucunda* (1.204),
subiratus (1.72), *subturpis* (2.264), etc.[76] Likewise, Tacitus does not generally go out of his way to include conversational words found in
Cicero's dialogues like *bellus*, though *fugitet* at 22.5 seems to be colloquial. Still, the dialogue form evokes certain colloquial turns of
phrase (examples are noted in the Index), and the repeated use of
the interjection *hercule* is plainly designed to imitate conversational
emphasis.[77]

We see an attempt to recapture the Ciceronian style in the use of
certain words. *autem*, for instance, is not in general a favourite –
there are only six occurrences in the *Annales*, but in this work it
is used over twenty times.[78] One striking characteristic of Cicero's
oratorical language which Tacitus imitates is the use of doublets,
sometimes even synonyms. These are very common, but it has been
noticed that Tacitus sometimes shows independence by reversing the
Ciceronian order.[79] This observation needs to be weighed carefully,
however, since Cicero himself does not use an invariable pattern for
his doublets,[80] and even where we find such a pattern, it may be de-
lusive, since we do not have all that Cicero wrote.

Another feature of Cicero's style was its balance, which he sometimes secured by the addition of words not strictly necessary to
the sense. Tacitus provides a nice example of this at 12.3, where
Maternus follows a reference to *bene facta* with one to *male admissa*;
male is not needed, except to secure balanced phrasing, since *admis-
sum* on its own means 'wrongdoing'. Likewise, at 31.2 *cognouit ... uim
uirtutum prauitatemque uitiorum et intellectum eorum quae...*, *prauitatem* does
not square with the two synonyms *uim* and *intellectum*, but has been

76 See too Zetzel on *Rep.* 1.9.1, or Douglas on *Brut.* 11, 29.

77 In fact, what we often find is *itaque hercule*, and it is only in this expression and only in *D.* that Tacitus uses *itaque*.

78 See *TLL* ii 1576. 57–8, 67–8 for figures.

79 See Gudeman (1894) 79, John (1899) 31, Güngerich (1980) 20, and nn.
on 10.6, 11.2, 36.1.

80 For example, the order of *sanctus* and *augustus* is different at *ND* 1.119
and 2.79.

added for the sake of verbal balance. This is just the sort of thing Tacitus eschews in his historical prose, which goes out of its way to avoid balance.

The word order too of the *Dialogus* shows an awareness of pre-ferred Ciceronian practice. For instance, Cicero, unlike Tacitus, generally did not begin sentences with *igitur*; Tacitus, outside this work, preferred to, but in the *Dialogus* he three times postpones it (8.4, 10.7, 20.6), a remarkably high incidence compared to his other works. In general the word order tends, as might be expected in a conversation, to be regular. For instance, only in the alembicated style of the historical works do we meet with the dislocation of words round a preposition, called anastrophe (see Woodman and Martin on *A.* 3.1.1 *litora ... contra* and 10.2 *iudice ab uno*); occurrences of this word order in the dialogue are formulaic (e.g. *ea de re*). That is in keeping with the more normal style of a conversation. On the other hand, a nice point, which again shows the influence of genre upon word order, was noticed by J. N. Adams,[81] which he called 'verbal hyperbaton': the verb separates a noun from its modifier. He found eighteen examples in the *Dialogus*, but only six in the much longer *Annales*; the reason he adduced was that history, but not oratory, eschewed this particular artificiality of style (a point made more generally by Norden (1909) I 332).

The style of oratory in which all of the interlocutors were trained was grander than that of everyday speech, and this is reflected in the way they talk. They use for instance a periodic structure, often elab-orated over three cola ('limbs'); instances are noted in the Index s.v. tricolon crescendo. The purpose of this structure is to distribute weight, and emphasize ideas. The rhetorical figure anaphora can also be used to add to the impressiveness, as in Maternus' peroration at 40.3. The habit of dividing sentences into cola and the charm of varied divisions are seen to perfection both in Aper's list of the faults of Ciceronian style (23.3), where his sentence is subdivided into three sections with a descending number of cola (3−2−1),[82] and in Maternus' *tour-de-force* double tricolon (36.4), where again ana-phora helps in the articulation.

---

81 'A type of hyperbaton in Latin prose', *PCPS* 17 (1971) 9.
82 The sentence was rightly singled out by Nägelsbach (1905) 712.

One of the leading characteristics of Cicero's oratorical prose was
its rhythmical quality, something noted by Aper at 22.2 *primus ...
adhibuit ... compositioni artem*, that is to say, Cicero first gave systematic attention to the rhythmical arrangement of words in the sentence. Formal Latin prose was rhythmically marked at cardinal
points, chiefly at the end of sentences and also (a more controversial
matter) at the end of internal cola.[83] In adopting a Ciceronian topic,
oratory, which was to be treated in a Ciceronian style, it was inevi-
table that Tacitus should have regard to a matter in which Cicero
was reckoned the first to take an informed interest.[84] Since moreover
his contemporaries, Pliny and Quintilian, took special care in this
department, Tacitus will not have wanted a work on this of all topics
to fall short in any stylistic refinement.[85] We should therefore attend
to how the final clausulae are composed so as to secure a satisfying
cadence.[86]

The commonest rhythmical cadences in this work are the double
cretic, and the cretic followed by a trochee or spondee; resolution of
a long into two shorts seems to have been felt not to spoil the rhythmic effect. Though the most noteworthy examples will be found in
the Index s.v. clausulae, attention may here be drawn to those which
serve to round off a speech, Aper's second, at 23.5–6. He there uses
the double cretic (*inuidia tardauerit*) (with resolution of the first long
syllable), the ditrochee (*planitas est, temperatis*), and the cretic (again

83 For general discussions of prose rhythm see Wilkinson (1963) 134–64,
esp. 162 for Tacitus, and 237–42 for a résumé of some modern theories; J. G.
F. Powell on 'prose-rhythm, Latin' in *OCD* 1261–2. R. G. M. Nisbet, 'Cola
and clausulae in Cicero's speeches' in E. M. Craik, ed., *Owls to Athens* (Oxford
1990) 349–59 discusses various points about rhythmical cola and how they
can be recognized (building upon Fraenkel's *Leseproben*), e.g. the use of *atque*
before a consonant.

84 For particular studies see H. Bornecque, 'La prose métrique et le Dialogue des orateurs', *Revue de Philologie* 23 (1899) 334–42, and A. Werber, *Der
Satzschlussrhythmus des Tacitus* (diss. Tübingen 1962), briefly noticed by Hanslik
(1974) 202, §180. That Tacitus in his historical works was indifferent to most
metrical clausulae is generally agreed; cf. Norden (1909) 332, Wilkinson (1963)
162.

85 For Pliny's practice in the *Panegyricus* see M. Durry, *Pline le Jeune, Pané-
gyrique de Trajan* (Paris 1938) 50–2; for Quintilian's doctrine see *Inst.* 9.4.

86 Güngerich (1980) shows particular care in this department.

with resolution of the first long syllable) + spondee (*genere dicendi, exprimitis affectus*), with which his whole speech ends (*posteri nostri*). Little wonder that Maternus received his remarks with such approbation.

The desire to produce agreeable rhythmic closure to a period sometimes prompts a slight dislocation of the normal word order. We see an example of this at 14.1 *altiorem inter eos esse sermonem*, where *sermonem* is postponed, and so produces a standard clausula, cretic + spondee. We may, on the other hand, notice how one undesirable cadence, that which ends the heroic hexameter, has been deliberately avoided by a slight hyperbaton at 33.6 *quae propriae esse oratorum uidentur*.

10. THE LAYOUT OF THE *DIALOGUS*

How did Tacitus plan the layout of the *Dialogus*?[87] It starts with an agreed presupposition: both Tacitus and his dedicatee, Fabius Justus, share the view that contemporary oratory is inferior to that of previous ages;[88] Fabius has, we are asked to believe, been badgering his friend for an explanation of the phenomenon. Tacitus undertakes to give the reason (or reasons) for this state of affairs. So the basic design is fixed: a question from the dedicatee and answer(s) from Tacitus. Now it was open to Tacitus to use a very simple format: Cicero had provided models in a number of his shorter works. The *Orator*, for instance, is a kind of letter to Brutus, in answer to a supposed request of his for an account of Cicero's opinion about the ideal orator; there is no discussion. There were also Cicero's dialogues on friendship (*Laelius*), on old age (*Cato maior*), and on the

87 Barwick (1929) is groundbreaking, and useful observations are to be found in R. Häussler, 'Zum Umfang und Aufbau des *Dialogus de oratoribus*', *Philol.* 113 (1969) 24–67, U. Hass-von Reitzenstein, *Beiträge zur gattungsgeschichtlichen Interpretation des Dialogus de oratoribus* (diss. Cologne 1970), K. Bringmann, 'Aufbau und Absicht des taciteischen *Dialogus de oratoribus*', *MH* 27 (1970) 164–78, Heubner *apud* Güngerich (1980) 203–6, and G. Wille, *Der Aufbau der Werke des Tacitus* (Amsterdam 1983) 118–217.

88 It should be noted that the indirect question in the first sentence stops at *retineat*; what follows is Tacitus' own observation in the indicative (note too the person of *appellamus*), and it corroborates the thesis of the question to the effect that oratory has declined.

history of Roman eloquence (*Brutus*), in all of which a distinguished
member of the élite set out his views on topics proposed by respectful younger men. Tacitus could have imitated these models, either
by answering Fabius' question personally or by describing, say, an
approach he made as a young man to Maternus for an account of
his reasons for turning from forensic oratory to poetry. He preferred
however a fuller, more dramatic, and more complex structure, a
debate. Planning the debate so that it should appear natural and
unforced could not have been all that easy, just because it was not to
be a free-wheeling discussion, designed to offer a variety of points of
view without reaching a resolution. It must build to a single answer.
For it is clear that Tacitus himself has one answer, which he regards
as superior to any others. Maternus will deliver it, and it naturally
must come last, to avoid anticlimax. So the artistic problem that
faced Tacitus was to design a dialogue that would defer Maternus'
answer over a reasonable span, and yet at the same time lead up to it
naturally in the course of conversation.[89] Let us try to reconstruct
the process by which Tacitus might have excogitated his design.

Since Maternus has the most satisfactory answer to the opening
question, he has to be kept out of the main discussion until Tacitus
is ready for him to give it. Hence the need for Messalla, who can
offer an answer that may go some way towards explaining the decline in oratory. His answer must come before Maternus'. Tacitus
then needed an antagonist in order to create a proper discussion, for
this is to be a dialogue, not a treatise: hence Aper's role. This is the
minimum number of speakers needed for a reasonable discussion of
the point at issue, and Tacitus economically confines the major ex-
positions to them. But as has already been postulated, deferral is
essential. If the discussion started with the precise point at issue, the
decline of oratory, laid before the speakers, it would turn out very
short, perhaps no more than three or four speeches. Tacitus hit upon
a most ingenious ploy: Messalla would not be present from the first,
and the point at issue would not be enunciated until 15.3, when he is

---

89 Virgil faced a similar problem in the second half of the *Aeneid*: his plot
required that Turnus be defeated, perhaps even killed, by Aeneas, so his
problem was to keep the heroes from encountering each other once battle
was engaged. He contrived this deferral over four books, 9–12.

brought in; it is his arrival which precipitates the question that prompted the composition of the *Dialogus* in the first place. But even then, Tacitus has need of deferral: though the precise question has at last been posed, the answers proper must not come at once. So Aper jumps in to defend contemporary oratorical style, and Messalla briefly replies to his position, before being reminded by Maternus of his real object, an answer to the question. But we cannot consider the central part of the discussion until we face an obvious question. Since the point at issue is not to be enunciated before Messalla's arrival, what is the purpose of the initial exchange between Aper and Maternus?[90]

Tacitus accepts, along with Fabius, that the oratory of the present day is inferior to that of the late Republic. He is also aware that others of his opinion, e.g. Quintilian, had analysed the issue and offered their own remedies. Tacitus' task therefore was not so much to cast his vote with others, but to redefine the point at issue so as to show (*a*) what, in his opinion, is really at stake, and (*b*) why the situation did not admit of radical improvement. The opening skirmish, it may be urged, was designed both to enlarge our view of what was implicit in the question and to remove Maternus from the discussion (some interjected conversation apart), until it was time for him to give his own assessment of the cause of decline. Let us now look at the first pair of speeches, bearing in mind that neither speaker has as yet the slightest interest in the question of decline.

Aper first. He is concerned not simply with oratory, but with 'eloquence': all verbal excellence is admirable to him (10.4). Now some men, like Maternus (though there can only ever be few like him), are in the happy position of being able to cast their talent in a variety of moulds, but they must choose which. Aper deplores Maternus'

90 Heubner *apud* Güngerich (1980) 203, among others, rightly rejects the view of Leo (1960) 278–9 and Reitzenstein (1915) 206–13 that the opening skirmish is not related to the central issue; nor is he happy with Barwick's suggestion (1929) 107–8 – reiterated in *Der Dialogus de oratoribus des Tacitus. Motive und Zeit seiner Entstehung* (Berichte der Sächsischen Akademie der Wissenschaften, Leipzig, phil.-hist. Kl. 101, 4; Berlin 1954) 22, 25 – that it is not much more than an airing of a subsidiary theme, a view recently restated by Fantham (1996) 193: 'a mere preliminary to his main concern'. Heubner's own account is set out in Güngerich (1980) 203–6.

choice to abandon forensic oratory for tragic poetry. So he stresses
the advantages success in oratory confers. (It should also be noted
that Tacitus puts the praises of oratory into Aper's mouth at this
stage to evoke the opening of a work that he is rivalling, viz. Cicero's
De oratore, which likewise began with Crassus' praise of the benefits
and power of oratory. But we are probably expected to notice one
major difference: no one in the *De oratore* refers to the fame attendant
upon success as itself a motive for excelling.) His point of view is
that of a careerist, and he asks which career rewards better. Put thus
his position is unassailable: oratory in Rome had always been more
rewarding than poetry, and it always would be. This helps us, the
absent audience at the debate, to see that once the question of decline is mooted, it will after all remain for men like Aper something
of an irrelevance. (We may compare Pliny's contemporary, Satrius
Rufus, who saw no reason to emulate Cicero in his contentedness
with the oratory of the day; *Ep.* 1.5.11.) Pliny, for example, may not
have turned himself into the Cicero of his day, but he had secured
wealth, prestige, office, and influence through his eloquence. What is
more, Aper lets fall insensibly, one does not have to be particularly
moral to secure these glittering prizes (8.3 *neuter moribus egregius*).

   That admission was a false step, and it becomes the dominant
note of Maternus' reply. He is not a careerist, but a good man, so
without more ado, at 12.2 he roundly condemns the whole of Rome's
oratorical tradition for its blood-stained greed. (This interpretation
depends on the force of *huius*,[91] but at the very least he is clearly
condemning the oratory of his own day.) Thus to Maternus as much
as to Aper the question of decline, once it has been opened up, is
strictly speaking a secondary issue. The good man regards the forensic profession as radically compromised, and he may prefer to avoid
it. On this assessment of their positions, neither man need be
exercised to any degree by the problem of decline, and indeed,
Maternus shows only an academic interest in the main debate. Tacitus has artfully raised him above the discussion, and so reserved him
as the mouthpiece for his own answer. By the same token, Tacitus
suggests to the absent audience that what men like Quintilian and

---

91 The interpretation of Wagenvoort (1926) 421, 435 is here accepted.

Pliny regarded as a burning issue, literary style in oratory, might
after all be of restricted relevance: neither Aper nor Maternus notices
it as a factor in deciding the sort of career a man should follow. Now
we need to ask how the question of decline is in fact introduced for
discussion.

It is still within the skirmish at the outset that the clue comes.
Aper had a number of topic headings to dilate upon in making his
case for oratory. He played his trump card last, reputation (8, 10):
orators beat poets in fame. The curious feature of Aper's exposition
of this topic is none the less of a piece with the careerist's point of
view: he seems to be content with a renown of purely contemporary
duration. Maternus does not directly confront this view of reputation, because as a good man he regards fame as of secondary importance. But in his reply to that part of Aper's speech he glances at a
wider perspective, and it is that which prepares the ground upon
which the argument of the dialogue as a whole can proceed. In
mentioning the fame of orators and poets Maternus sounds a deeper
note. At 12.5, for instance, he refers to the regard in which Homer
and Demosthenes are held *apud posteros*. Aper had said nothing of the
opinion of succeeding generations, for he seemed content with a renown circumscribed within his own time. Maternus however appeals
to posterity, and with a single word, *hodie* at 12.6, points to the control posterity exercises over reputation: 'nowadays' Virgil is less re-
probated than Cicero. Maternus at a stroke kindles new lights on the
issue, the influence of time, and the literary canon. He has referred
to texts handed down from one generation to another, not so much
as cultural icons, but as living models for literary imitation. This interest in texts comes to shape the whole question of fame in the
course of debate. It is the texts of past speeches to which appeal will
in due course be made by those who debate the issue of decline
in contemporary oratory. Now Maternus, as a good man, is not so
much interested in that problem at this stage, but he again provides
the key word, *liber*, at 12.6, where it means 'a speech published as a
book'. It is that which unlocks the door to the main point at issue,
why modern oratory has declined. Tacitus wants to answer that
question, because he has his own special understanding of what
is really at issue, and because he believes others, like Pliny and
Quintilian, fell short of grasping the nub. But he also saw that the

question of decline was not by any means the whole story. To a
careerist like Aper or to a good man like Maternus the question was
largely academic. You could prove to Aper that modern oratorical
style was inferior, but he would reply that since it was uniformly so
and since the best of even a bad lot must prevail, then so long as
Rome needed barristers, forensic oratory would secure wealth and
fame to its practitioners. Maternus on the other hand had repudiated oratory in its entirety not because its style was undistinguished,[92]
but because it was morally bankrupt. The opening skirmish then is
arguably designed by Tacitus to circumscribe the importance of the
question posed at the outset; he gives it a perspective so that it does
not necessarily occupy the foreground. Still, it deserves an answer
(but not, we surmise, the answer of a Quintilian), and we must move
from the preliminary debate to a posing of the question. Hints as to
the scope of the question are lodged artfully in that initial debate.
We note Maternus' reference to posterity at 12.5, but should also
have been struck by his expression at 12.3 *perpetuitate famae*, and by
his concluding reference to his own tomb memorial. Fame is an
issue, after all, and its continuance beyond one's death depends
on the right kind of success. We may now recall that we first saw
Maternus sitting in his chamber, book in hand: the book of the
tragedy he had recited the day before, which he intends to publish.
The book is the vehicle of posthumous fame, and it sets the standard
of criticism. This becomes a leitmotiv in the *Dialogus*, and references
to books henceforth become frequent.

To sum up to this point. The opening skirmish is not an irrelevance, nor does it merely set the scene by offering a subsidiary issue
for debate. It is designed to provide alternative models in which the
question of oratorical decline is of no great significance. Tacitus
thus reduced the question to a realistic scale (as he conceived it),
and, thanks to Maternus' casual references to the continuation of
fame and the book as its vehicle, he hints that the problem is in
essence literary. Only if one regards forensic oratory as a literary

92 Martin (1981) 61 says that it was because of oratory's decline that Maternus had transferred his talent and energies to the writing of poetry; the
text of his speech does not support this contention, unless moral decline is
taken to be the point at issue. But Aper never picks up that point.

form does the question of decline arise at all. The stylistic issue had then to be faced. But it would now be inappropriate for Maternus to argue the point, because his convictions clearly lay elsewhere; he might be conceived of as having a view on the issue, but since he has given oratory up (and not for literary reasons) he is not the best man for the job. Hence the need for Messalla.

The arrival of Messalla – and it is perhaps the only artistic weakness in Tacitus' plotting that it is not motivated in any way – resolves the aporia, and gives the argument a push in the direction of its main question. Messalla's deferred arrival is not in the least clumsy.[93] Let us imagine his presence from the outset: how would the question of decline be posed by him or anyone else after the initial (and necessary) debate between Aper and Maternus? Messalla would have seen that it was of secondary importance to both of them. Tacitus has brilliantly arranged it that Messalla should know of the opening debate only what Secundus briefly tells him at 14.2, namely that Aper had been speaking *ad causas agendas* and Maternus *pro carminibus suis*. He has no idea of the details, nor, more importantly, does he know what they have said against each other's propositions. (It is worth noting in this context a piece of Tacitean urbanity, uncovered by Wagenvoort (1926) 428: another reason for keeping Messalla out of the earlier debate was to spare his hearing Maternus' implicit denunciation of the *delatores*, among whom one of the most feared and eminent had been his own half-brother, Regulus.)

---

93 It has often been noted that this 'interruption' has a sort of model in Plato's *Symposium*, where Alcibiades appears late at Agathon's party, but he plausibly explains that he has come to help celebrate his friend's success in the dramatic competition. So not only the interruption but the circumstances of the two works are up to a point similar: both Agathon and Maternus are tragic poets, and the dialogues take place in the poet's home the day after the 'performance' of one of his works (see E. Fraenkel, *Horace* (Oxford 1957) 136 n. 1). Otherwise the tone is quite different: the atmosphere of the *Dialogus* is severe and even worried, at least at the outset. R. Hirzel pointed out in *Der Dialog. Ein literarhistorischer Versuch* (Leipzig 1895) I 220–1 how exceptional it was for a new arrival in a dialogue to change the direction of the conversation: again, Tacitus is different from Plato, whose Alcibiades merely joins in the conversation. For more speculative discussion of the relation between the works see now J. W. Allison, 'Tacitus' Dialogus and Plato's Symposium', in *Hermes* 127 (1999) 479–92.

Messalla thus enters, all unaware of what is at issue, beyond the bare
outline provided by Secundus. He is adroitly but naturally manipu-
lated by Tacitus into broaching a new topic, which becomes the
centrepiece of debate.

Messalla is devoted to literature, and to oratory as a literary form;
he applauds the disputants for occupying themselves not just with
the business of oratory, but with learning and literature. He goes on
to confirm his own predilection for the wider aspects of literary
activity by praising Secundus for writing the biography of a contemporary orator, and thus unconsciously he reflects the lights kindled
by Maternus: he looks forward to more books from Secundus (but
not books of speeches), and of course one writes biographies only of
worthy men whose fame deserves to survive them. Finally, and cru-
cially, he ironically praises Aper for being addicted to merely contemporary practices, and for ignoring the culture of the orators of
old. Aper rises to the taunt, and the main topic is about to emerge in
conversation.

Aper rounds upon Messalla for habitually running down the present out of regard for the past, and this in spite of his own renown,
gloria, in the field of forensic eloquence. We again recall the special
twist Maternus had given to the question of renown, namely its per-
manence. Messalla does not deny his success, but as a literary man
he is constantly driven to compare the present with the past, both in
Greece and in Rome. He finds an unbridgeable gap between the
best now and that of former days, and he expresses the hope that
someone will investigate and give an account of the causes of it
(15.2). He sets no store by contemporary fame: Nicetes Sacerdos
is currently a star in Asia Minor, but he cannot hold a candle to
Demosthenes. This was not the sort of consideration that Aper had
taken into account when he first broached the topic of an orator's
fame, but Maternus had given the topic a push in this direction in
his reply: fame is something that can last, and Secundus' biography
of the orator Julius Africanus shows that men still hope for something more than ephemeral renown. It is that of which Messalla is
so cripplingly aware (cf. 34.5 *magnam illam et <u>duraturam</u> eloquentiae
famam*). His anxiety is nurtured upon books, the monuments of past
excellence to be studied and imitated; they presented a standing

challenge to contemporary speakers to rival their excellence. The classic literature of oratory humbled successors in the field.[94] That feeling will dominate what he has to say in due course, and move the debate to its conclusion.

But, as was pointed out above, Tacitus still needed to defer Messalla's answers. His invention in securing the delay is once again equal to the demand made upon it. Messalla has at last broached the question of causes. He says that he himself has given the matter much thought, and that is a cue for Secundus to invite him to air his views. If this were not to be a debate, Tacitus might have cut to the chase and had Messalla give the answer which now begins at 28. But he constructs the brief conversation in such a way as to bring about a fuller debate of the literary problem.

Messalla engages to offer his answer, provided he is assured of the support of Secundus and Maternus (he clearly anticipates Aper's opposition). This request for support is artfully designed to produce two effects. First, it prepares us for some sort of supplement to Messalla's answer, in fact the concluding remarks of Maternus.[95] Secondly, Maternus, in promising his support, picks up Messalla's presumption that Aper will oppose, and draws attention to how he is already girt for battle. That is Aper's cue. We must at this point not forget that the ethos of the whole dialogue is that of a trial, and thanks to Messalla's intervention the accused turns out to be 'Modern Eloquence'. Now if we moved at once to the causes of decline, we would in effect be taking it for granted, as Messalla insists everyone does (15.2), that decline is an agreed fact. To put that into forensic terms, the accused stands condemned without a hearing. That to a fair-minded Roman was intolerable; a case must be made

94 Antonius in Cic. *De orat.* 2.92 remarked upon the paucity of written speeches in early Roman oratory, so no such anxiety existed for Cicero and his generation. Tacitus certainly felt a similar anxiety as an historian (see p. 11 above).

95 Some commentators used to think that it also paved the way to remarks by Secundus, now lost in the lacuna between 37.8 and 38 (discussed in §12 below). We cannot be sure: Secundus may have been invited to speak at that point, but presumably he declined and handed the task over to Maternus, since the lacuna is now agreed to have been quite short.

for the accused, even if the *patronus* is not himself entirely convinced of its merits.[96] (Tacitus himself, for instance, praised Messalla for standing by the reprehensible Regulus, even though it went against the grain (*Hist.* 4.42.2 *non causam neque reum tueri*); *pietas* demanded the show of loyalty.) Aper therefore, like a conscientious barrister, refuses to let a defendant be condemned without defence. That would be a perversion of justice, as his friends clearly appreciate. The 'prosecution' – Messalla, Maternus, and Secundus – have not of course formally spoken against Aper's 'client', but rather have presumed guilt, so their plea can be taken for granted. In a Roman court, as in ours, defence follows prosecution; Aper does not after all jump the gun, but takes his turn as the defendant's *patronus*, and satisfies the requirements of due process. It is his *continua oratio* which defers Messalla's answer. When Aper has finished, Maternus invites Messalla not to reply to him, but to give his deferred account of the cause of oratorical decline (24.2). Messalla assents, but none the less cannot resist a brief riposte (25–6), and, if the similitude of a trial may be pressed somewhat, this could be regarded as a truncated *altercatio*, which followed the set-piece pleas (see 34.2n.). He has to be reined in by Maternus (27.1). Then and only then do we settle to the proper business of the dialogue, expounding the reasons for decline. This seems to be the large-scale plan that Tacitus adopted for developing his theme within the confines of a basic question-and-answer format. There are in addition some points that should be attended to in the main debates.

The form Aper's argument takes is hardly accidental. Tacitus has him develop the historical issue that in due course Maternus himself will address to conclude their debate. Aper begins not wholly facetiously by questioning the concept of antiquity; he wants to unpack it and show the difficulty of demarcating precisely where the ancients stop and the moderns begin. Take Cicero, whom Maternus had introduced into his first speech (17.2): he died a mere hundred and twenty or so years before the date of their own conversation.

---

96 The point that all the speakers, trained orators to a man, were presenting a case, is elegantly brought out by Luce (1993) 28–31.

Did that really entitle him to be ranged among the ancients? We must here pay attention to the way in which Aper calculates that period of one hundred and twenty years. Cicero was executed in the year Octavian became suffect-consul, 43 BC. Now the whole of Aper's calculation is made up of imperial reigns (and, as was noted above in the discussion of authenticity, Tacitus and Tacitus alone uses the date of his first consulship to mark the beginning of Augustus' rule). This method of calculation is for Aper merely convenient, but for Maternus, listening on the sidelines, it is of central importance, and Tacitus designs it so that Maternus himself at 24.3, when reminding Messalla of his undertaking, adverts to it by recalling that only one hundred and twenty years separate them from Cicero's death. Those years, calculated by imperial reigns, will enable Maternus to answer the question posed by the dialogue, by pointing out that it is the imperial system of government which has wrought a change in oratory at Rome. So Aper unwittingly prepares the way for Maternus, and the second half of the debate is illuminated by this chronological consideration. What Aper meant as a flight of fancy (where in fact does antiquity end?) is taken in earnest by Maternus: the death of Cicero was symbolic of the end, because it happened in the year the principate began, and the change in constitution tolled the knell of traditional oratory.

All three speakers agree that change has taken place, but each assesses its impact differently. Aper remains the careerist, and sees no mileage in aping Cicero nowadays. Whatever his literary merits (which Aper is prepared to denigrate, 22–3), his style would hardly succeed in a modern trial (20). But Aper makes a sort of concession to a theme that is becoming dominant in the debate, namely the survival of one's fame, and, just as in his first speech, he makes a false move, which again it is for Maternus to pick up. In his concluding remarks he refers to the renown his friends may hope to secure from *posteri nostri* (23.6), but that implies comparison, and Maternus, who now seems to be in charge, dismisses this suggestion (24.2): we cannot compare ourselves to the ancients. We might ask at this point if Tacitus himself would agree with that position, at least so far as concerns literary style. It may be that with regard to the literary aspects of oratory he shared somewhat more of Aper's opinion than do the other interlocutors.[97] In that case, the middle pair of speeches would have to be regarded as ending in a draw; aesthetic arguments never admit of complete resolution. However that may be, without more ado Maternus hands the reins to Messalla, who in substance sticks to the literary lines pursued by Aper, but corrects what he feels is a superficial assessment. He accepts the existence of variety in the styles of the past, but insists upon a fundamental *sanitas*, tone of health, common to all of them (25.4). Once again he appeals to the books (25.4, 26.4) which enshrine their achievements. He also makes the damaging point that Aper has adduced no examples by name to set alongside the greats of the past. This is telling just because Messalla himself had commended Secundus for his biography of a contemporary orator, Julius Africanus (14.4). In effect, the literary issue is thus decided, and Messalla can duly address himself to the causes of decline as he sees them.

His explanation presumably owes something to Quintilian's recent publications (recent for Tacitus and his audience, not of course available to the interlocutors in the dialogue). Messalla's tone is hardly optimistic and he simply makes comparisons between child-rearing and educational practice then and now. He does not, in what is left of his speech, suggest that reform is possible or likely. Tacitus is thus arguably playing Messalla off against Quintilian. Their assessment of the inferiority of modern eloquence is correct so far as it goes. But they do not ask themselves what a reformed oratory would be designed to achieve. It is that short-sightedness which Maternus exposes.

In effect Maternus' final speech is a gloss on Aper's appeal to change in the taste of audiences. Aper had not explained why their taste changed; he gave effects, not causes. Maternus goes deeper, and expounds upon the pre-eminence of oratory in the life of the late Republic, when trials were political issues (36–7). That, he hints, is hardly their function nowadays, and there is a consequent lack of significance in the courts. He notes too the damaging changes in legal procedure (38). This undermines what Messalla had said about the need for careful preparation; the modern court has no time for

97 So C. D. N. Costa, 'The "Dialogus"', in T. A. Dorey, ed., *Tacitus* (London 1969) 31.

that (39.3). Maternus too appeals to the classic texts to show that the now irrecoverable forensic procedure of the past encouraged the production of immortal oratorical prose (39.5). After all, it was not entirely a question of that shared health of style that Messalla insisted upon. The legal system then and now has much to do with the issue.

Finally, Maternus resumes the moral argument he had used at the outset in his skirmish with Aper. Much as he admires the oratory of old, he cannot forget that he condemned it in comparison with the Golden Age (12.2). So he condemns it again as the product of strife for which the state and its leaders often paid too dear a price (40.4). Oratory feeds upon human wrong-doing and misfortune. The closer our constitution can draw to perfection, the less we shall need barristers. It is, he tactfully puts it, as much the extinction of political life as the procedural changes in the courts (which the emperors introduced) which have curtailed forensic eloquence.

There is considerable debate about the tone of Maternus' final remarks: a contradiction is detected between his warm acceptance of the new dispensation and his fancied criticism of it in his dramas (though it is hard to see why one should not be able to find fault in what one basically admires). Is he therefore now being ironical?[98] Not necessarily: Maternus openly acknowledges, for instance, that the peace of the principate had been secured at the cost of more than forensic oratory when he deplores on two occasions the loss of free speech, *libertas*, at 13.4 and 27.3. A possible way to reconcile his apparent inconsistency is to remember that this is a debate among trained professional barristers, whose special function is to state their position. Now in both of his speeches Maternus is replying to what has been said before by Aper and by Messalla respectively. His views are therefore coloured by his adversarial position.[99] Messalla praised the society of old, in order to explain the success of its oratory;

98 See above all A. Köhnken, 'Das Problem der Ironie bei Tacitus', *MH* 30 (1973) 32–50; others who urge this view are conveniently listed by S. Döpp, 'Zeitverhältnisse und Kultur im Taciteischen Dialogus', in B. Kühnert *et al.*, eds., *Prinzipat und Kultur im 1. und 2. Jahrhundert* (Bonn 1995) 223 n. 29.

99 This is the approach to the problem persuasively urged by Lier (1996) 58–9 n. 6, and 62–3. His discussion nicely complements that of Luce (1993).

Maternus must show that that success was dearly bought in terms of social upheaval, now happily settled. Irony seems out of place.

Aper has the final word, which he uses to show that he appreciates the force of Maternus' argument. As the party breaks up amid good-will there is the promise of a 'return match'. Aper says he will accuse Maternus before the professional teachers of oratory (42.2): if men agree with Maternus' assessment, then the rhetoricians will be out of a job.

11. CHARACTERS AND CHARACTERIZATION

One of the attractions for Tacitus of the conversational form must have been the opportunity it offered to give verbal characterization to the interlocutors.[100] As an orator himself Tacitus was trained in the practice of ethopoieia, and a dialogue enabled him to indulge that skill (as he would indulge it later in his historical works).[101] We find him therefore providing the reader with clues to the tone of the discourse, e.g. at 4.1 *seueritate*, 11.1 *acrius ... intento ore, remissus et subridens*, 14.1 *concitatus et uelut instinctus*, and 24.1 *uim et ardorem*. The style of the utterances so delivered would have to be appropriate to the characters in that situation.

Nothing beyond what we see in this work is known of two of the chief characters, M. Aper and Curiatius Maternus.[102] Vipstanus

---

100 Gugel (1969) is particularly astute on this matter. See also Heubner *apud* Güngerich (1980) 198–200.

101 For the historical speeches see Syme (1958) 192–3, 316–17, 320, 476, 539.

102 Syme (1979) 701–2 noted some possible relations of Aper. Even Maternus' praenomen is unknown. Norden (1909) 324–5 believed that Tacitus' Maternus was identical with a sophist killed by Domitian in 91, according to Dio, but then gave up that position, on the strength of Gudeman's arguments (Nachträge 19); 'sophist' was hardly the term to use of a senator. J. Stroux, 'Vier Zeugnisse zur römischen Literaturgeschichte der Kaiserzeit I. Maternus, Redner und Dichter', *Philol.* 86 (1931) 338 n. 1 also denied the identity, as did Güngerich (1980), and T. D. Barnes, 'Curiatius Maternus', *Hermes* 109 (1981) 382–4 (though he considered the issue afresh in 'The significance of Tacitus' *Dialogus de Oratoribus*', *HSCP* 90 (1986) 239–43). A. Cameron, 'Tacitus and the date of Curiatius Maternus' death', *CR* 17 (1967) 258–61 revived the identification. But after all, it cannot be urged that the shadow of death reached back over fifteen years, from 91 to 75, the date of the conversation.

Messalla, however, figures in Tacitus' *Historiae*, where he is warmly appreciated (see 14.1n.). Fantham (1996) 198 has rightly styled him a 'Young Fogey'; this appears in his frequent appeals to the historical past, and in his somewhat out-dated pretence that the term 'rhetor' is not yet at home in Latin (that may have done for Cicero's Crassus in *De orat.* 1.52, 3.54, but was hardly true of the reign of Vespasian). His Ciceronianism may perhaps peep out in his use of *infinitus*, a word common in *De oratore*. But he is robust, and not afraid of giving offence (in which he is clearly at one with Maternus). Tacitus praised his eloquence in the *Historiae*, and is bound therefore to give him an impressive style, which is exemplified by the impassioned tone of his argument as it rises to a definition of the true orator at 30.4–5. Messalla deploys a number of rhetorical devices: exclamation (*hercule*), anaphora of *non* and of *ille*, repetition of *ita*, the climactic array of adjectives of number (*multa, plurimis, omnium*), the use of synonymous expression to secure weight (*exundat et exuberat*), the careful balancing of clauses, rhythmic clausulae, and the variety of prepositions (*pro ... ad ... cum*). Tacitus was equal to the task of realistically substantiating the judgement he made of his interlocutors.

Aper is not mentioned by either Pliny or Quintilian, so Tacitus seems to have chosen as the paladin of modern oratory one whose own fame proved ephemeral. None the less, he regards him as one of the most renowned speakers of his day (2.1), and, more importantly, had carried out his *tirocinium fori* under Aper's care, so *pietas* will ensure that any words put into his mouth will display that skill for which he was once noted, and which Tacitus himself aspired to acquire. (It should also be remembered that Aper performs something of the role of Antonius in Cicero's *De oratore*, and of Hortensius in the dialogue named after him; both are robustly practical men, who despised formal doctrine, so Aper has something of that about him (2.2).)

Aper is the champion of the modern day; not surprisingly then he is made to harp upon it emphatically, by using the synonymous doublet *nouus et recens* (cf. 6.5 and 8.1); on the other hand, he alone refers to the antiquated with the word, *oblitteratus* (8.1, 22.5), and, as examples of his brutalist attack, he uses such remarkable critical terms as *impexam* (20.3), *ueternus* (20.5), and *olentia* (22.5) to describe what he does not like. We detect in his speeches a fondness for similes and metaphors, particularly of a military nature, which suggest his own combativeness. His similes are agricultural (6.6), architectural (20.7, 22.4), and biological (21.8). Gudeman (1894) 79 noted a high incidence of synonymous doublets in Aper's speeches, and reckoned they gave his style an unusual fullness of expression. Epigrammatic point was the chief ornament of the rhetorical eloquence of the time, and Aper shows a ready turn of phrase at, e.g., 8.4 *opes, quas facilius inuenies qui uituperet quam qui fastidiat*, and 10.1 *mediocris poetas nemo nouit, bonos pauci* (among many others). His somewhat hectoring manner is revealed by his fondness for the expression 'I won't allow' (5.4, 10.5, 16.4). But perhaps what most especially characterizes Aper is his fondness for the phrase *natus ad* ... (5.4, 6.2, 10.5), and his appeal to Maternus' own nature (10.5, 10.6). Tacitus had stressed in his opening description of Aper his reliance upon his own *ingenium* and *uis naturae* (2.1); these expressions therefore give voice to his inmost beliefs about the importance of being true to one's nature.

It is generally agreed among the other interlocutors that Aper does not hold with the case he urges (so Messalla at 15.2 and Maternus at 24.2, 28.1 <u>omnes sentimus</u>), and Aper neither assents to the charge (as did Antonius at Cic. *De orat.* 2.40) nor, more tellingly, does he deny it.[103] Why does Tacitus stress this point? It may be that the answer lies outside the dialogue itself. We must not forget Tacitus' personal attachment to Aper, who was as it were his 'pupil master'. Loyalty required that he not be put in a bad light. Now since everyone – Tacitus, Fabius Justus, the other characters in the dialogue – are all agreed about the inferiority of modern eloquence, it would suggest a perverted judgement in Aper if he alone stood out against them in finding contemporary oratory the match of antiquity. It was more respectful of his judgement to stress that he was basically in agreement with all the others. His defence of the modern style, an aesthetic issue, is still honourable to him for the reasons given above.

Curiatius Maternus was also, in addition to being a barrister, in

103 So Luce (1993) 19 n. 26; further discussions of Aper's role: W. Deuse, 'Zur advocatus diaboli-Funktion Apers im *Dialogus* und zur Methode ihrer Deutung', *Grazer Beiträge* 3 (1975) 51–68, and the critique of Luce (1993) 19–20; S. Goldberg, 'Appreciating Aper: the defence of modernity in Tacitus' *Dialogus de Oratoribus*', *CQ* 49 (1999) 224–37, esp. 233.

the Senate (cf. 11.4). He is up to a point the mouth-piece of the author himself, but, on the other hand, he may strike the reader as somewhat naive when he speaks, so soon after the reign of Nero, of his confidence that he is secure (13.5–6), or that the Princeps is very wise, as if by definition (41.4). As one given up to poetry, his verbal characterization is also appropriate. He quotes verse (13.5), and his syntax is given lightly poetic colour (13.6). But he too is a man of his time, and like Aper, can use bold similes (36.1), and epigram (13.4 *tantum posse liberti solent*). Since he stands accused of withdrawing from legal practice, he emphasized the notion of the poet's retirement by often deploying words that begin with a *se-* prefix: *securitatem* (11.4), *secretum* (12.1), *secedit* (12.1), and, emphatically, *securum . . . secessum* (13.1).

The essential feature of the conversation is that all of the speakers are friends, and the tone of their discourse is respectful, however candid. Since moreover they are all trained pleaders, they conceive it to be their purpose to present a case (as was noted above on p. 43). This may entail exaggeration, inconsistency, or the deliberate glossing over of weak points. No one character therefore wholly represents the views of Tacitus himself, and any one may speak for an aspect of his complex character. In Aper, for instance, the remarkable expression of the joys of pleading at 6–7 seems to flow from the author's personal experience.[104]

12. THE TRANSMISSION OF THE TEXT

In 1425 a monk of Hersfeld informed Poggio Bracciolini that he knew of a MS containing, among other texts, the *Agricola*, *Germania*, and *Dialogus* – texts the very existence of which no humanist had hitherto suspected, let alone that they might be unrecorded works by Tacitus.[105] Poggio tried long but unsuccessfully to secure the book, but it was not until 1455 that Enoch of Ascoli retrieved it, at the

104 The point is made by W. Den Boer, 'Die gegenseitigen Verhältnisse der Personen im *Dialogus de oratoribus* und die Anschauung des Tacitus', *Mnemosyne* 7 (1939) 193–224, R. Güngerich, *Gnomon* 27 (1955) 441 n. 1, Syme (1958) 109, and R. H. Martin, *CR* 22 (1972) 357.

105 For discussion see Heubner *apud* Güngerich (1980) 186–8, Winterbottom (1986), Römer (1991), and above all Kaster (1992) 1–3, 6–10, with a stemma at 7, Fig. 2.

behest of Pope Nicolas V, who was stocking the newly organized
Vatican library.[106] It is now generally agreed that Enoch kept the
Hersfeld MS, rather than took a copy of it, and that he detached
from it, with a view to separate sale, the *Agricola*; at any rate a MS
found at Jesi in this century contains a ninth-century quaternion of
that text.[107] Though debate has raged over its origin, there seems to
be a developing consensus that this quaternion is indeed part of the
Hersfeld MS;[108] we thus have an idea of the sort of MS from which
the humanist copies of the *Agricola* derived.[109] Unfortunately the rest
of it, which contained the *Dialogus*, was lost, not, however, before
being repeatedly copied. Thus all of the extant MSS upon which this
text is founded date from after 1455.

   The Hersfeld MS, from which the humanists transcribed their own,
was itself heavily corrected by the first scribe, and carried variants
and corrections by a subsequent writer (as we can see from Till's
photocopy), which the transcribers tended to choose between.[110]

---

106 See Sabbadini (1967) I 108–9 for Poggio, and 140–1 for Enoch; cf. *Di-
zionario biografico degli Italiani* XLII 696–7 (though it was wrong to say that the
Hersfeld MS is extant in Leiden). The early correspondence about the Hersfeld MS is tabulated by Merklin (1991) 2257–9.

107 See the account by R. M. Ogilvie in his edn of the *Agricola* (Oxford
1967) 80–7.

108 Römer (1991), among others, is inclined on balance to believe that it is.
If it is not, we are faced with a paradox enunciated by Winterbottom (1986)
411: 'our *Agricola* texts descend from the Jesi manuscript, but our *Germania*
⟨and⟩ *Dialogus* ... texts from the Hersfeldensis: even though the Hersfeldensis
contained the *Agricola* ...' There does seem to be one too many MSS here.

109 See R. Till, *Handschriftliche Untersuchungen zu Tacitus Agricola und Germania (Der Codex Aesinas)* (Berlin–Dahlem 1943), which has a photographic re-
production. The Jesi MS disappeared from sight until very recently, and is
now in Rome (see F. Niutta, 'Sul codice Esinate di Tacito, ora Vitt. Em. 1631
della Biblioteca Nazionale di Roma', in *Quad. Storia* 43 (1996) 173–202).

110 An example: at *Agr.* 32.3 the scribe of the Jesi/Hersfeldensis wrote *itam
deserent ... quam*, but marked the *i* for removal; in the margin, however, the
corrector has written *deserent ... tamquam*, and this reading was accepted by all
the humanist scribes, and so appeared in printed texts until the discovery of
the Jesi MS. Kaster (1992) 33 stresses that the Hersfeldensis and the copy/
copies of it which are the source of all our humanist MSS were very poor
witnesses indeed, and that the author's words can often be recovered only by
conjecture (see further his edn of Suetonius, *De rhetoribus et grammaticis* (Oxford
1995) lviii).

Moreover, our extant MSS were generally produced by scholars whose knowledge of Latin enabled them to correct obvious (and sometimes less obvious) errors as they wrote (for instance Guarnieri, who wrote out additional leaves to supplement the Jesi MS, corrected the text of the *Agricola* on the Hersfeld MS itself at 29.4 *uiridis*). In these circumstances it is very difficult to produce a traditional stemma, demonstrating more or less discrete lines of tradition, and textual critics still argue what shape such a stemma might take.[111] All, however, agree that the extant MSS do not derive directly from the Hersfeldensis, but from lost humanist copies of it.[112] The text required substantial correction, and the first scribes themselves often provided it. Subsequent scholars have cleared away many more of the difficulties, and many of their conjectures have secured almost universal assent. Since the present is not a critical edition, many of those generally accepted corrections are here printed without comment; Güngerich (1980) usually gives an account of the more significant conjectures and the reasons for accepting them, and where there is no comment here, it may be assumed that his arguments are accepted. On the other hand, we must not lose sight of the fact that our text is the product of much philological toil, and so some account is given of difficulties that seem to defy solution, or that raise interesting issues of transmission. (Here regret must be expressed that the late C. O. Brink did not survive to complete his projected edition of this work for the Cambridge Classical Texts and Commentaries series.)

The most serious defect in the text is the lacuna at 35.5, which was noticed by those who first transcribed the text – that is to say, it was already present in the Hersfeld MS; its extent remains the subject of debate, since, if it was large, we might have to suppose that a whole speech, possibly delivered by Secundus, has been

---

111 In addition to Kaster's stemma (see n. 105), most recently C. Brink has discussed the issue in 'A bipartite stemma of Tacitus' *Dialogus de Oratoribus* and some transmitted readings', *ZPE* 102 (1994) 131–52. On the other hand M. D. Reeve has suggested that stemmatics in such a tradition are of less importance than the identity of the scribes, whose writing habits, if identified, might throw more interesting light upon the transmission (cf. *JRS* 90 (2000) 205).

112 See Murgia (1977), and Kaster (1992) 8–10.

lost.[113] On the other hand, if it was small, then we probably have a fair idea of the shape and scope of the overall argument. That the lacuna was not great, six columns, or one-and-a-half folia, was the view of Barwick (1929) 102–6; he regarded the remarks of Decembrio, a humanist who described the length of the lacuna, as erroneous.[114] Murgia, however, observed that Barwick was misled by Gudeman's apparatus,[115] and yet he confessed himself unable to explain why Decembrio had said the lacuna was six folia long in the Hersfeld MS.[116] Still he accepted that the lacuna was short, a single folium, which therefore contained little more than the end of Messalla's speech, and the beginning of Maternus', with some intervening chit-chat, and this now seems to be the orthodoxy.

The present text does not reproduce exactly that of any earlier edition, though it owes much to the editorial work of Winterbottom (1975), whose MSS sigla are adopted, as well as to the critical discussions in the commentary of Güngerich (1980). No apparatus criticus is provided since those of the Oxford Classical Text and of Köstermann's Teubner (1970) provide the main information.

113 P. Steinmetz, 'Secundus im *Dialogus de oratoribus* des Tacitus', *RM* 131 (1988) 342–57 seeks to establish that there was a gap of sufficient length to contain a contribution by Secundus, but the absence of any reference to a speech of his in the closing scene works against that suggestion, which is generally scouted (see Luce (1993) 12 n. 8).

114 He had discussed the issue earlier in 'Der Umfang der Lücke in Tacitus' *Dialogus de oratoribus*', *RM* 68 (1913) 279–85, 638–9.

115 'The length of the lacuna in Tacitus' *Dialogus*', *CSCA* 12 (1979) 221–40; his views are not accepted, however, by R. Häussler, 'Aktuelle Probleme der Dialogus-Rezeption: Echtheitserweise und Lückenumgang', *Philol.* 130 (1986) 75–6. See also Heubner *apud* Güngerich (1980) 193–4, and Merklin (1991) 2271–5.

116 For Decembrio's terminology see S. Rizzo, *Il lessico filologico degli umanisti* (Rome 1973) 33.

CORNELI TACITI
DIALOGVS DE ORATORIBVS

CORNELI TACITI
DIALOGVS DE ORATORIBVS

1.1 Saepe ex me requiris, Iuste Fabi, cur, cum priora saecula tot eminentium oratorum ingeniis gloriaque floruerint, nostra potissimum aetas deserta et laude eloquentiae orbata uix nomen ipsum oratoris retineat; neque enim ita appellamus nisi antiquos, horum autem temporum diserti causidici et aduocati et patroni et quiduis potius quam oratores uocantur. **1.2** cui percontationi tuae respondere, et tam magnae quaestionis pondus excipere ut aut de ingeniis nostris male existimandum ⟨sit⟩ si idem assequi non possumus aut de iudiciis si nolumus, uix hercule auderem si mihi mea sententia proferenda ac non disertissimorum, ut nostris temporibus, hominum sermo repetendus esset, quos eandem hanc quaestionem pertractantes iuuenis admodum audiui. **1.3** ita non ingenio sed memoria et recordatione opus est, ut quae a praestantissimis uiris et excogitata subtiliter et dicta grauiter accepi, cum singuli diuersas quidem sed probabiles causas afferrent, dum formam sui quisque et animi et ingenii redderent, isdem nunc numeris isdemque rationibus prosequar, seruato ordine disputationis; **1.4** neque enim defuit qui diuersam quoque partem susciperet ac multum uexata et irrisa uetustate nostrorum temporum eloquentiam antiquorum ingeniis anteferret.

2.1 Nam postero die quam Curiatius Maternus Catonem recitauerat, cum offendisse potentium animos diceretur, tamquam in eo tragoediae argumento sui oblitus tantum Catonem cogitasset, eaque de re per Vrbem frequens sermo haberetur, uenerunt ad eum M. Aper et Iulius Secundus, celeberrima tum ingenia fori nostri, quos ego utrosque non modo in iudiciis studiose audiebam, sed domi quoque et in publico assectabar mira studiorum cupiditate et quodam ardore iuuenili, ut fabulas quoque eorum et disputationes et arcana semotae dictionis penitus exciperem, quamuis maligne plerique opinarentur nec Secundo promptum esse sermonem et Aprum ingenio potius et ui naturae quam institutione et litteris famam eloquentiae consecutum. **2.2** nam et Secundo purus et pressus et, in quantum satis erat, profluens sermo non defuit, et Aper omni eruditione imbutus contemnebat potius litteras quam nesciebat, tamquam maiorem industriae et laboris gloriam habiturus, si ingenium eius nullis alienarum artium adminiculis inniti uideretur.

3.1 Igitur ut intrauimus cubiculum Materni, sedentem ipsum⟨que⟩ quem pridie recitauerat librum inter manus habentem deprehendimus.

3.2 Tum Secundus 'nihilne te,' inquit, 'Materne, fabulae malignorum terrent quo minus offensas Catonis tui ames? an ideo librum istum apprehendisti ut diligentius retractares et, sublatis si qua prauae interpretationi materiam dederunt, emitteres Catonem non quidem meliorem, sed tamen securiorem?'

3.3 Tum ille: 'leges tu quid Maternus sibi debuerit, et agnosces quae audisti. quod si qua omisit Cato, sequenti recitatione Thyestes dicet: hanc enim tragoediam disposui iam et intra me ipse formaui. atque ideo maturare libri huius editionem festino ut dimissa priore cura nouae cogitationi toto pectore incumbam.'

3.4 'Adeo te tragoediae istae non satiant' inquit Aper 'quo minus omissis orationum et causarum studiis omne tempus modo circa Medeam, ecce nunc circa Thyesten consumas, cum te tot amicorum causae, tot coloniarum et municipiorum clientelae in forum uocent, quibus uix suffeceris, etiam si non nouum tibi ipse negotium importasses, ⟨ut⟩ Domitium et Catonem, id est nostras quoque historias et Romana nomina, Graeculorum fabulis aggregares.'

4.1 Et Maternus: 'perturbarer hac tua seueritate nisi frequens et assidua nobis contentio iam prope in consuetudinem uertisset. nam nec tu agitare et insequi poetas intermittis et

ego, cui desidiam aduocationum obicis, cotidianum hoc patrocinium defendendae aduersus te poeticae exerceo. **4.2** quo
laetor magis oblatum nobis iudicem qui me uel in futurum
uetet uersus facere uel, quod iam pridem opto, sua quoque
auctoritate compellat ut omissis forensium causarum angustiis, in quibus mihi satis superque sudatum est, sanctiorem
illam et augustiorem eloquentiam colam.'

5.1 'Ego uero,' inquit Secundus, 'antequam me iudicem
Aper recuset, faciam quod probi et modesti iudices solent, ut
in iis cognitionibus excusent in quibus manifestum est alteram apud eos partem gratia praeualere. **5.2** quis enim nescit
neminem mihi coniunctiorem esse et usu amicitiae et assiduitate contubernii quam Saleium Bassum, cum optimum uirum
tum absolutissimum poetam? porro si poetica accusatur, non
alium uideo reum locupletiorem.'

5.3 'Securus sit' inquit Aper 'et Saleius Bassus et quisquis
alius studium poeticae et carminum gloriam fouet cum causas
agere non possit. **5.4** [et] ego enim, quatenus arbitrum litis
huius ⟨non⟩ inuenimus, non patiar Maternum societate plurium defendi, sed ipsum solum apud uos arguam, quod natus
ad eloquentiam uirilem et oratoriam, qua parere simul et
tueri amicitias, asciscere necessitudines, complecti prouincias
possit, omittit studium quo non aliud in ciuitate nostra uel ad
utilitatem fructuosius ⟨uel ad uoluptatem dulcius⟩ uel ad dignitatem amplius uel ad Vrbis famam pulchrius uel ad totius
imperii atque omnium gentium notitiam illustrius excogitari
potest.

5.5 'Nam si ad utilitatem uitae omnia consilia factaque
nostra derigenda sunt, quid est tutius quam eam exercere
artem qua semper armatus praesidium amicis, opem alienis,
salutem periclitantibus, inuidis uero et inimicis metum et terrorem ultro ferat, ipse securus et uelut quadam perpetua
potentia ac potestate munitus? **5.6** cuius uis et utilitas rebus
prospere fluentibus aliorum perfugio et tutela intellegitur; sin
proprium periculum increpuit, non hercule lorica et gladius

in acie firmius munimentum quam reo et periclitanti eloquentia, praesidium simul ac telum quo propugnare pariter
et incessere siue in iudicio siue in senatu siue apud principem
possis. **5.7** quid aliud infestis patribus nuper Eprius Marcellus
quam eloquentiam suam opposuit, qua accinctus et minax
disertam quidem sed inexercitatam et eius modi certaminum
rudem Heluidi sapientiam elusit? plura de utilitate non dico,
cui parti minime contra dicturum Maternum meum arbitror.

6.1 'Ad uoluptatem oratoriae eloquentiae transeo, cuius
iucunditas non uno aliquo momento, sed omnibus [prope]
diebus ac prope omnibus horis contingit. **6.2** quid enim dulcius libero et ingenuo animo et ad uoluptates honestas nato
quam uidere plenam semper et frequentem domum suam
concursu splendidissimorum hominum, idque scire non pecuniae, non orbitati, non officii alicuius administrationi, sed sibi
ipsi dari, ipsos quin immo orbos et locupletes et potentes
uenire plerumque ad iuuenem et pauperem ut aut sua aut
amicorum discrimina commendent? **6.3** ullane tanta ingen-
tium opum ac magnae potentiae uoluptas quam spectare
homines ueteres et senes et totius orbis gratia subnixos in
summa rerum omnium abundantia confitentes id quod optimum sit se non habere? **6.4** iam uero qui togatorum comitatus
et egressus, quae in publico species, quae in iudiciis ueneratio,
quod illud gaudium consurgendi assistendique inter tacentes
et in unum conuersos, coire populum et circumfundi coram
et accipere adfectum quemcumque orator induerit! **6.5** uulgata dicentium gaudia et imperitorum quoque oculis expo-
sita percenseo. illa secretiora et tantum ipsis orantibus nota
maiora sunt. siue accuratam meditatamque profert orationem, est quoddam sicut ipsius dictionis ita gaudii pondus et
constantia; siue nouam et recentem curam non sine aliqua tre-
pidatione animi attulerit, ipsa sollicitudo commendat euen-
tum et lenocinatur uoluptati; **6.6** sed extemporalis audaciae atque ipsius temeritatis uel praecipua iucunditas est; nam
⟨in⟩ ingenio quoque, sicut in agro, quamquam alia diu ser-

antur atque elaborentur, gratiora tamen quae sua sponte nascuntur.

7.1 'Equidem, ut de me ipso fatear, non eum diem laetiorem egi quo mihi latus clauus oblatus est, uel quo homo nouus et in ciuitate minime fauorabili natus quaesturam aut tribunatum aut praeturam accepi quam eos quibus mihi pro mediocritate huius quantulaecumque in dicendo facultatis aut reum prospere defendere aut apud centumuiros causam aliquam feliciter orare aut apud principem ipsos illos libertos et procuratores principum tueri et defendere datur. **7.2** tum mihi supra tribunatus et praeturas et consulatus ascendere uideor, tum habere quod si non in animo oritur nec codicillis datur nec cum gratia uenit.

7.3 'Quid? fama et laus cuius artis cum oratorum gloria comparanda est? qui illustriores sunt in Vrbe non solum apud negotiosos et rebus intentos sed etiam apud [iuuenes et] adulescentes, quibus modo recta est indoles et bona spes sui? **7.4** quorum nomina prius parentes liberis suis ingerunt? quos saepius uulgus quoque imperitum et tunicatus hic populus transeuntes nomine uocat et digito demonstrat? aduenae quoque et peregrini iam in municipiis et coloniis suis auditos, cum primum Vrbem attigerunt, requirunt ac uelut agnoscere concupiscunt. **8.1** ausim contendere Marcellum hunc Eprium, de quo modo locutus sum, et Crispum Vibium (libentius enim nouis et recentibus quam remotis et oblitteratis exemplis utor) non minus ⟨notos⟩ esse in extremis partibus terrarum quam Capuae aut Vercellis, ubi nati dicuntur.

8.2 'Nec hoc illis ⟨alterius bis⟩, alterius ter milies sestertium praestat, quamquam ad has ipsas opes possunt uideri eloquentiae beneficio uenisse, ⟨sed⟩ ipsa eloquentia, cuius numen et caelestis uis multa quidem omnibus saeculis exempla edidit ad quam usque fortunam homines ingenii uiribus peruenerint, sed haec, ut supra dixi, proxima et quae non auditu cognoscenda sed oculis spectanda haberemus. **8.3** nam quo sordidius et abiectius nati sunt quoque notabilior

paupertas et angustiae rerum nascentes eos circumsteterunt,
eo clariora et ad demonstrandam oratoriae eloquentiae utilitatem illustriora exempla sunt, quod sine commendatione na-
talium, sine substantia facultatum, neuter moribus egregius,
alter habitu quoque corporis contemptus, per multos iam
annos potentissimi sunt ciuitatis ac, donec libuit, principes
fori, nunc principes in Caesaris amicitia agunt feruntque
cuncta atque ab ipso principe cum quadam reuerentia dili-
guntur, quia Vespasianus, uenerabilis senex et patientissimus
ueri, bene intellegit ceteros quidem amicos suos iis niti quae
ab ipso acceperint quaeque ipsi accumulare et in alios con-
gerere promptum sit, Marcellum autem et Crispum attulisse
ad amicitiam suam quod non a principe acceperint nec accipi
possit. **8.4** minimum inter tot ac tanta locum obtinent imagines ac tituli et statuae, quae neque ipsa tamen negleguntur,
tam hercule quam diuitiae et opes, quas facilius inuenies qui
uituperet quam qui fastidiat. his igitur et honoribus et orna-
mentis et facultatibus refertas domos eorum uidemus qui se
ab ineunte adulescentia causis forensibus et oratorio studio
dederunt.

9.1 'Nam carmina et uersus, quibus totam uitam Maternus
insumere optat (inde enim omnis fluxit oratio), neque dignitatem ullam auctoribus suis conciliant neque utilitates alunt;
uoluptatem autem breuem, laudem inanem et infructuosam
consequuntur. **9.2** licet haec ipsa et quae deinde dicturus sum
aures tuae, Materne, respuant, cui bono est si apud te Agamemnon aut Iason diserte loquitur? quis ideo domum defensus et tibi obligatus redit? quis Saleium nostrum, egregium
poetam uel, si hoc honorificentius est, praeclarissimum ua-
tem, deducit aut salutat aut prosequitur? **9.3** nempe si amicus
eius, si propinquus, si denique ipse in aliquod negotium inciderit, ad hunc Secundum recurret aut ad te, Materne, non
quia poeta es neque ut pro eo uersus facias; hi enim Basso
domi nascuntur, pulchri quidem et iucundi, quorum tamen
hic exitus est, ut cum toto anno, per omnes dies, magna noc-

tium parte unum librum excudit et elucubrauit, rogare ultro
et ambire cogatur ut sint qui dignentur audire, et ne id quidem gratis: nam et domum mutuatur et auditorium exstruit
et subsellia conducit et libellos dispergit. **9.4** et ut beatissimus
recitationem eius euentus prosequatur, omnis illa laus intra
unum aut alterum diem, uelut in herba uel flore praecerpta,
ad nullam certam et solidam peruenit frugem, nec aut amicitiam inde refert aut clientelam aut mansurum in animo
cuiusquam beneficium, sed clamorem uagum et uoces inanes
et gaudium uolucre. **9.5** laudauimus nuper ut miram et ex-
imiam Vespasiani liberalitatem, quod quingenta sestertia
Basso donasset. pulchrum id quidem, indulgentiam principis
ingenio mereri: quanto tamen pulchrius, si ita res familiaris
exigat, se ipsum colere, suum genium propitiare, suam ex-
periri liberalitatem! **9.6** adice quod poetis, si modo dignum
aliquid elaborare et efficere uelint, relinquenda conuersatio
amicorum et iucunditas Vrbis, deserenda cetera officia utque
ipsi dicunt, in nemora et lucos, id est in solitudinem, re-
cedendum est.

    10.1 'Ne opinio quidem et fama, cui soli seruiunt et quod
unum esse pretium omnis laboris sui fatentur, aeque poetas
quam oratores sequitur, quoniam mediocres poetas nemo
nouit, bonos pauci. **10.2** quando enim rarissimarum recita-
tionum fama in totam Vrbem penetrat, nedum ut per tot
prouincias innotescat? quotus quisque, cum ex Hispania uel
Asia, ne quid de Galliis nostris loquar, in Vrbem uenit, Saleium Bassum requirit? atque adeo si quis requirit, ut semel
uidit, transit et contentus est, ut si picturam aliquam uel statuam uidisset.

    10.3 'Neque hunc meum sermonem sic accipi uolo tam-
quam eos quibus natura sua oratorium ingenium denegauit
deterream a carminibus, si modo in hac studiorum parte
oblectare otium et nomen inserere possunt famae. **10.4** ego
uero omnem eloquentiam omnesque eius partes sacras et
uenerabiles puto, nec solum coturnum uestrum aut heroici

carminis sonum, sed lyricorum quoque iucunditatem et ele-
gorum lasciuias et iamborum amaritudinem et epigrammatum lusus et quamcumque aliam speciem eloquentia habeat
anteponendam ceteris aliarum artium studiis credo. **10.5** sed
tecum mihi, Materne, res est, quod, cum natura tua in ipsam
arcem eloquentiae ferat, errare mauis et summa adept⟨ur⟩us
in leuioribus subsistis. ut si in Graecia natus esses, ubi ludicras quoque artes exercere honestum est, ac tibi Nicostrati
robur ac uires di dedissent, non paterer immanes illos et
ad pugnam natos lacertos leuitate iaculi aut iactu disci
uanescere, sic nunc te ab auditoriis et theatris in Forum et ad
causas et ad uera proelia uoco, cum praesertim ne ad illud
quidem confugere possis quod plerisque patrocinatur, tamquam minus obnoxium sit offendere poetarum quam oratorum studium: **10.6** efferuescit enim uis pulcherrimae naturae
tuae, nec pro amico aliquo, sed, quod periculosius est, pro
Catone offendis. nec excusatur offensa necessitudine officii
aut fide aduocationis aut fortuitae et subitae dictionis impetu:
meditatus uideris [aut] elegisse personam notabilem et cum
auctoritate dicturam. **10.7** sentio quid responderi possit: hinc
ingentes †ex his† assensus, haec in ipsis auditoriis praecipue
laudari et mox omnium sermonibus ferri. tolle igitur quietis
et securitatis excusationem, cum tibi suma aduersarium super-
iorem. **10.8** nobis satis sit priuatas et nostri saeculi con-
trouersias tueri, in quibus [expressis] si quando necesse sit
pro periclitante amico potentiorum aures offendere et probata sit fides et libertas excusata.'

11.1 Quae cum dixisset Aper acrius, ut solebat, et intento
ore, remissus et subridens Maternus 'parantem' inquit 'me
non minus diu accusare oratores quam Aper laudauerat (fore
enim arbitrabar ut a laudatione eorum digressus detrectaret
poetas atque carminum studium prosterneret) arte quadam
mitigauit, concedendo iis qui causas agere non possent ut
uersus facerent. **11.2** ego autem sicut in causis agendis efficere aliquid et eniti fortasse possum, ita recitatione trag-

oediarum. et ingredi famam auspicatus sum, cum quidem im⟨perante⟩ Nerone improbam et studiorum quoque sacra profanantem Vatini potentiam fregi; hodie si quid in nobis notitiae ac nominis est, magis arbitror carminum quam orationum gloria partum. **11.3** ac iam me deiungere a forensi labore constitui, nec comitatus istos et egressus aut frequentiam salutationum concupisco, non magis quam aera et imagines, quae etiam me nolente in domum meam irruperunt. **11.4** nam statum cuiusque ac securitatem melius innocentia tuetur quam eloquentia; nec uereor ne mihi umquam uerba in senatu nisi pro alterius discrimine facienda sint.

12.1 'Nemora uero et luci et secretum ipsum, quod Aper increpabat, tantam mihi afferunt uoluptatem ut inter praecipuos carminum fructus numerem quod non in strepitu nec sedente ante ostium litigatore nec inter sordes ac lacrimas reorum componuntur, sed secedit animus in loca pura atque innocentia fruiturque sedibus sacris. **12.2** haec eloquentiae primordia, haec penetralia; hoc primum habitu cultuque commoda mortalibus in illa casta et nullis contacta uitiis pectora influxit: sic oracula loquebantur. nam lucrosae huius et sanguinantis eloquentiae usus recens et ex malis moribus natus atque, ut tu dicebas, Aper, in locum teli repertus. **12.3** ceterum felix illud et, ut more nostro loquar, aureum saeculum, et oratorum et criminum inops, poetis et uatibus abundabat, qui bene facta canerent, non qui male admissa defenderent.

12.4 'Nec ullis aut gloria maior aut augustior honor primum apud deos, quorum proferre responsa et interesse epulis ferebantur, deinde apud illos dis genitos sacrosque reges, inter quos neminem causidicum sed Orphea et Linum ac, si introspicere altius uelis, ipsum Apollinem accepimus. **12.5** uel si haec fabulosa nimis et composita uidentur, illud certe mihi concedes, Aper, non minorem honorem Homero quam Demostheni apud posteros, nec angustioribus terminis famam Euripidis aut Sophoclis quam Lysiae aut Hyperidis includi.

12.6 plures hodie reperies qui Ciceronis gloriam quam qui Vergili detrectent; nec ullus Asini aut Messallae liber tam illustris est quam Medea Ouidi aut Vari Thyestes.

13.1 'Ac ne fortunam quidem uatum et illud felix contubernium comparare timuerim cum inquieta et anxia oratorum uita. licet illos certamina et pericula sua ad consulatus euexerint, malo securum et quietum Vergili secessum, in quo tamen neque apud diuum Augustum gratia caruit neque apud populum Romanum notitia. **13.2** testes Augusti epistulae, testis ipse populus, qui auditis in theatro Vergili uersibus surrexit uniuersus et forte praesentem spectantemque Vergilium ueneratus est sic quasi Augustum. **13.3** ne nostris quidem temporibus Secundus Pomponius Afro Domitio uel dignitate uitae uel perpetuitate famae cesserit. **13.4** nam Crispus iste et Marcellus, ad quorum exempla me uocas, quid habent in hac sua fortuna concupiscendum: quod timent, an quod timentur? quod, cum cotidie aliquid rogentur, ii quibus praestant indignantur? quod alligati omni adulatione nec imperantibus umquam satis serui uidentur nec nobis satis liberi? quae haec summa eorum potentia est? tantum posse liberti solent.

13.5 ' "Me uero dulces", ut Vergilius ait, "Musae", remotum a sollicitudinibus et curis et necessitate cotidie aliquid contra animum faciendi, in illa sacra illosque fontes ferant; nec insanum ultra et lubricum forum famamque fallacem trepidus experiar. **13.6** non me fremitus salutantium nec anhelans libertus excitet, nec incertus futuri testamentum pro pignore scribam, nec plus habeam quam quod possim cui uelim relinquere, quandoque [enim] fatalis et meus dies ueniat; statuarque tumulo non maestus et atrox, sed hilaris et coronatus, et pro memoria mei nec consulat quisquam nec roget.'

14.1 Vixdum finierat Maternus, concitatus et uelut instinctus, cum Vipstanus Messalla cubiculum eius ingressus est, suspicatusque ex ipsa intentione singulorum altiorem inter.

eos esse sermonem 'num parum tempestiuus' inquit 'inter-
ueni secretum consilium et causae alicuius meditationem
tractantibus?'

14.2 'Minime, minime,' inquit Secundus, 'atque adeo uellem maturius interuenisses; delectasset enim te et Apri nostri
accuratissimus sermo, cum Maternum ut omne ingenium ac
studium suum ad causas agendas conuerteret exhortatus est,
et Materni pro carminibus suis laeta utque poetas defendi dec-
ebat audentior et poetarum quam oratorum similior oratio.'

14.3 'Me uero' inquit '[et] sermo iste infinita uoluptate
adfecisset, atque id ipsum delectat, quod uos, uiri optimi et
⟨optimi⟩ temporum nostrorum oratores, non forensibus tantum negotiis et declamatorio studio ingenia uestra exercetis,
sed eius modi etiam disputationes assumitis quae et ingenium
alunt et eruditionis ac litterarum iucundissimum oblectamen-
tum cum uobis qui illa disputatis adferunt, tum etiam iis ad
quorum aures peruenerint. **14.4** itaque hercule non minus
probari uideo in te, Secunde, quod Iuli Africani uitam componendo spem hominibus fecisti plurium eius modi librorum,
quam in Apro quod nondum ab scholasticis controuersiis re-
cessit et otium suum mauult nouorum rhetorum more quam
ueterum oratorum consumere.'

15.1 Tum Aper: 'non desinis, Messalla, uetera tantum et
antiqua mirari, nostrorum autem temporum studia irridere
atque contemnere. nam hunc tuum sermonem saepe excepi,
cum oblitus et tuae et fratris tui eloquentiae neminem hoc
tempore oratorem esse contenderes [antiquis], eo credo aud-
acius quod malignitatis opinionem non uerebaris, cum eam
gloriam quam tibi alii concedunt ipse tibi denegares.'

15.2 'Neque illius' inquit 'sermonis mei paenitentiam ago,
neque aut Secundum aut Maternum aut te ipsum, Aper,
quamquam interdum in contrarium disputes, aliter sentire
credo. ac uelim impetratum ab aliquo uestrum ut causas
huius infinitae differentiae scrutetur ac reddat, quas mecum
ipse plerumque conquiro. **15.3** et quod quibusdam solacio est

mihi auget quaestionem, quia uideo etiam Graiis accidisse ut longius absit ⟨ab⟩ Aeschine et Demosthene Sacerdos iste Nicetes et si quis alius Ephesum uel Mytilenas concentu scholasticorum et clamoribus quatit quam Afer aut Africanus aut uos ipsi a Cicerone aut Asinio recessistis.'

16.1 'Magnam' inquit Secundus 'et dignam tractatu quaestionem mouisti. sed quis eam iustius explicabit quam tu, ad cuius summam eruditionem et praestantissimum ingenium cura quoque et meditatio accessit?'

16.2 Et Messalla 'aperiam' inquit 'cogitationes meas, si illud a uobis ante impetrauero, ut uos quoque sermonem hunc nostrum adiuuetis.'

16.3 'Pro duobus' inquit Maternus 'promitto; nam et ego et Secundus exsequemur eas partes quas intellexerimus te non tam omisisse quam nobis reliquisse. Aprum enim solere dissentire et tu paulo ante dixisti et ipse satis manifestus est iam dudum in contrarium accingi nec aequo animo perferre hanc nostram pro antiquorum laude concordiam.'

16.4 'Non enim' inquit Aper 'inauditum et indefensum saeculum nostrum patiar hac uestra conspiratione damnari. sed hoc primum interrogabo, quos uocetis antiquos, quam oratorum aetatem significatione ista determinetis. **16.5** ego enim cum audio antiquos, quosdam ueteres et olim natos intellego, ac mihi uersantur ante oculos Vlixes et Nestor, quorum aetas mille fere et trecentis annis saeculum nostrum antecedit; uos autem Demosthenen et Hyperiden profertis, quos satis constat Philippi et Alexandri temporibus floruisse, ita tamen ut utrique superstites essent. **16.6** ex quo apparet non multo plures quam trecentos annos interesse inter nostram et Demosthenis aetatem. quod spatium temporis si ad infirmitatem corporum nostrorum referas, fortasse longum uideatur, si ad naturam saeculorum ac respectum immensi huius aeui, perquam breue et in proximo est. **16.7** nam si, ut Cicero in Hortensio scribit, is est magnus et uerus annus quo

eadem positio caeli siderumque quae cum maxime est rursum
existet, isque annus horum quos nos uocamus annorum duo-
decim milia nongentos quinquaginta quattuor complectitur,
incipit Demosthenes [uidetur], quem uos ueterem et antiquum fingitis, non solum eodem anno quo nos, sed etiam
eodem mense extitisse.

17.1 'Sed transeo ad Latinos oratores, in quibus non Menenium ut puto Agrippam, qui potest uideri antiquus, nostrorum
temporum disertis anteponere soletis, sed Ciceronem et Caesarem et Caelium et Caluum et Brutum et Asinium et Messal-
lam: quos quid antiquis temporibus potius adscribatis quam
nostris, non uideo. **17.2** nam ut de Cicerone ipso loquar,
Hirtio nempe et Pansa consulibus, ut Tiro libertus eius scrip-
sit, VII idus ⟨Decembres⟩ occisus est, quo anno diuus Augustus in locum Pansae et Hirti se et Q. Pedium consules
suffecit. **17.3** statue sex et quinquaginta annos, quibus mox
diuus Augustus rem publicam rexit; adice Tiberi tres et
uiginti, et prope quadriennium Gai, ac bis quaternos denos
Claudi et Neronis annos, atque illum Galbae et Othonis et
Vitelli longum et unum annum, ac sextam iam felicis huius
principatus stationem qua Vespasianus rem publicam fouet;
centum et uiginti anni ab interitu Ciceronis in hunc diem
colliguntur, unius hominis aetas. **17.4** nam ipse ego in Bri-
tannia uidi senem qui se fateretur ei pugnae interfuisse qua
Caesarem inferentem arma Britanni arcere litoribus et pel-
lere aggressi sunt. ita si eum, qui armatus C. Caesari restitit,
uel captiuitas uel uoluntas uel fatum aliquod in Vrbem pertra-
xisset, aeque idem et Caesarem ipsum et Ciceronem audire
potuit et nostris quoque actionibus interesse. **17.5** proximo
quidem congiario ipsi uidistis plerosque senes qui se a diuo
quoque Augusto semel atque iterum accepisse congiarium
narrabant; **17.6** ex quo colligi potest et Coruinum ab illis
et Asinium audiri potuisse; nam Asinius in medium usque
Augusti principatum, Coruinus paene ad extremum durauit:

ne diuidatis saeculum et antiquos ac ueteres uocitetis oratores quos eorundem hominum aures agnoscere ac uelut coniungere et copulare potuerunt.

18.1 'Haec ideo praedixi ut si qua ex horum oratorum fama gloriaque laus temporibus acquiritur, eam docerem in medio sitam et propiorem nobis quam Seruio Galbae aut C. Carboni quosque alios merito antiquos uocauerimus; sunt enim horridi et impoliti et rudes et informes et quos utinam nulla parte imitatus esset Caluus uester aut Caelius aut ipse Cicero. **18.2** agere enim fortius iam et audentius uolo si illud ante praedixero, mutari cum temporibus formas quoque et genera dicendi. sic Catoni seni comparatus C. Gracchus plenior et uberior, sic Graccho politior et ornatior Crassus, sic utroque distinctior et urbanior et altior Cicero, Cicerone mitior Coruinus et dulcior et in uerbis magis elaboratus. **18.3** nec quaero quis disertissimus: hoc interim probasse contentus sum, non esse unum eloquentiae uultum, sed ⟨in⟩ illis quoque quos uocatis antiquos plures species deprehendi, nec statim deterius esse quod diuersum est, uitio autem malignitatis humanae uetera semper in laude, praesentia in fastidio esse. **18.4** num dubitamus inuentos qui pro Catone Appium Caecum magis mirarentur? satis constat ne Ciceroni quidem obtrectatores defuisse, quibus inflatus et tumens nec satis pressus, sed supra modum exsultans et superfluens et parum Atticus uideretur. **18.5** legistis utique et Calui et Bruti ad Ciceronem missas epistulas, ex quibus facile est deprehendere Caluum quidem Ciceroni uisum exsanguem et attritum, Brutum autem otiosum atque diiunctum; rursusque Ciceronem a Caluo quidem male audisse tamquam solutum et eneruem, a Bruto autem, ut ipsius uerbis utar, tamquam "fractum atque elumbem". **18.6** si me interroges, omnes mihi uidentur uerum dixisse, sed mox ad singulos ueniam, nunc mihi cum uniuersis negotium est.

19.1 'Nam quatenus antiquorum admiratores hunc uelut terminum antiquitatis constituere solent qui ⟨...⟩ usque ad

Cassium ⟨...⟩ quem reum faciunt, quem primum adfirmant flexisse ab illa uetere atque derecta dicendi uia, non infirmitate ingenii nec inscitia litterarum transtulisse se ad illud dicendi genus contendo, sed iudicio et intellectu. **19.2** uidit namque, ut paulo ante dicebam, cum condicione temporum et diuersitate aurium formam quoque ac speciem orationis esse mutandam. facile perferebat prior ille populus, ut imperitus et rudis, impeditissimarum orationum spatia atque id ipsum laudabat, si dicendo quis diem eximeret. **19.3** iam uero longa principiorum praeparatio et narrationis alte repetita series et multarum diuisionum ostentatio et mille argumentorum gradus et quidquid aliud aridissimis Hermagorae et Apollodori libris praecipitur, in honore erat; quod si quis odoratus philosophiam uideretur atque ex ea locum aliquem orationi suae insereret, in caelum laudibus ferebatur. **19.4** nec mirum; erant enim haec noua et incognita, et ipsorum quoque oratorum paucissimi praecepta rhetorum aut philosophorum placita cognouerant. **19.5** at hercule peruulgatis iam omnibus, cum uix in corona quisquam assistat quin elementis studiorum, etsi non instructus, at certe imbutus sit, nouis et exquisitis eloquentiae itineribus opus est, per quae orator fastidium aurium effugiat, utique apud eos iudices qui ui et potestate, non iure et legibus cognoscunt, nec accipiunt tempora sed constituunt, nec exspectandum habent oratorem dum illi libeat de ipso negotio dicere, sed saepe ultro admonent atque alio transgredientem reuocant et festinare se testantur. **20.1** quis nunc feret oratorem de infirmitate ualetudinis suae praefantem, qualia sunt fere principia Coruini? quis quinque in Verrem libros exspectabit? quis ⟨de⟩ exceptione et formula perpetietur illa immensa uolumina quae pro M. Tullio aut Aulo Caecina legimus? **20.2** praecurrit hoc tempore iudex dicentem et, nisi aut cursu argumentorum aut colore sententiarum aut nitore et cultu descriptionum inuitatus et corruptus est, auersatur [dicentem]. **20.3** uulgus quoque assistentium et affluens et uagus auditor assueuit iam

exigere laetitiam et pulchritudinem orationis, nec magis perfert in iudiciis tristem et impexam antiquitatem quam si quis
in scaena Rosci aut Turpionis [aut] Ambiui exprimere gestus uelit. **20.4** iam uero iuuenes et in ipsa studiorum incude
positi, qui profectus sui causa oratores sectantur, non solum
audire sed etiam referre domum aliquid illustre et dignum
memoria uolunt, traduntque in uicem ac saepe in colonias ac
prouincias suas scribunt, siue sensus aliquis arguta et breui
sententia effulsit, siue locus exquisito et poetico cultu enituit.
20.5 exigitur enim iam ab oratore etiam poeticus decor, non
Acci aut Pacuui ueterno inquinatus, sed ex Horati et Vergili
et Lucani sacrario prolatus. **20.6** horum igitur auribus et
iudiciis obtemperans nostrorum oratorum aetas pulchrior et
ornatior exstitit. neque ideo minus efficaces sunt orationes
nostrae quia ad aures iudicantium cum uoluptate perueniunt.
20.7 quid enim si infirmiora horum temporum templa credas
quia non rudi caemento et informibus tegulis exstruuntur sed
marmore nitent et auro radiantur?

21.1 'Equidem fatebor uobis simpliciter me in quibusdam
antiquorum uix risum, in quibusdam autem uix somnum tenere. nec unum de populo †ganuti aut atti de furnio et coranio† quique alii in eodem ualetudinario haec ossa et hanc
maciem probant: ipse mihi Caluus, cum unum et uiginti ut
puto libros reliquerit, uix in una aut altera oratiuncula satis
facit. **21.2** nec dissentire ceteros ab hoc meo iudicio uideo:
quotus enim quisque Calui in Asicium aut in Drusum legit? at
hercule in omnium studiosorum manibus uersantur accusationes quae in Vatinium inscribuntur, ac praecipue secunda
ex his oratio; est enim uerbis ornata et sententiis, auribus
iudicum accommodata, ut scias ipsum quoque Caluum intellexisse quid melius esset, nec uoluntatem ei, quo ⟨minus⟩
sublimius et cultius diceret, sed ingenium ac uires defuisse.

21.3 'Quid? ex Caelianis orationibus nempe eae placent,
siue uniuersae ⟨siue⟩ partes earum, in quibus nitorem et altitudinem horum temporum agnoscimus. **21.4** sordes autem

illae uerborum et hians compositio et inconditi sensus redolent antiquitatem; nec quemquam adeo antiquarium puto ut Caelium ex ea parte laudet qua antiquus est.

21.5 'Concedamus sane C. Caesari ut propter magnitudinem cogitationum et occupationes rerum minus in eloquentia effecerit quam diuinum eius ingenium postulabat, tam hercule quam Brutum philosophiae suae relinquamus; nam in orationibus minorem esse fama sua etiam admiratores eius fatentur. **21.6** nisi forte quisquam aut Caesaris pro Deci⟨di⟩o Samnite aut Bruti pro Deiotaro rege ceterosque eiusdem lentitudinis ac teporis libros legit, nisi qui et carmina eorundem miratur: fecerunt enim et carmina et in bibliothecas rettulerunt, non melius quam Cicero, sed felicius, quia illos fecisse pauciores sciunt.

21.7 'Asinius quoque, quamquam propioribus temporibus natus sit, uidetur mihi inter Menenios et Appios studuisse. Pacuuium certe et Accium non solum tragoediis sed etiam orationibus suis expressit, adeo durus et siccus est. **21.8** oratio autem, sicut corpus hominis, ea demum pulchra est in qua non eminent uenae nec ossa numerantur, sed temperatus ac bonus sanguis implet membra et exsurgit toris ipsosque neruos rubor tingit et decor commendat. **21.9** nolo Coruinum insequi, quia non per ipsum stetit quo minus laetitiam nitoremque nostrorum temporum exprimeret; uidemus enim quam iudicio eius uis aut animi aut ingenii suffecerit.

22.1 'Ad Ciceronem uenio, cui eadem pugna cum aequalibus suis fuit quae mihi uobiscum est: illi enim antiquos mirabantur, ipse suorum temporum eloquentiam anteponebat; nec ulla re magis eiusdem aetatis oratores praecurrit quam iudicio. **22.2** primus enim excoluit orationem, primus et uerbis delectum adhibuit et compositioni artem, locos quoque laetiores attemptauit et quasdam sententias inuenit, utique in iis orationibus quas senior iam et iuxta finem uitae composuit, id est postquam magis profecerat usuque et experimentis didicerat quod optimum dicendi genus esset. **22.3** nam

priores eius orationes non carent uitiis antiquitatis: lentus est
in principiis, longus in narrationibus, otiosus circa excessus;
tarde commouetur, raro incalescit; pauci sensus apte et cum
quodam lumine terminantur. nihil excerpere, nihil referre
possis, et uelut in rudi aedificio firmus sane paries et duratu-
rus, sed non satis expolitus et splendens. **22.4** ego autem oratorem, sicut locupletem ac lautum patrem familiae, non eo
tantum uolo tecto tegi quod imbrem ac uentum arceat sed
etiam quod uisum et oculos delectet, non ea solum instrui
supellectile quae necessariis usibus sufficiat, sed sit in apparatu eius et aurum et gemmae, ut sumere in manus et aspic-
ere saepius libeat. **22.5** quaedam uero procul arce⟨a⟩ntur ut
iam oblitterata et olentia; nullum sit uerbum uelut rubigine
infectum, nulli sensus tarda et inerti structura in morem
annalium componantur; fugitet foedam et insulsam scurrilitatem, uariet compositionem nec omnes clausulas uno et eodem
modo determinet.

23.1 'Nolo irridere "rotam Fortunae" et "ius uerrinum" et
illud tertio quoque sensu in omnibus orationibus pro sententia positum "esse uideatur". nam et haec inuitus rettuli et
plura omisi, quae tamen sola mirantur atque exprimunt ii qui
se antiquos oratores uocant. **23.2** neminem nominabo, genus
hominum significasse contentus; sed uobis utique uersantur
ante oculos isti qui Lucilium pro Horatio et Lucretium pro
Vergilio legunt, quibus eloquentia Aufidi Bassi aut Seruili
Noniani ex comparatione Sisennae aut Varronis sordet, qui
rhetorum nostrorum commentarios fastidiunt oderunt, Calui
mirantur, **23.3** quos more prisco apud iudicem fabulantes
non auditores sequuntur, non populus audit, uix denique
litigator perpetitur, adeo maesti et inculti illam ipsam quam
iactant sanitatem non firmitate sed ieiunio consequuntur.
23.4 porro ne in corpore quidem ualetudinem medici probant quae animi anxietate contingit. parum est aegrum non
esse: fortem et laetum et alacrem uolo. prope est ab infirmitate in quo sola sanitas laudatur.

23.5 'Vos uero, disertissimi ⟨uiri⟩, ut potestis, ut facitis, illustrate saeculum nostrum pulcherrimo genere dicendi. **23.6** nam et te, Messalla, uideo laetissima quaeque antiquorum imitantem, et uos, Materne ac Secunde, ita grauitati sensuum nitorem et cultum uerborum miscetis, ea electio inuentionis, is ordo rerum, ea quotiens causa poscit ubertas, ea quotiens permittitur breuitas, is compositionis decor, ea sententiarum planitas est, sic exprimitis affectus, sic libertatem temperatis, ut etiam si nostra iudicia malignitas et inuidia tardauerit, uerum de uobis dicturi sint posteri nostri.'

24.1 Quae cum Aper dixisset, 'agnoscitisne' inquit Maternus 'uim et ardorem Apri nostri? quo torrente, quo impetu saeculum nostrum defendit! quam copiose ac uarie uexauit antiquos! quanto non solum ingenio ac spiritu sed etiam eruditione et arte ab ipsis mutuatus est per quae mox ipsos incesseret! **24.2** tuum tamen, Messalla, promissum immutasse non debet. neque enim defensorem antiquorum exigimus nec quemquam nostrum, quamquam modo laudati sumus, iis quos insectatus est Aper comparamus. ac ne ipse quidem ita sentit, sed more uetere et a nostris philosophis saepe celebrato sumpsit sibi contra dicendi partes. **24.3** igitur exprome nobis non laudationem antiquorum (satis enim illos fama sua laudat), sed causas cur in tantum ab eloquentia eorum recesserimus, cum praesertim centum et uiginti annos ab interitu Ciceronis in hunc diem effici ratio temporum collegerit.'

25.1 Tum Messalla: 'sequar praescriptam a te, Materne, formam; neque enim diu contra dicendum est Apro, qui primum ut opinor nominis controuersiam mouit, tamquam parum proprie antiqui uocarentur quos satis constat ante centum annos fuisse. **25.2** mihi autem de uocabulo pugna non est; siue illos antiquos siue maiores siue quo alio mauult nomine appellet, dummodo in confesso sit eminentiorem illorum temporum eloquentiam fuisse.

'Ne illi quidem parti sermonis eius repugno, qua fatetur plures formas dicendi etiam isdem saeculis, nedum diuersis

extitisse. **25.3** sed quo modo inter Atticos oratores primae
Demostheni tribuuntur, proximum [autem] locum Aeschines
et Hyperides et Lysias et Lycurgus obtinent, omnium autem
concessu haec oratorum aetas maxime probatur, sic apud nos
Cicero quidem ceteros eorundem temporum disertos ante-
cessit, Caluus autem et Asinius et Caesar et Caelius et Brutus
iure et prioribus et sequentibus anteponuntur. **25.4** nec refert
quod inter se specie differunt, cum genere consentiant. astrictior Caluus, neruosior Asinius, splendidior Caesar, amarior
Caelius, grauior Brutus, uehementior et plenior et ualentior
Cicero: omnes tamen eandem sanctitatem eloquentiae seruant, ut si omnium pariter libros in manum sumpseris, scias
quamuis in diuersis ingeniis esse quandam iudicii ac uoluntatis similitudinem et cognationem.

   25.5 'Nam quod in uicem se obtrectauerunt (et sunt aliqua
epistulis eorum inserta, ex quibus mutua malignitas deteg-
itur), non est oratorum uitium, sed hominum. **25.6** nam et
Caluum et Asinium et ipsum Ciceronem credo solitos [et
inuidere] et liuere et ceteris humanae infirmitatis uitiis adfici;
solum inter hos arbitror Brutum non malignitate nec inuidia
sed simpliciter et ingenue iudicium animi sui detexisse. an
ille Ciceroni inuideret qui mihi uidetur ne Caesari quidem
inuidisse?

   25.7 'Quod ad Seruium Galbam et C. Laelium attinet et si
quos alios antiqu⟨i⟩orum agitare ⟨Aper⟩ non destitit, non
exigit defensorem, cum fatear quaedam eloquentiae eorum
ut nascenti adhuc nec satis adultae defuisse. **26.1** ceterum
si omisso optimo illo et perfectissimo genere eloquentiae elig-
enda sit forma dicendi, malim hercule C. Gracchi impetum
aut L. Crassi maturitatem quam calamistros Maecenatis aut
tinnitus Gallionis, adeo melius est orationem uel hirta toga
induere quam fucatis et meretriciis uestibus insignire. **26.2**
neque enim oratorius iste, immo hercule ne uirilis quidem
cultus est quo plerique temporum nostrorum actores ita
utuntur ut lasciuia uerborum et leuitate sententiarum et

licentia compositionis histrionales modos exprimant; **26.3** quodque uix auditu fas esse debeat, laudis et gloriae et ingenii loco plerique iactant cantari saltarique commentarios suos. unde oritur illa foeda et praepostera, sed tamen frequens †sicut his clam et† exclamatio, ut oratores nostri tenere dicere, histriones diserte saltare dicantur.

26.4 'Equidem non negauerim Cassium Seuerum, quem solum Aper noster nominare ausus est, si iis comparetur qui postea fuerunt, posse oratorem uocari, quamquam in magna parte librorum suorum plus bilis habeat quam sanguinis. primus enim contempto ordine rerum, omissa modestia ac pudore uerborum, ipsis etiam quibus utitur armis incompositus et studio feriendi plerumque deiectus, non pugnat, sed rixatur. **26.5** ceterum, ut dixi, sequentibus comparatus et uarietate eruditionis et lepore urbanitatis et ipsarum uirium robore multum ceteros superat.

'Quorum neminem Aper nominare et uelut in aciem educere sustinuit. **26.6** ego autem exspectabam ut incusato Asinio et Caelio et Caluo aliud nobis agmen produceret pluresque uel certe totidem nominaret, ex quibus alium Ciceroni, alium Caesari, singulis deinde singulos opponeremus. **26.7** nunc detrectasse nominatim antiquos oratores contentus neminem sequentium laudare ausus est nisi in publicum et in commune, ueritus credo ne multos offenderet, si paucos excerpsisset. **26.8** quotus enim quisque scholasticorum non hac sua persuasione fruitur, ut se ante Ciceronem numeret, sed plane post Gabinianum? at ego non uerebor nominare singulos, quo facilius propositis exemplis appareat quibus gradibus fracta sit et deminuta eloquentia.'

27.1 'Parce' inquit Maternus 'et potius exsolue promissum. neque enim hoc colligi desideramus, disertiores esse antiquos, quod apud me quidem in confesso est, sed causas exquirimus, quas te solitum tractare paulo ante ⟨dixisti⟩, plane mitior et eloquentiae temporum nostrorum minus iratus, antequam te Aper offenderet maiores tuos lacessendo.'

27.2 'Non sum' inquit 'offensus Apri mei disputatione, nec uos offendi decebit si quid forte aures uestras perstringet, cum sciatis hanc esse eius modi sermonum legem, iudicium animi citra damnum affectus proferre.'

27.3 'Perge' inquit Maternus 'et cum de antiquis loquaris, utere antiqua libertate, ⟨a⟩ qua uel magis degenerauimus quam ab eloquentia.'

28.1 Et Messalla: 'non reconditas, Materne, causas requiris nec aut tibi ipsi aut huic Secundo uel huic Apro ignotas, etiam si mihi partes assignatis proferendi in medium quae omnes sentimus. **28.2** quis enim ignorat et eloquentiam et ceteras artes desciuisse ab illa uetere gloria non inopia hominum, sed desidia iuuentutis et neglegentia parentum et inscientia praecipientium et obliuione moris antiqui? quae mala primum in Vrbe nata, mox per Italiam fusa, iam in prouincias manant. **28.3** quamquam uestra uobis notiora sunt: ego de Vrbe et his propriis ac uernaculis uitiis loquar, quae natos statim excipiunt et per singulos aetatis gradus cumulantur, si prius de seueritate ac disciplina maiorum circa educandos formandosque liberos pauca praedixero.

28.4 'Nam pridem suus cuique filius, ex casta parente natus, non in cella emptae nutricis, sed gremio ac sinu matris educabatur, cuius praecipua laus erat tueri domum et inseruire liberis. eligebatur autem maior aliqua natu propinqua, cuius probatis spectatisque moribus omnis eiusdem familiae suboles committeretur; coram qua neque dicere fas erat quod turpe dictu neque facere quod inhonestum factu uideretur. **28.5** ac non studia modo curasque, sed remissiones etiam lususque puerorum sanctitate quadam ac uerecundia temperabat. sic Corneliam Gracchorum, sic Aureliam Caesaris, sic Atiam Augusti [matrem] praefuisse educationibus ac produxisse principes liberos accepimus. **28.6** quae disciplina ac seueritas eo pertinebat ut sincera et integra et nullis prauatibus detorta unius cuiusque natura toto statim pectore arriperet artes honestas et, siue ad rem militarem siue ad iuris

scientiam siue ad eloquentiae studium inclinasset, id solum
ageret, id uniuersum hauriret.

29.1 'At nunc natus infans delegatur Graeculae alicui
ancillae, cui adiungitur unus aut alter ex omnibus seruis,
plerumque uilissimus nec cuiquam serio ministerio accom-
modatus. horum fabulis et erroribus [et] uirides [teneri] statim et rudes animi imbuuntur; nec quisquam in tota domo
pensi habet, quid coram infante domino aut dicat aut faciat.
29.2 quin etiam ipsi parentes non probitati neque modestiae
paruulos adsuefaciunt, sed lasciuiae et dicacitati, per quae
paulatim impudentia irrepit et sui alienique contemptus.

29.3 'Iam uero propria et peculiaria huius Vrbis uitia
paene in utero matris concipi mihi uidentur, histrionalis
fauor et gladiatorum equorumque studia: quibus occupatus et
obsessus animus quantulum loci bonis artibus relinquit? quotum quemque inuenies qui domi quicquam aliud loquatur?
quos alios adulescentulorum sermones excipimus, si quando
auditoria intrauimus? **29.4** ne praeceptores quidem ullas cre-
briores cum auditoribus suis fabulas habent; colligunt enim
discipulos non seueritate disciplinae nec ingenii experimento,
sed ambitione salutationum et illecebris adulationis.

30.1 'Transeo prima discentium elementa, in quibus et
ipsis parum laboratur. nec in auctoribus cognoscendis nec in
euoluenda antiquitate nec in notitia uel rerum uel hominum
uel temporum satis operae insumitur. **30.2** sed expetuntur
quos rhetoras uocant: quorum professio quando primum in
hanc urbem introducta sit quamque nullam apud maiores
nostros auctoritatem habuerit, statim dicturus, ⟨prius⟩ re-
feram necesse est animum ad eam disciplinam qua usos esse
eos oratores accepimus quorum infinitus labor et cotidiana
meditatio et in omni genere studiorum assiduae exercitationes ipsorum etiam continentur libris.

30.3 'Notus est uobis utique Ciceronis liber qui Brutus
inscribitur, in cuius extrema parte (nam prior commemora-
tionem ueterum oratorum habet) sua initia, suos gradus, suae

eloquentiae uelut quandam educationem refert: se apud Q. Mucium ius ciuile didicisse, apud Philonem Academicum, apud Diodotum Stoicum omnes philosophiae partes penitus hausisse; neque iis doctoribus contentum quorum ei copia in Vrbe contigerat, Achaiam quoque et Asiam peragrasse, ut omnem omnium artium uarietatem complecteretur.

30.4 'Itaque hercule in libris Ciceronis deprehendere licet non geometriae, non musicae, non grammaticae, non denique ullius ingenuae artis scientiam ei defuisse. ille dialecticae subtilitatem, ille moralis partis utilitatem, ille rerum motus causasque cognouerat. **30.5** ita est enim, optimi uiri, ita: ex multa eruditione et plurimis artibus et omnium rerum scientia exundat et exuberat illa admirabilis eloquentia; neque oratoris uis et facultas sicut ceterarum rerum angustis et breuibus terminis clauditur, sed is est orator qui de omni quaestione pulchre et ornate et ad persuadendum apte dicere pro dignitate rerum, ad utilitatem temporum, cum uoluptate audientium possit.

31.1 'Hoc sibi illi ueteres persuaserant, ad hoc efficiendum intellegebant opus esse non ut in rhetorum scholis declamarent nec ut fictis nec ullo modo ad ueritatem accedentibus controuersiis linguam modo et uocem exercerent, sed ut [in] iis artibus pectus implerent in quibus de bonis ac malis, de honesto et turpi, de iusto et iniusto disputatur; haec enim est oratori subiecta ad dicendum materia. **31.2** nam in iudiciis fere de aequitate, in deliberationibus ⟨de utilitate, in laudationibus⟩ de honestate disserimus, ita ⟨tamen⟩ ut plerumque haec ipsa in uicem misceantur. de quibus copiose et uarie et ornate nemo dicere potest, nisi qui cognouit naturam humanam et uim uirtutum prauitatemque uitiorum et intellectum eorum quae nec in uirtutibus nec in uitiis numerantur. **31.3** ex his fontibus etiam illa profluunt, ut facilius iram iudicis uel instiget uel leniat qui scit quid ira, et promptius ad miserationem impellat qui scit quid sit misericordia et quibus animi motibus concitetur. **31.4** in his artibus exercitationibusque uersatus orator, siue apud infestos siue apud cupidos siue apud inuidentes siue apud tristes siue apud timentes dicendum habuerit, tenebit uenas animorum et, prout cuiusque natura postulabit, adhibebit manum et temperabit orationem, parato omni instrumento et ad omnem usum reposito.

31.5 'Sunt apud quos astrictum et collectum et singula statim argumenta concludens dicendi genus plus fidei meretur: apud hos dedisse operam dialecticae proficiet. alios fusa et aequalis et ex communibus ducta sensibus oratio magis delectat: ad hos permouendos mutuabimur a Peripateticis aptos et in omnem disputationem paratos iam locos. **31.6** dabunt Academici pugnacitatem, Plato altitudinem, Xenophon iucunditatem; ne Epicuri quidem et Metrodori honestas quasdam exclamationes assumere iisque, prout res poscit, uti alienum erit oratori. **31.7** neque enim sapientem informamus neque Stoicorum comitem, sed eum qui quasdam artes haurire, omnes libare debet. ideoque et iuris ciuilis scientiam ueteres oratores comprehendebant et grammatica musica [et] geometria imbuebantur. **31.8** incidunt enim causae, plurimae quidem ac paene omnes quibus iuris notitia desideratur, pleraeque autem in quibus haec quoque scientia requiritur.

32.1 'Nec quisquam respondeat sufficere ut ad tempus simplex quiddam et uniforme doceamur. primum enim aliter utimur propriis, aliter commodatis, longeque interesse manifestum est possideat quis quae profert an mutuetur. deinde ipsa multarum artium scientia etiam aliud agentes nos ornat atque ubi minime credas eminet et excellit: **32.2** idque non doctus modo et prudens auditor sed etiam populus intellegit, ac statim ita laude prosequitur ut legitime studuisse, ut per omnes eloquentiae numeros isse, ut denique oratorem esse fateatur. quem non posse aliter existere nec extitisse umquam confirmo nisi eum qui, tamquam in aciem omnibus armis instructus, sic in Forum omnibus artibus armatus exierit.

32.3 'Quod adeo neglegitur ab horum temporum disertis ut in actionibus eorum huius quoque cotidiani sermonis foeda

ac pudenda uitia deprehendantur, ut ignorent leges, non teneant senatus consulta, ius ciuitatis ultro derideant, sapientiae
uero studium et praecepta prudentium penitus reformident.
32.4 in paucissimos sensus et angustas sententias detrudunt
eloquentiam uelut expulsam regno suo, ut quae olim omnium
artium domina pulcherrimo comitatu pectora implebat, nunc
circumcisa et amputata, sine apparatu sine honore, paene
dixerim sine ingenuitate, quasi una ex sordidissimis artificiis
discatur.

32.5 'Ergo hanc primam et praecipuam causam arbitror
cur in tantum ab eloquentia antiquorum oratorum recesserimus. si testes desiderantur, quos potiores nominabo quam
apud Graecos Demosthenen, quem studiosissimum Platonis
auditorem fuisse memoriae proditum est? **32.6** et Cicero
his ut opinor uerbis refert, quidquid in eloquentia effecerit,
id se non "rhetorum ⟨officinis⟩", sed "Academiae spatiis"
consecutum.

32.7 'Sunt aliae causae, magnae et graues, quas ⟨a⟩ uobis
aperiri aequum est, quoniam quidem ego iam meum munus
expleui et, quod mihi in consuetudine est, satis multos
offendi, quos, si forte haec audierint, certum habeo dicturos
me, dum iuris et philosophiae scientiam tamquam oratori
necessariam laudo, ineptiis meis plausisse.'

33.1 Et Maternus 'mihi quidem' inquit 'susceptum a te
munus adeo peregisse nondum uideris ut incohasse tantum et
uelut uestigia ac liniamenta quaedam ostendisse uidearis.
33.2 nam quibus ⟨artibus⟩ instrui ueteres oratores soliti sint
dixisti differentiamque nostrae desidiae et inscientiae aduersus acerrima et fecundissima eorum studia demonstrasti:
cetera exspecto, ut quem ad modum ex te didici quid aut illi
scierint aut nos nesciamus, ita hoc quoque cognoscam, quibus
exercitationibus iuuenes iam et Forum ingressuri confirmare
et alere ingenia sua soliti sint. **33.3** neque enim solum arte et
scientia, sed longe magis facultate et ⟨usu⟩ eloquentiam contineri nec tu puto abnues et hi significare uultu uidentur.'

33.4 Deinde cum Aper quoque et Secundus idem adnuissent, Messalla quasi rursus incipiens: 'quoniam initia et semina ueteris eloquentiae satis demonstrasse uideor docendo quibus artibus antiqui oratores institui erudirique soliti sint, persequar nunc exercitationes eorum. **33.5** quamquam ipsis artibus inest exercitatio, nec quisquam percipere tot tam uarias ac reconditas res potest, nisi ut scientiae meditatio, meditationi facultas, facultati usus [eloquentiae] accedat; per quae colligitur eandem esse rationem et percipiendi quae proferas et proferendi quae perceperis. **33.6** sed si cui obscuriora haec uidentur isque scientiam ab exercitatione separat, illud certe concedet, instructum et plenum his artibus animum longe paratiorem ad eas exercitationes uenturum quae propriae esse oratorum uidentur.

34.1 'Ergo apud maiores nostros iuuenis ille qui foro et eloquentiae parabatur, imbutus iam domestica disciplina, refertus honestis studiis, deducebatur a patre uel a propinquis ad eum oratorem qui principem in ciuitate locum obtinebat. **34.2** hunc sectari, hunc prosequi, huius omnibus dictionibus interesse siue in iudiciis siue in contionibus assuescebat, ita ut altercationes quoque exciperet et iurgiis interesset utque sic dixerim pugnare in proelio disceret. **34.3** magnus ex hoc usus, multum constantiae, plurimum iudicii iuuenibus statim contingebat, in media luce studentibus atque inter ipsa discrimina, ubi nemo impune stulte aliquid aut contrarie dicit quo minus et iudex respuat et aduersarius exprobret, ipsi denique aduocati aspernentur.

34.4 'Igitur uera statim et incorrupta eloquentia imbuebantur, et, quamquam unum sequerentur, tamen omnes eiusdem aetatis patronos in plurimis et causis et iudiciis cognoscebant, habebantque ipsius populi diuersissimarum aurium copiam, ex qua facile deprehenderent quid in quoque uel probaretur uel displiceret. **34.5** ita nec praeceptor deerat, optimus quidem et electissimus, qui faciem eloquentiae, non imaginem praestaret, nec aduersarii et aemuli ferro non rudibus dimicantes, nec auditorium semper plenum, semper nouum, ex inuidis et fauentibus, ut nec bene ⟨nec male⟩ dicta dissimularentur. scitis enim magnam illam et duraturam eloquentiae famam non minus in diuersis subselliis parari quam suis: inde quin immo constantius surgere, ibi fidelius corroborari.

34.6 'Atque hercule sub eius modi praeceptoribus iuuenis ille de quo loquimur, oratorum discipulus, fori auditor, sectator iudiciorum, eruditus et assuefactus alienis experimentis, cui cotidie audienti notae leges, non noui iudicum uultus, frequens in oculis consuetudo contionum, saepe cognitae populi aures, siue accusationem susceperat siue defensionem, solus statim et unus cuicumque causae par erat. **34.7** nono decimo aetatis anno L. Crassus C. Carbonem, uno et uicesimo Caesar Dolabellam, altero et uicesimo Asinius Pollio C. Catonem, non multum aetate antecedens Caluus Vatinium iis orationibus insecuti sunt quas hodieque cum admiratione legimus.

35.1 'At nunc adulescentuli nostri deducuntur in scholas istorum qui rhetores uocantur, quos paulo ante Ciceronis tempora extitisse nec placuisse maioribus nostris ex eo manifestum est quod a Crasso et Domitio censoribus claudere, ut ait Cicero, "ludum impudentiae" iussi sunt. **35.2** sed, ut dicere institueram, deducuntur in scholas: ⟨in⟩ quibus non facile dixerim utrumne locus ipse an condiscipuli an genus studiorum plus mali ingeniis afferant. **35.3** nam in loco nihil reuerentiae est, in quem nemo nisi aeque imperitus intrat; in condiscipulis nihil profectus, cum pueri inter pueros et adulescentuli inter adulescentulos pari securitate et dicant et audiantur; ipsae uero exercitationes magna ex parte contrariae. **35.4** nempe enim duo genera materiarum apud rhetoras tractantur, suasoriae et controuersiae. ex his suasoriae quidem tamquam plane leuiores et minus prudentiae exigentes pueris delegantur, controuersiae robustioribus assignantur, quales per fidem et quam incredibiliter compositae. sequitur autem ut materiae abhorrenti a ueritate declamatio quoque adhibeatur. **35.5** sic fit ut tyrannicidarum praemia aut uitiatarum electiones aut pestilentiae remedia aut incesta matrum aut quidquid in schola cotidie agitur, in foro uel raro uel numquam, ingentibus uerbis prosequantur. cum ad ueros iudices uentum ***'

36.1 '*** rem cogitare, nihil humile, nihil abiectum eloqui poterat. magna eloquentia, sicut flamma, materia alitur et motibus excitatur et urendo clarescit. eadem ratio in nostra quoque ciuitate antiquorum eloquentiam prouexit. **36.2** nam etsi horum quoque temporum oratores ea consecuti sunt quae composita et quieta et beata re publica tribui fas erat, tamen illa perturbatione ac licentia plura sibi assequi uidebantur, cum mixtis omnibus et moderatore uno carentibus tantum quisque orator saperet quantum erranti populo persuaderi poterat. **36.3** hinc leges assiduae et populare nomen, hinc contiones magistratuum paene pernoctantium in rostris, hinc accusationes potentium reorum et assignatae etiam domibus inimicitiae, hinc procerum factiones et assidua senatus aduersus plebem certamina. **36.4** quae singula etsi distrahebant rem publicam, exercebant tamen illorum temporum eloquentiam et magnis cumulare praemiis uidebantur, quia quanto quisque plus dicendo poterat, tanto facilius honores assequebatur, tanto magis in ipsis honoribus collegas suos anteibat, tanto plus apud principes gratiae, plus auctoritatis apud patres, plus notitiae ac nominis apud plebem parabat. **36.5** hi clientelis etiam exterarum nationum redundabant, hos ituri in prouincias magistratus reuerebantur, hos reuersi colebant, hos et praeturae et consulatus uocare ultro uidebantur, hi ne priuati quidem sine potestate erant, cum et populum et senatum consilio et auctoritate regerent. **36.6** quin immo sibi ipsi persuaserant neminem sine eloquentia aut assequi posse in ciuitate aut tueri conspicuum et eminentem locum. **36.7** nec mirum, cum etiam inuiti ad populum producerentur, cum parum esset in senatu breuiter censere, nisi quis ingenio

et eloquentia sententiam suam tueretur, cum in aliquam inuidiam aut crimen uocati sua uoce respondendum haberent,
cum testimonia quoque in ⟨iudiciis⟩ publicis non absentes
nec per tabellam dare, sed coram et praesentes dicere coge-
rentur. **36.8** ita ad summa eloquentiae praemia magna etiam
necessitas accedebat, et quo modo disertum haberi pulchrum
et gloriosum, sic contra mutum et elinguem uideri deforme
habebatur. **37.1** ergo non minus rubore quam praemiis sti-
mulabantur ne clientulorum loco potius quam patronorum
numerarentur, ne traditae a maioribus necessitudines ad alios
transirent, ne tamquam inertes et non suffecturi honoribus
aut non impetrarent aut impetratos male tuerentur.

37.2 'Nescio an uenerint in manus uestras haec uetera quae
et in antiqu⟨ari⟩orum bibliothecis adhuc manent et cum
maxime a Muciano contrahuntur ac iam undecim, ut opinor,
Actorum libris et tribus Epistularum composita et edita sunt.
37.3 ex his intellegi potest Cn. Pompeium et M. Crassum
non uiribus modo et armis, sed ingenio quoque et oratione
ualuisse; Lentulos et Metellos et Lucullos et Curiones et
ceteram procerum manum multum in his studiis operae
curaeque posuisse, nec quemquam illis temporibus magnam
potentiam sine aliqua eloquentia consecutum.

37.4 'His accedebat splendor reorum et magnitudo causarum, quae et ipsa plurimum eloquentiae praestant. nam
multum interest utrumne de furto aut formula et interdicto
dicendum habeas an de ambitu comitiorum, de expilatis
sociis et ciuibus trucidatis. **37.5** quae mala sicut non accidere
melius est isque optimus ciuitatis status habendus est in quo
nihil tale patimur, ita cum acciderent ingentem eloquentiae
materiam subministrabant. crescit enim cum amplitudine rerum uis ingenii, nec quisquam claram et illustrem orationem
efficere potest nisi qui causam parem inuenit. **37.6** non, opinor, Demosthenen orationes illustrant quas aduersus tutores
suos composuit, nec Ciceronem magnum oratorem P. Quinctius defensus aut Licinius Archias faciunt: Catilina et Milo et

Verres et Antonius hanc illi famam circumdederunt; non quia
tanti fuerit rei publicae malos ferre ciues ut uberem ad dicendum materiam oratores haberent, sed, ut subinde admoneo, quaestionis meminerimus sciamusque nos de ea re
loqui quae facilius turbidis et inquietis temporibus exstitit.
37.7 quis ignorat utilius ac melius esse frui pace quam bello
uexari? plures tamen bonos proeliatores bella quam pax
ferunt. **37.8** similis eloquentiae condicio: nam quo saepius
steterit tamquam in acie quoque plures et intulerit ictus et
exceperit quoque maiores aduersarios acrioresque pugnas sibi
ipsa desumpserit, tanto altior et excelsior et illis nobilitata
⟨dis⟩criminibus in ore hominum agit, quorum ea natura est,
ut secura uelint ⟨...⟩.

38.1 'Transeo ad formam et consuetudinem ueterum iudiciorum: quae etsi nunc aptior est ueritati, eloquentiam tamen
illud Forum magis exercebat in quo nemo intra paucissimas
horas perorare cogebatur et liberae comperendinationes
erant et modum dicendo sibi quisque sumebat et numerus
neque dierum neque patronorum finiebatur. **38.2** primus
haec tertio consulatu Cn. Pompeius astrinxit imposuitque
ueluti frenos eloquentiae, ita tamen ut omnia in Foro, omnia
legibus, omnia apud praetores gererentur: apud quos quanto
maiora negotia olim exerceri solita sint quod maius argumentum est quam quod causae centumuirales, quae nunc
primum obtinent locum, adeo splendore aliorum iudiciorum
obruebantur ut neque Ciceronis neque Caesaris neque Bruti
neque Caeli neque Calui, non denique ullius magni oratoris
liber apud centumuiros dictus legatur, exceptis orationibus
Asini quae pro heredibus Vrbiniae inscribuntur, ab ipso tamen Pollione mediis diui Augusti temporibus habitae, postquam longa temporum quies et continuum populi otium et
assidua senatus tranquillitas et maxima principis disciplina
ipsam quoque eloquentiam sicut omnia depacauerat?

39.1 'Paruum et ridiculum fortasse uide⟨bi⟩tur quod dicturus sum, dicam tamen, uel ideo ut rideatur. quantum

humilitatis putamus eloquentiae attulisse paenulas istas quibus astricti et uelut inclusi cum iudicibus fabulamur? quantum uirium detraxisse orationi auditoria et tabularia credimus in quibus iam fere plurimae causae explicantur? **39.2** nam quo modo nobiles equos cursus et spatia probant, sic est aliquis oratorum campus per quem nisi liberi et soluti ferantur debilitatur ac frangitur eloquentia. **39.3** ipsam quin immo curam et diligentis stili anxietatem contrariam experimur, quia saepe interrogat iudex ⟨ante⟩quam incipias, et ex interrogatione eius incipiendum est, frequenter probationibus et testibus silentium [patronus] indicit. unus inter haec dicenti aut alter assistit, et res uelut in solitudine agitur. **39.4** oratori autem clamore plausuque opus est et uelut quodam theatro, qualia cotidie antiquis oratoribus contingebant, cum tot pariter ac tam nobiles Forum coartarent, cum clientelae quoque ac tribus et municipiorum etiam legationes ac pars Italiae periclitantibus assisteret, cum in plerisque iudiciis crederet populus Romanus sua interesse quid iudicaretur. **39.5** satis constat C. Cornelium et M. Scaurum et T. Milonem et L. Bestiam et P. Vatinium concursu totius ciuitatis et accusatos et defensos, ut frigidissimos quoque oratores ipsa certantis populi studia excitare et incendere potuerint. itaque hercule eius modi libri extant ut ipsi quoque qui egerunt non aliis magis orationibus censeantur. **40.1** Iam uero cont⟨ent⟩iones assiduae et datum ius potentissimum quemque uexandi atque ipsa inimicitiarum gloria, cum se plurimi disertorum ne a P. quidem Scipione aut Sulla aut Cn. Pompeio abstinerent et ad incessendos principes uiros, ut est natura inuidiae, †populi quoque et histriones auribus uterentur†, quantum ardorem ingeniis, quas oratoribus faces admouebant!

40.2 'Non de otiosa et quieta re loquimur et quae probitate et modestia gaudeat, sed est magna illa et notabilis eloquentia alumna licentiae, quam stulti libertatem uocant, comes seditionum, effrenati populi incitamentum, sine obsequio, sine seueritate, contumax temeraria arrogans, quae in bene constitutis ciuitatibus non oritur. **40.3** quem enim oratorem Lacedaemonium, quem Cretensem accepimus? quarum ciuitatum seuerissima disciplina et seuerissimae leges traduntur. ne Macedonum quidem ac Persarum aut ullius gentis quae certo imperio contenta fuerit eloquentiam nouimus. Rhodii quidam, plurimi Athenienses oratores exstiterunt, apud quos omnia populus, omnia imperiti, omnia, ut sic dixerim, omnes poterant. **40.4** nostra quoque ciuitas, donec errauit, donec se partibus et dissensionibus et discordiis confecit, donec nulla fuit in Foro pax, nulla in senatu concordia, nulla in iudiciis moderatio, nulla superiorum reuerentia, nullus magistratuum modus, tulit sine dubio ualentiorem eloquentiam, sicut indomitus ager habet quasdam herbas laetiores. sed nec tanti rei publicae Gracchorum eloquentia fuit ut pateretur et leges, nec bene famam eloquentiae Cicero tali exitu pensauit.

41.1 'Sic quoque quod superest [antiquis oratoribus] forum non emendatae nec usque ad uotum compositae ciuitatis argumentum est. **41.2** quis enim nos aduocat nisi aut nocens aut miser? quod municipium in clientelam nostram uenit, nisi quod aut uicinus populus aut domestica discordia agitat? quam prouinciam tuemur nisi spoliatam uexatamque? atqui melius fuisset non queri quam uindicari. **41.3** quod si inueniretur aliqua ciuitas in qua nemo peccaret, superuacuus esset inter innocentes orator sicut inter sanos medicus. quo modo tamen minimum usus minimumque profectus ars medentis habet in iis gentibus quae firmissima ualetudine ac saluberrimis corporibus utuntur, sic minor oratorum honor, obscurior[que] gloria est inter bonos mores et in obsequium regentis paratos. **41.4** quid enim opus est longis in senatu sententiis, cum optimi cito consentiant? quid multis apud populum contionibus, cum de re publica non imperiti et multi deliberent, sed sapientissimus et unus? quid uoluntariis accusationibus, cum tam raro et tam parce peccetur? quid inuidiosis et excedentibus modum defensionibus, cum clementia cognoscentis obuiam periclitantibus eat?

41.5 'Credite, optimi et in quantum opus est disertissimi uiri, si aut uos prioribus saeculis aut illi quos miramur his nati essent ac deus aliquis uitas ac [uestra] tempora repente mutasset, nec uobis summa illa laus et gloria in eloquentia neque illis modus et temperamentum defuisset: nunc, quoniam nemo eodem tempore assequi potest magnam famam et magnam quietem, bono saeculi sui quisque citra obtrectationem alterius utatur.'

42.1 Finierat Maternus, cum Messalla: 'erant quibus contra dicerem, erant de quibus plura dici uellem, nisi iam dies esset exactus.'

'Fiet' inquit Maternus 'postea arbitratu tuo, et si qua tibi obscura in hoc meo sermone uisa sunt, de iis rursus conferemus.' **42.2** ac simul assurgens et Aprum complexus 'ego' inquit 'te poetis, Messalla antiquariis criminabimur.'

'At ego uos rhetoribus et scholasticis' inquit.

Cum arrisissent, discessimus.

COMMENTARY

1–2 Dedication

An author in antiquity followed certain traditional strategies to introduce a prose treatise. His chief aim was to elucidate the scope of the work more fully than the bare title could do, and he usually suggested that its theme had been determined by someone who serves in effect as the dedicatee of the work. In addition, the dedicatee's alleged interest in the topic and in the work's publication relieved the author of some responsibility: he did not thrust his views upon his readers, but had notionally been invited to write by a friend, whose compulsion was not to be resisted. Compared, however, with the proems of Cicero, the proem to *D.* is short, an example of contemporary stylistic brevity.

The question Fabius Justus is imagined to have posed is basically an historical one, for he noticed a difference between the past and the present, and asked for an explanation of the process underlying it (see A. D. Leeman, 'Structure and meaning in the prologues of Tacitus', *YCS* 23 (1973) 171). The historically founded answer will be given by Maternus at 40.2–42, the change in the form of government at Rome. (It is noteworthy that the introduction to the *Agricola* also dwells upon the difference between former times and the present day as regards the writing of biography.)

1.1 Saepe ['repeatedly'] **... requiris:** cf. Cic. *Orat.* 1–3 *saepius idem roganti, saepius rogas, quaeris ... saepius* (Cicero to Brutus, who has supposedly asked for his views on the ideal orator). Such expressions were long a commonplace of authors, who sought to account for publication by claiming that a friend had urged it; cf. the introduction to a lost treatise on dinner parties by Chaerepho, ἐπειδή μοι πολλάκις ἐπέστειλας 'since you often bade me ...' (Callim. fr. 434 Pf.). Pliny tells an amusing story of a legal wit's subversion of the formula at *Ep.* 6.15 (see O. Hiltbrunner, 'Prisce, iubes ...', *ZRG* 96 (1979) 40–2). For *D.* see T. Janson, *Latin prose prefaces: studies in literary conventions* (Stockholm 1964) 60–4; P. White, *Promised verse* (Cambridge, Mass. 1993) 73 compares its opening to Varro, *RR, Rhet. Her.*, Cic. *Top.* and Quint. *Inst.*

Iuste Fabi: L. Fabius Justus (*cos. suff.* in 102) was also a friend of the younger Pliny, who wrote two notes to him (Sherwin-White on *Ep.* 1.5.8). In due course he took up consular commands in lower Moesia (105) and Syria (109); public administration had more to offer than legal practice (see Sherwin-White on Plin. *Ep.* 2.14.2). For Fabius' career see Syme (1970) 110–18 = *Danubian papers* (Bucharest 1971) 122–34 and *RP* III index s.v. The *nomen gentilicium* and *cognomen* are here reversed, originally a poetic practice, e.g. Pl. *Merc.* 10 *Macci Titi* (see N–H on Hor. *C.* 2.2.3 *Crispe Sallusti*), but more common-place in first-century AD prose (Goodyear on *A.* 1.8.3 discerns 'no clearly recognizable principle'; a view seconded by B. Salway, *JRS* 84 (1994) 130: 'little more than a stylistic device', Kraus on Livy 6.18.4, Woodman and Martin on *A.* 3.21.3).   **cum priora sae-cula ... floruerint** 'whereas [*OLD cum²* 7b] in previous ages ora-tors flourished'; Latin readily used expressions for time as the subject (Nägelsbach (1905) 610 compares Cic. *Fam.* 5.17.1 *quod priora tempora in ruinis reip. nostrisque iacuerunt*, to which may be added *Brut.* 320 *pri-mus et secundus annus et tertius tantum quasi de picturae ueteris colore detrax-erat*, Hor. *Epist.* 2.2.55 *singula de nobis anni praedantur euntes*, and *Agr.* 7.1 *sequens annus graui uulnere animum domumque adflixit*). *priora saecula* will be 'echoed' by Maternus in his summing-up at 41.5, an example of ring-composition, which brings the work full circle. Throughout the work such references to anything 'older' or 'of former times' (e.g. 14.4 *ueterum*, 19.2 *prior ille populus*) indicate the time of the late Re-public.   **ingeniis gloriaque:** not necessarily an instance of hendiadys, since an individual talent may not be recognized, and re-nown may not be based on merit (so Longhi). The notion that *ingenia* are not what they used to be is also enunciated at the beginning of the *Historiae*: *postquam bellatum apud Actium ... magna illa ingenia cessere* (T. refers only to historians), a remarkable community of concept between these works.   **deserta** 'barren' keeps up the metaphor of *floruerint*.   **horum ... temporum diserti:** the expression will be recalled at 32.3, when Messalla belittles contemporary pleaders. *diserti* 'accomplished speakers' is the subject word. Cicero had differ-entiated the *disertus* from the *eloquens* at *De orat.* 1.94–5 (Douglas on *Brut.* 39.27, p. 30, has an important note on Cicero's usage; cf. Quint. *Inst.* 1.10.8 and Colson on *Inst.* 1.8.4). But T. only ever used *eloquens* of historical writers (see *Agr.* 10.3, quoted at 23.2).   **cau-sidici** 'professional pleaders' (Austin on Quint. *Inst.* 12.1.25); the word often sounded a pejorative note (cf. Sen. *Apocol.* 12.3.54 *causidici, uenale genus*) because 'according to old Roman custom a man's legal interests would be looked after by his *patronus*'; the name 'suggests taking money for what ought to be an *officium*' (Courtney on Juv. 7.106). For less critical usage see Crook (1995) 152.   **aduo-cati** were originally 'supporters' of the parties in a lawsuit (Douglas on Cic. *Brut.* 289; this sense is found at 34.3), but they became in course of time themselves professional 'counsel' (Crook (1995) 148–9). Quintilian used the word often, only sometimes of inferior pleaders (Austin on *Inst.* 12.1.13; Peterson on *Inst.* 10.1.111 contrasts Ciceronian usage). The point of this string of names is that oratory is now practically confined to the lawcourts, and has lost its place in the Senate and before the Roman people.   **oratores:** at *A.* 6.20.1 T., relating a witticism of C. Sallustius Crispus Passienus, styles him *orator* (see Furneaux *ad loc.* for references to the quality of his oratory), the only public speaker of the Empire to be set implicitly on the same level as the classic speakers of the Republic, Cicero, Hortensius, Pollio and Messalla Corvinus (cf. *A.* 2.37.3, 11.6.7, 13.34.2). In his second speech in this work Aper is not afraid to use the word, just as he used *eloquentia* in his first; for him its representatives still exist. But it should be borne in mind, as Crook (1995) 149 with n. 185 argues, that *orator* never was the common word for counsel, and that in this passage the usage is grandiose and 'normative'.

1.2 T. follows a common strategy and places responsibility for the notions to be expressed upon others rather than himself.   **tam magnae** = *tantae*, but more emphatic (H–S 848, Nachträge to 206b Zus. β).   ⟨**sit**⟩ was added by Lipsius; it was omitted by haplography (writing once what should be written twice) before *si*.   **iudiciis** 'judgements', though we should probably translate it with our metaphor 'tastes' (Nägelsbach (1905) 54). Latin did not use *gustus* metaphorically, because for the Romans 'taste' was an intellectual rather than a purely aesthetic or emotional concept, and so could be expected to give a rational account of itself. *iudicium* and *ingenium* 'ability' are often combined or contrasted (19.1, 21.9, 25.4). At this stage, as Reitzenstein (1915) 270 n. noted, T. indulges in some coat-trailing, since he seems to assume that the cause for decline is to be sought in deficiencies on the part of contemporary orators, rather than in the change of political system at Rome.   **si mihi mea sententia:** for word order cf. Cic. *Verr.* 5.35 *ita mihi meam uoluntatem* ...   **disertissimorum, ut nostris temporibus, hominum:** the alert reader might have recalled that Cicero, using a similar ploy to introduce his *De oratore*, had referred to the interlocutors of that dialogue as *hominum eloquentissimorum* (1.24). T. has not only changed the epithet, because he does not believe that any orator is any longer *eloquens*, but he has also added a restriction (*OLD ut* 22) to the preceding superlative, which strikes a warning note, not least because here it gives T.'s own opinion; it will be 'echoed' by Maternus at 41.5.   **repetendus:** without *memoria* (*OLD* 6c).   **iuuenis admodum:** T., born 55/6, was about 19 years old; the allusion to his age accounts for his modest silence in the presence of his elders.   **audiui** establishes a fiction, which ultimately derives from the Platonic dialogue, that a particular conversation is to be reproduced by one who was present (cf. Cic. *Fam.* 9.8.1 *puto fore ut, cum legeris, mirere nos id locutos esse inter nos quod numquam locuti sumus; sed nosti morem dialogorum*). That fiction was propagated by Cicero in his *De oratore* and *De re publica* (1.13.2), though he does not profess to have been present at the conversations, but to record what others told him.

1.3 memoria et recordatione: a Ciceronian phrase, in which the words are not exact synonyms: *memoria* is the mental faculty which stores the past, *recordatio* the activity of fishing out information from that store (Wilkins on *De orat.* 1.228).   **accepi** 'I heard' (*OLD* 18).   **subtiliter** 'precisely' (*OLD* 5).   **grauiter** 'with conviction' (*OLD* 10). Precision and conviction are characteristics of the best sort of oratory, since careful argumentation informs, impassioned delivery moves the audience (cf. Cic. *Brut.* 89).   **diuersas** 'different'.   **quidem** is found in the MS V, perhaps as a conjecture, and it is defended by Murgia (1978) 172; for the phraseology cf. Quint. *Inst.* 11.3.82 *diuersa quidem sed pari deformitate*. The MS tradition, *B*Γ*N, read *uel easdem* for *quidem*, but this (?gloss) gives no satisfactory sense, and though editors have variously tried to tidy up the phrasing by deletion or emendation, a totally convincing solution is elusive.   **causas** 'pleas' (*OLD* 2b).   **dum** is subordinate

to *cum*, 'and in so doing …'.   **redderent** 'reproduce' (*OLD* 7); the
subjunc. is assimilated to *afferrent* (K–S ΙΙ 377–8; cf. 28.6 *inclinasset*).
Since *quisque* refers to individuals within a group the plural of the
verb is regular (G–L §211 EXCEPTIONS (a)).   **et animi** ['tempera-
ment' (*OLD* 14)] **et ingenii** form a common pair (cf. Cic. *Brut.*
93 with Douglas's n., and *De orat.* 1.113 for oratorical contexts), cf.
21.9. *forma* ['outline'] *ingenii* is a Ciceronian expression (*Brut.* 294, 327
and cf. Quint. *Inst.* 12.10.1), but *forma animi* is Tacitean (cf. *Agr.* 46.3
formamque ac figuram animi).   **numeris** 'steps', 'stages' (*OLD* 12, cf.
32.2).   **rationibus** 'arguments'.

1.4 neque enim defuit qui …: Aper is meant.   **diuersam**
here means 'opposite'; *uexata et irrisa* will be accounted for at 24.1
uexauit (Aper is subject) and 23.1 *irridere* (Aper is speaking) respectively.   **eloquentiam:** here virtually synonymous with *ingeniis*,
which in the context implies a talent for oratory; cf. Cic. *Brut.* 318
non ut ingenium et eloquentiam meam perspicias.

2.1 Nam 'Well then'; expository (*OLD* 6).   **postero die
quam … uenerunt:** this echoes the beginning of Cic. *De orat.* 2.12
postero igitur die quam illa erant acta … repente eo Q. Catulus … uenit, but
the setting is markedly different from the model. Cicero's conversations were usually placed outside Rome in the gardens of the
country estates of leading figures in public life (the *Brutus* seems to be
exceptional: Cicero is at home (*domi* 10), but none the less *otiosus* and
out of doors); the interlocutors are friends or relatives at leisure –
the occasion is generally specified as a holiday, e.g. *De orat.* 2.12 *etenim uides esse ludos* (for discussion see E. Becker, *Technik und Szenerie des
ciceronischen Dialogs* (Osnabrück 1938)). Conversation is for them intellectual relaxation. *D.* on the contrary is set in Rome itself, and the
conversation is held indoors (*cubiculum*, 3.1; cf. the scene in the home
of Silius Italicus sketched at Plin. *Ep.* 3.7.4: *salutabatur colebatur, mul-
tumque in lectulo iacens cubiculo semper … doctissimis sermonibus dies trans-
igebat*). The spirit of the conversation, at any rate at the outset, is
urgent, not relaxed; Maternus' friends have been upset on his behalf
and have come to warn him to be more cautious. The occasion of
the conversation therefore is a matter closely affecting the well-being
of one of the speakers. This is not a topic for disinterested discussion, but goes to the heart of a man's chosen way of life.   **Curiatius Maternus** was a senator (11.4); he is known only from this

work. See Intro. 44.   **Catonem:** the protagonist was presumably the younger M. Porcius Cato, Julius Caesar's implacable rival and the paladin of *libertas*, a virtue of which Maternus deplores the loss at 27.3. His reputation was to some extent rehabilitated under Augustus (Syme (1958) 430, 557), and he became a type of absolute integrity for declaimers (there is a discussion by V. Tandoi, *Maia* 18 (1966) 20–41). Thrasea Paetus had recently composed a biography of him, and so behind Cato might have been glimpsed the contemporary martyr, the elder Helvidius Priscus ('It was not until the accession of Trajan that the ghost of Cato was laid at last': Syme (1958) 28). It is significant that the play was a *praetexta*, i.e. one based not on Greek myth but on Roman history.   **recitauerat:** the public reading of a literary work by the author himself was designed to elicit advance criticism so that the author could revise his work for publication (for general information on this practice see *OCD* s.v. recitatio, and Mayor on Juv. 3.9, 7.38). The situation described here is realistic: Pliny at *Ep.* 9.27 relates that the friends of someone unnamed (but often thought to be T. himself: Syme (1958) 120), who had interrupted a recitation from his history of the contemporary period, tried to discourage him from carrying out his intention of reciting publicly any more.   **offendisse:** drama was traditionally regarded as a potential medium for the criticism of authority at Rome. Republican audiences had been quick to detect topical references (even anachronistically), and the tradition survived into the Principate, if only as a means of incriminating the innocent (cf. Suet. *Tib.* 61.3, and the fate of Scaurus referred to at 3.3 *Thyestes* n.). That Maternus was running a risk at this time (AD 75/6) is plausible, since the elder Helvidius Priscus, a persistent critic of the regime, had recently been relegated, and perhaps even by now executed with the connivance of Titus (Levick (1999) 86–7, 89, 93, and 192; see 5.7n.); subsequently, Domitian had the younger Helvidius executed *c.* 93 *quasi scaenico exodio sub persona Paridis et Oenones diuortium suum cum uxore taxasset* (Suet. *Dom.* 10.4). As Sherwin-White observed in his nn. on Plin. *Epp.* 2.18.5 and 3.9.26, Roman society at this time was fussy in the extreme about *offensae*, and Pliny at any rate always took care to avoid giving offence, or only risked it where loyalty was at stake (see *Ep.* 4.17.11). We may also recall Juvenal's elaborate precautions in his first satire against attacking the living. Contemporary history was a particular danger (*Ep.* 5.8.12 *graues offensae*), but T. obviously was prepared to take the chance.   **potentium:** i.e. members of the imperial court.   **tamquam** commonly in first-century Latin gives a reason or cause a subjective colour, without suggesting that it is false (*OLD* 7, G–L §602 N. 4); Winterbottom's translation brings this out: 'It was felt that ...'   **eo:** as usual, the pronominal adjective, which here refers to the tragedy, is attracted from the gen. to the case of the leading noun (*TLL* VII 2.481.57; K–S I 64–6).   **sui oblitus** 'he had forgotten his own situation' (Winterbottom); Maternus refused to reckon with the consequences.   **Catonem cogitasset** 'had only the character of Cato in mind' (*OLD* 8, 9).   **per Vrbem:** Rome, like modern Washington, was a hive of political gossip, cf. *A.* 11.27.1 *in ciuitate omnium gnara et nihil reticente*, 13.6.2 *in Vrbe sermonum auida.*   **uenerunt ad eum:** the next piece of action is deferred until *intrauimus* (3.1), because T. digresses to describe his attachment to the two orators.   **M. Aper:** unknown apart from his appearance here.   **Iulius Secundus** was praised by Quintilian for his *elegantia* (*Inst.* 12.10.11, and cf. 10.1.120, 3.12). He was *ab epistulis* to Otho (Plut. *Otho* 9), a post requiring literary accomplishment.   **tum** hints that these men were dead when T. composed this work.   **assectabar:** it was clearly still the practice (despite what Messalla says at 34.1) for young men who intended to enter public life to attend daily upon a prominent man as he conducted business (20.4; see Cic. *Am.* 1, Plin. *Ep.* 2.14.10, Quint. *Inst.* 10.5.19).   **fabulas** 'conversations' (*OLD* 1, but the word is not found with this sense before the first century AD).   **arcana semotae dictionis** 'the secrets of their intimate discourse' seems to refer to the *secretae exercitationes* referred to by Seneca the Elder, *Con.* 7 pr. 1 or by Cic. *De orat.* 1.157. These will have been practice speeches, perhaps declamations (*OLD dictio* 4), delivered not in public, but to a select circle.   **plerique** 'very many' (*OLD plerusque* 4), a usage of the later first century (i.e. not in Sen.).   **nec Secundo promptum esse sermonem:** this perhaps provides a reason for his not taking part in the debate (for interesting speculations on that head see T. Köves-Zulauf, 'Reden und Schweigen im taciteischen *Dialogus*', *RM* 135 (1992) 316–41). For *promptus* 'ready' as an oratorical virtue cf. the *prompta ac profluens ... eloquentia* of Augustus (*A.* 13.3.2).   **ingenio potius et ui naturae:** see 2.2n.   **institutione et**

litteris 'academic training in literature', hendiadys. This is the only occurrence in the work of *institutio*, and Winterbottom (1964) 94 suggested that it might have been chosen to hint at the work of Quintilian, the sort of thing Aper felt he could appear to do without.

2.2 nam explains *maligne*. T. regards the imputations of weakness as unfounded.   **purus** 'unadorned' rather than 'unadulterated' Latin; for the usage see Sandys on Cic. *Orat.* 53, 79 (*De orat.* 3.29).   **pressus** 'concise', 'close' (18.4): for this term see Sandys on Cic. *Orat.* 20. The two occur together at Plin. *Ep.* 7.9.8, where they characterize an epistolary style.   **in quantum:** *OLD quantum*[1] 7d, cf. 24.3n.   **profluens:** a favourable term also at Cic. *De orat.* 2.159 and used of Augustus' oratory (see 1n.); but since the term could be pejorative (Nägelsbach (1905) 562n.) T. adds the qualification *in quantum satis erat.*   **omni** 'manifold' (*OLD* 6a).   **imbutus** 'grounded in', rather than possessing a profound (or professional) knowledge of, a variety of subjects; the sense is particularly common with reference to literary knowledge (19.5, 31.7; *OLD imbuo* 4). This description of Aper recalls that of Cicero's Crassus at *De orat.* 2.4, esp. *despicere* and *contemnere.*   **tamquam ... habiturus:** see 2.1n.   **industriae ... ingenium ... artium:** this traditional triad of terms (or variants of them, as listed below) encapsulates an ideal rooted in Hellenic culture, namely that to realize our talents we need both systematic instruction and practice. This ideal was taken over by Cicero, and became part of the tradition in accounts of oratorical education (see Douglas on *Brut.* 22 and p. xxviii, Austin on Quint. *Inst.* 12.1.9); cf. too what Messalla says at 33.5. Words related to *ingenium*, which has the absolute sense of our word 'genius' from the time of Horace (*S.* 1.4.43, 2.4.47; Lejay p. 102; *TLL* VII 1.1527), are *uis* (24.1), *ardor* (24.1), *spiritus* (24.1), *impetus* (10.6n.), *natura* (2.1), *facultas* (7.1). Those related to *ars* are *eruditio* (16.1, 24.1), and *scientia* (33.3); finally, those synonymous with *industria* are *cura* (16.1), *exercitatio* (30.2, 33.2), *meditatio* (16.1, 30.2, 33.5), *studium* (8.4), *labor* (as here, 30.2), *usus* (22.2, 33.5). Their balanced combination, as found in Messalla (16.1), revealed the true master.   **industriae et laboris:** a long-standing common pair of synonyms (*TLL* VII 1.1274.62–4). Aper, like the young Cicero (*Brut.* 318 *ut laborem et industriam* [*meam perspicias*]), took on a number of cases and prepared them diligently.

eius: used instead of *suum* (*OLD is* B 5c; Roby §2268b).   **aliena-rum** 'superfluous' (*OLD* 9); his talent was sufficiently practised to need no further accomplishments, e.g. a knowledge of music, geometry, or philosophy.   **adminiculis:** a Ciceronian word (*Am.* 88; cf. *A.* 12.5.3, 14.54.2 (Seneca)).   **uideretur** 'was seen to'.

3–5.2 Introduction to the debate

The reason for the visit of Maternus' friends is now explained: they have come to encourage him to abandon covert reflections upon contemporary political life in his tragedies. When prudent admonitions fail, Aper takes a more radical line and attacks the poetic calling of his friend.

3.1 Igitur resumes the narrative (*OLD* 4, 5), which was broken off after *uenerunt ad eum* ... (2.1).   **intrauimus:** contrast 42.2 *discessimus*; these are the only verbs to include T. himself. **ipsum⟨que⟩:** a reviewer of Walther's edition in 1833 added *que*, which would have been swallowed up by haplography of the following *quem*.   **inter manus:** *in manibus* would be commoner (*OLD manus* 12), but cf. *A.* 3.16.1. The book was probably a papyrus roll, so of course it had to be held in both hands, and was seen 'between' them.

3.2 offensas 'offensive remarks' (*OLD* 5a), cf. *offendisse*, 2.1n.; presumably these were anti-tyrannical, since the younger Cato had committed suicide after the battle of Thapsus at Utica in 46 BC rather than live under the sole rule of Julius Caesar.   **sublatis si qua:** for the form of abl. absolute in which the subject of the perf. part. pass. is a clause see Roby §1252, K–S I 773 A.7.   **non quidem meliorem:** Secundus is courteous: improvement of the literary quality would be impossible, though political safety is possible.   **securiorem:** for the adj. used in this sense cf. *Agr.* 30.1, *H.* 1.1.4.

3.3 leges tu 'you will indeed read ...' The personal pronoun following its verb is not emphatic, but helps to focus the word it is attached to (see J. N. Adams, in J. N. Adams and R. G. Mayer, eds., *Aspects of the language of Latin poetry* = *PBA* 93 (1999) 109 n. 11, and idem, 'Wackernagel's law and the position of unstressed personal pronouns in classical Latin', *Trans. Phil. Soc.* 92 (1994) 142). *leges*

promises publication of the just-recited play, whilst *agnosces* corrects
Secundus' hope that it might be revised.   **Maternus:** self-
reference by name was a rhetorical figure called *emphasis* or *affectus*
(see Austin on Virg. *Aen.* 6.510, Mayer on Lucan 8.80), which we can
render with the indefinite article: 'a Maternus'. Its effect depends
upon context: here it expresses, above all, pride: Maternus will
undertake to improve the finish of his poem, but as a Roman gentle-
man he will also speak his mind unreservedly. (T. admired the self-
possession of the poet, as we see from his description of the death of
Lucan at *A.* 15.70.1.)   **Thyestes:** a perennial favourite, 'useful for
invective against palace and dynasty, for maxims of subversive statecraft' (Syme (1958) 362, and see A. La Penna, 'Atreo e Tieste sulle
scene romane', in *Fra teatro, poesia e politica romana* (Turin 1979) 127–
41); under Tiberius the *Atreus* of the consular orator Aemilius Scaurus proved his undoing (*A.* 6.29.3 and Dio 58.24.3–4). There was a
famous *Thyestes* by Varius (12.6n.); Seneca's is extant. A play about
the rival brothers, Atreus and Thyestes, might indeed have seemed
topical at this time, when Vespasian's elder son, Titus, was con-
solidating his position as heir to the detriment of his younger
brother Domitian.   **disposui** suggests *dispositio*, the careful arrangement of the parts of an integrated literary work (cf. Plut. on
Menander, *Moral.* 348A: the comic poet had arranged the plot, but
not yet written down the words).   **maturare ... festino:** pleonasm is not uncommon with words expressing speed (Persson (1927)
5–7; K–S II 569).   **cura:** the trouble taken over a literary work,
cf. 6.5n.   **toto pectore** 'wholeheartedly'; a colloquial expression
(Otto §1368; *OLD pectus* 4b; 28.6), found with *incumbere* at Cic. *Ad fam.*
10.10.2.

3.4 Secundus has failed to induce his friend to mitigate his outspokenness, the object of his visit. So Aper now changes tack (to a
familiar topic, cf. 4.1) in order to achieve their original purpose, and
tries to belittle Maternus' devotion to poetry in its entirety. This will
provide the transition to the theme of the discourse (so Longhi).   **Adeo ... consumas** 'so far are your current tragedies
from satisfying you, that you employ all your time on ...'   **quo
minus:** the context implies prevention (we stop once we are satisfied), so that *quo minus* virtually has the sense of *quin* (cf. 34.3n.).
Aper also seems to be echoing Secundus' *nihilne te ... terrent quo minus*

... **omissis ... studiis:** Aper's complaint is strictly *ad hominem* and he will return to this point at 10.3–8: he minds that Maternus is neglecting an aspect of his nature (cf. *natus ad* 5.4n.). **modo** 'just recently'. **nunc:** because they have just this moment heard of it. **Thyesten:** Winterbottom's introduction of the Greek acc. form of proper names is followed here and at 16.5. The usage accords with that of T.'s contemporaries, Quintilian and Pliny. **coloniarum et municipiorum:** the combination designated the towns of Italy generally (Goodyear on *A.* 1.79.1). **clientelae:** cf. 5.5; A. Lintott, *Imperium Romanum* (London 1993) 171–2 discusses this sort of patronage (but a senator was not essential), and on p. 130 the *coloniae et municipia*. **suffeceris:** potential perf. subjunc. (*LS* §119, G–L §257.2, NOTE 1). **etiam si non ... importasses** 'even without your having inflicted'. Composing a Roman tragedy was harder than adapting a Greek one because its plot had to be devised *de nouo*. **⟨ut⟩**, added by Niebuhr, is explanatory (*OLD* 39, *NLS* §168), and gives the substance of the *negotium*; its presence also helps to signpost the construction. **Domitium:** perhaps Nero's great-great-grandfather, well treated in Lucan's *Bellum Ciuile*, and pictured, contrary to historical fact, as a resolute opponent of Caesar; that was, to be sure, flattery of the poet's friend (see Mayer on Lucan 8, p. 7 and 'On Lucan and Nero', *BICS* 25 (1978) 85–8). Maternus' play might, on the other hand, have been about his son, *cos.* 32, who defected at Actium from Antony to Octavian, and then committed suicide (cf. Syme (1958) 110). In either case the hero might have been made out to be opposed to tyranny, as Cato certainly was. **historias ... fabulis:** 'history' is contrasted with 'myths'; cf. *fabulosa* at 12.5. **Graeculorum:** the diminutive here and at 29.1 is slighting.

4.1 frequens et assidua: a very common doublet (*TLL* II 887.9–10); for *assidua contentio*, another common phrase, see *TLL* II 885.9–12. **uertisset** 'develop into' (*OLD* 21). **insequi** 'hound' (*OLD* 4, cf. 21.9). **aduocationum** 'duties of advocacy' (*OLD* 2). **patrocinium defendendae ... poeticae:** a slight pleonasm is detectable here in the use of the gen. of definition. Maternus is amused, ironical: how can he be charged with idleness as a pleader, when he is defending his client, Poetry, on a daily basis?

4.2 Maternus develops the judicial image he has just used, so that the ensuing discussion is turned into a sort of private trial. **iudicem:** such a role is not usual in a dialogue, and so the eristic tone of a trial is established at the outset. T. presumably introduced Secundus into the dialogue in order to create this situation. **qui ... :** a consecutive relative clause (*NLS* §156).   **omissis ... angustiis:** the phraseology parodies and corrects Aper's expression in 3.4 *omissis ... causarum studiis*, making a point to which Maternus himself will return at 39. Modern oratory is 'confined' to law courts (*forensium*). The Republic had offered vast and various public places and audiences to oratory – the Senate, the Rostra, *contiones, iudicia populi* and *quaestiones* (see J.-M. David, *Le patronat judiciaire au dernier siècle de la République romaine* (1992)). In the Empire senatorial business was reduced in importance, though it had also become more of a court of justice. The real reduction in oratorical activity was in the political sphere.   **mihi:** dat. of agent.   **sanctiorem** 'grander' = σεμνός (Quint. *Inst.* 8.3.6, 24; Norden (1909) I 330 n. 1); 'purer' (in literary sense) according to H. Nettleship, *Contributions to Latin lexicography* (Oxford 1889) s.v.; cf. *sanctitatem* 25.4n. Cicero noted at *Arch.* 18 that Ennius called poets *sanctos* and there may be an allusion here to the notion of their divine inspiration (see 21.5n.).   **augustiorem** forms a Ciceronian doublet with *sanctiorem* (*TLL* II 1379.70–1); cf. 12 below for the reason why these terms are appropriate, used of poetry.   **eloquentiam** 'gift of utterance'. Aper agrees that any verbal skill, including poetry, can achieve its own *eloquentia* (10.4).

5.1 Secundus feels in duty bound to declare an interest. **iudicem** 'as judge', a secondary predicate.   **recuset** 'can refuse'; the potential subjunc. is usual after *antequam* where the action is anticipated (*OLD* 2).   **probi et modesti:** a doublet found also at Ter. *Ad.* 930 and Cic. *Off.* 2.70. The nouns of similar meaning will be impressively reiterated in the speeches of Messalla (29.2) and Maternus (40.2).   **ut:** 3.4n.   **cognitionibus** 'judicial enquiries' (*OLD* 3).   **excusent** 'offer excuses'; the verb in this sense is usually, but not invariably, reflexive (K–S I 95; cf. *Agr.* 42.2).

5.2 Saleius Bassus, a natural poetic talent of considerable force, wrote epic (no longer extant), and enjoyed financial support from Vespasian (9.5; Juvenal noted his slender means, 7.80 *tenui*); he died young (Quint. *Inst.* 10.1.90).   **optimum uirum** subtly paves the way to the moral issue in the use of language; Aper will not be troubled by this at 8.3 *neuter moribus egregius*.   **porro** 'and indeed' develops the argument (cf. Ogilvie and Richmond on *Agr.* 15.5, *OLD* 6b).   **locupletiorem** 'creditworthy' i.e. he can give security (*OLD* 4). Secundus, in offering his friend Bassus as the best defendant of poetry, misconceives the point of Aper's attack: it was not directed at poetry and poets as such, but at one who preferred poetry as an activity to oratory, Maternus. His case is exceptional, and the introductory duel is mounted to elicit that point.

5.3–10.8 The first speech of Aper

Aper's speech is carefully blocked out into discrete sections, *partitio*; its structure is ably analysed by Luce (1993) 27, and its aristocratic social values by C. Champion, '*Dialogus* 5.3–10.8: a reconsideration of the character of Marcus Aper', *Phoenix* 48 (1994) 152–63, esp. 155. This is the only set speech in the dialogue, and Secundus remarks upon its premeditation (14.2 *accuratissimus sermo*; but Maternus had already indicated at 4.1 that the matter was often discussed between them). Aper's eulogy is not unreminiscent of the first speech in Plato's *Symposium*, on Eros, but Cicero's praise of oratory at *De orat.* 1.31 and 2.33–6 and of the study of law at *De orat.* 1.185–203, which is also carefully laid out, served as the model. The parody of a trial and the implicit invitation at 4.1 prompt him to adopt the tone of a prosecutor (to which he draws attention with *ultro* §5). His comparison of orator and poet (and the similar strategy in Maternus' reply) reflects a long-standing tradition within rhetorical schools of comparing professions. For instance, one of the minor declamations ascribed to Quintilian, §268, pits a doctor against a philosopher and an orator; a couple of his lines of argument against the latter's profession are not dissimilar to what we find in our pair of speeches (see Winterbottom's notes on 268.18 and 22).

We do not arrive at the issue of Fabius Justus' imagined question (1.1) in the speech of Aper, but the reply of Maternus (11–13) will give an important new turn to the direction of the debate. It should be noted that Aper focuses entirely upon the contemporary scene, and indeed draws attention to his lack of interest in (though not lack of knowledge of) the past: *nouis et recentibus* (8.1).

5.3 sit: the common predicate of two subjects, esp. if it precedes the first, is regularly singular (G–L §285 EXCEPTION 1).   **gloriam:** Aper himself unconsciously introduces what will become an important theme in the debate.   **cum causas agere non possit:** the crucial issue, which corrects Secundus' misapprehension and redirects the charge at Maternus.

5.4 enim explains Aper's position further.   **quatenus** 'seeing that' (*OLD* 8).   ⟨**non**⟩ **inuenimus:** the transmitted text *inueniri* is clearly faulty, but the correct course to take for emendation, which depends upon our understanding of the whole context, is much debated. The chief question is whether Aper accepts or rejects Secundus' refusal to act as arbiter in a trial of poetry on the grounds of bias. Murgia (1978) 173–4 urged that without the assurance that he had found a judge, Aper's following declaration that he will confine the case to Maternus is unmotivated; Güngerich *ad loc.* noted that Aper has just corrected Secundus' misconception of the point at issue in '*this* case' (*litis huius*), and so smoothed the way to his acting as arbitrator after all. Their views notwithstanding, the argument of M. Possanza, 'A crux in Tacitus *Dialogus* 5.3–4', *Phoenix* 49 (1995) 131–9 is here accepted in essence: Aper acknowledges that there is to be no expert (*arbiter*) to judge the proceedings, hence the need for the addition of *non*. It should also be noted that Maternus' remark at 16.3 would hardly be suitable if Secundus were still seen as an impartial arbitrator of the discussion. The form of the verb is also problematic, and here the conjecture of A. Wagener is accepted *exempli gratia*; other solutions have been proposed.   **societate plurium defendi** looks to the proverb pithily expressed by Lucan, *quod multis peccatur inultum est* (5.260), and Juvenal, *sed illos | defendit numerus* (2.45–6); cf. *H.* 2.52.2 *inter multos societate culpae tutior*, *A.* 14.49.3 *plures numero tuti*. Maternus remains in Aper's view a special case, hence *ipsum solum.*   **uos**, referring not only to Secundus but to Tacitus, is the conjecture of Lipsius for the impossible *eos* of the tradition (probably due to recollection of *apud eos* in 1). Certainty is impossible.   **natus** '*though* born', a concessive idea is understood. Aper alone in the dialogue uses the phrase *natus ad*, and that some three times (here, 6.2, 10.5), always referring to oratory (for which cf. Cic. *Balb.* 3 *homine nato ad dicendi ... facultatem*).   **eloquentiam uirilem:** Aper picks up Maternus' word from 4.2, but adds the telling

epithet, for public speaking is an élite Roman male's proper function.   **oratoriam:** cf. 6.1, 8.3; there are other 'gifts of speech'
(cf. 10.4).   **amicitias ... necessitudines:** as we should say
nowadays, a successful pleader built up a 'network' of professional
friendships in his practice.   **complecti prouincias:** prestige
was gained from representing the legal interests of the provinces, as
Pliny had done in the trial of the henchmen of Caecilius Classicus
(*Ep.* 3.9.4 *in Classicum tota prouincia incubuit*). For further discussion see
Brunt (1990) 53–95, esp. 82–4 on *patroni*, and 86 on the results of extortion trials (with addenda on 487–506). The accusers were or could
be provincials, acting through *legati*, and Pliny was an *aduocatus* on
behalf of Baetica (*Ep.* 3.4 and 9).   **omittit studium** picks up the
charge at 3.4.   **quo:** the rest of the sentence forms a climax,
in which Aper lists the topics he intends to develop.   ⟨**uel ad
uoluptatem dulcius**⟩ is the supplement of Schultingh, revised by
Ritter. Since at 6.1 Aper turns to discuss the orator's pleasure (and at
9.1 the poet's), most editors suppose that he mentioned the topic at
this point, but that the phrase was omitted in the MSS because, like
all the others, it ended with a comparative adverb, and a scribe's eye
skipped from one similar ending to another (called by textual critics
'saut du même au même').   **Vrbis ... imperii ... gentium:**
the genitives indicate that fame and notoriety are secured in an ever-
widening circuit. *totius* and *omnium* further enhance Aper's claims.

5.5 Aper's first step is arguably faulty, since a conscientious man
would not be guided entirely (*omnia*) by considerations of expediency
(*utilitas*) alone (though Quintilian too glances at that argument, *Inst.*
12.11.29); moralists insisted upon the part played by integrity (*honestas*). Discussion of these issues takes up the third book of Cicero's *De
officiis*.   **tutius:** Brunt (1990) 86 draws attention to the dangers
incurred by *patroni* and *aduocati* who acted as prosecutors.   **armatus:** cf. Cic. *De orat.* 1.32 for a very similar plea on behalf of oratorical skill. Trials in antiquity were commonly described in military
metaphors, and the participants in this debate, Aper above all, regularly employ the terminology of battle (or sometimes gladiatorial
combat, an exclusively Roman activity) to characterize forensic oratory. The metaphor is particularly useful to Aper in his attack upon
the comparative slightness of Maternus' chosen activity; cf. 10.5
ad pugnam natos lacertos ... ad uera proelia. But it will be exposed as

hollow and inapplicable to contemporary circumstances by Messalla
at 37.7–8. (For the metaphor in *D.* see the Intro. to Peterson's
comm., lxi–lxii; more generally see Mayor's n. and addenda [1 454–
5] on Juv. 7.173 *ad pugnam qui descendit*, and Crook (1995) 5, 15; for
Quintilian's usage see Austin on *Inst.* 12.9.2 (he cited G. Assfahl, *Ver-
gleich und Metapher bei Quintilian* (Stuttgart 1932) 83–100) or the Intro.
to Peterson's comm. on Book x, lvi–lvii.)   **amicis:** cf. Stat. *Silu.*
4.5.50–2 *uenale sed non eloquium tibi,* | *ensisque uagina quiescit* | *stringere ni
iubeant amici*, with Coleman's n.   **alienis:** cf. 3.4.   **periclitantibus** 'standing trial' (*OLD* 5).   **metum et terrorem:** not a
common synonymous doublet (*TLL* VIII 912.6, cf. Cic. *Sest.* 34).
ultro: i.e. as prosecutor. In general acting for the defence had long
been reckoned as more creditable (cf. 10.8 below, Douglas's introduction to Cic. *Brut.*, xli, Quint. *Inst.* 12.7.1, and Suillius' reported
rebuke to Seneca in *A.* 13.42.3 *uiuidam et incorruptam eloquentiam tuendis
ciuibus exercerent*; Quintilian also reckoned defence a severer test of
advocacy, *Inst.* 5.13.3). Prosecution had moreover come by this time
to be associated with the *delatores*, and a man's reputation suffered
for it (cf. Sherwin-White on Pliny's treatment of Regulus in *Ep.* 1.5.1,
pp. 93–5). Cassius Severus, who will be seen as the pivotal figure in
the history of Roman forensic oratory, had however already shown a
preference for it (19.1, 26.4, Quint. *Inst.* 11.1.57).   **ferat** has a different sense in English with the various objects; with the last it
means 'inflict'. The indefinite third pers. subject 'one' is readily
understood from the context (see H–S 412, and cf. Wilkins on Cic.
De orat. 1.30 *neque uero mihi quicquam praestabilius uidetur, quam posse
dicendo tenere hominum mentes ... impellere quo uelit, unde autem uelit dedu-
cere*). This holds good even when an indefinite second pers. follows
(*possis* below (6)); cf. Cic. *Brut.* 209 *cum autem difficile sit in longa oratione
non aliquando aliquid ita dicere ut sibi ipse non conueniat, quanto difficilius
cauere ne quid dicas quod non conueniat eius orationi qui ante te dixerit?* (see
Kroll *ad loc.*).   **uelut quadam** apologizes for the use of a metaphorical expression (cf. also *A.* 3.55.5 quoted on 18.2n. and *uelut*
26.5). The Romans felt metaphorical usages of their language more
strongly than we do in ours, and commonly qualified any novel departure. The alliteration is remarkable.   **potentia ac potestate:** the first term is general, the second refers to power legally
conferred. A magistrate could not be tried during his term of office,

so Aper regards the successful pleader as enjoying a virtually (*uelut*) perpetual legal inviolability.

5.6 uis 'efficacy' (*OLD* 14, 15). **periculum:** specifically of legal risks (*OLD* 3). **increpuit** of dangers or alarms first thus in Cic. (*OLD* 1b). **lorica et gladius = praesidium ... ac telum** (in apposition to *eloquentia*) respectively; the imagery is traditional, as noted on *armatus* in 5. **siue in iudicio siue in senatu siue apud principem:** three or four types of process are here envisaged. *iudicium* signifies a lawsuit either before a *praetor* or in the centumviral court; the Senate now tried its own members; the Princeps both adjudicated disputes in private with a council to advise and exercised an increasingly important function as an appeals court.

5.7 As usual after a general discussion, a particular example is provided to clinch the point. **Eprius Marcellus** (T. Clodius) had an impressive career, despite the humble origins at which *quid aliud* hints (for further details and bibliography see *OCD*). He became urban praetor-for-a-day under Claudius on 30 December 48 (*A.* 12.4.3), and in 57 was arraigned on a charge of extortion in Lycia, but secured a notoriously unjust acquittal in a trial conducted before the Senate (*A.* 13.33.3). He was then *cos. suff.* under Nero, possibly in 62 and violently attacked Thrasea Paetus in 66 (see 8.2n.). He became strongly attached to Vespasian and prospered under him: proconsul of Asia for three years, an extraordinary honour, and a second consulship in 74; he was also co-opted into prestigious priesthoods. Eprius was not a good man (cf. 8.3n.), and represented for T. the perversion of great gifts (cf. the description of his impassioned oratory at *A.* 16.29.1); he thus provides a double-edged example of oratorical prowess, and reference to him disables Aper's case before it is well under way (for a similar lapse cf. Scaurus' choice of models for his undertaking a prosecution at *A.* 3.66.1: they all lost!). If T. subscribed to the traditional definition of the orator as *uir bonus dicendi peritus* (Winterbottom (1964) 90) then Aper's case is weakened, because Eprius was so far from being himself *bonus* that he attacked a good man like Thrasea Paetus. Even into late antiquity Eprius seems to have remained the type of a *delator* (see Sidonius Apollinaris, *Ep.* 5.7.3). **accinctus** sustains the martial metaphor (5n.); cf. *succinctus* at Quint. *Inst.* 12.4.1. **minax:** also of Eprius at *A.*

16.29.1.   **Heluidi:** the elder Helvidius Priscus won T.'s highest
praise as a *ciuis, senator, maritus, gener, amicus, cunctis uitae officiis aequa-
bilis, opum contemptor, recti peruicax, constans aduersus metus* (*H.* 4.5.2; *PIR*²
H 59; *RE* VIII 216–21). To vindicate his father-in-law, Thrasea Paetus, he had mounted an attack in the Senate against Eprius in 69
under Galba; this failed, not because Helvidius was a poor speaker –
T. refers to *egregiis utriusque orationibus*, *H.* 4.6.2 – but because Galba's
inclination was uncertain and the Senate divided. In effect, it was
not eloquence, in the historian's opinion, that rescued Eprius on that
occasion. A second attack, presumably the one alluded to here by
nuper, was made under Vespasian in 69/70; it too was successfully
fought off (T. fully reports their exchange at *H.* 4.6–8, for which see
Levick (1999) 82–3, 85 and esp. J. Pigoń, 'Helvidius Priscus, Eprius
Marcellus, and *Iudicium Senatus*: observations on Tacitus, *Histories*
4.7–8', *CQ* 42 (1992) 235–46). Priscus tried yet a third time to van-
quish Marcellus (*H.* 4.43), but again in vain. For Helvidius' own fate
see 2.1 *offendisse* n.   **sapientiam** 'philosophical wisdom'.   **elusit** 'foiled', perhaps a technical term of gladiatorial combat (Mayer
on Hor. *Epist.* 1.17.18).   **meum:** the possessive pronoun displays
warmth of affection (*OLD* 2b), cf. 27.2. This statement prepares us
for Maternus' neglect of the topic, though he hints that he has after
all little 'use' for such oratory at 11.4 (*securitatem*) and 13.6.

   6.1 uoluptatem: the line of argument adopted in this section of
Aper's speech is perhaps unexpected; he is not concerned with the
pleasure oratory gives its audience, but with the advocate's private
thrill at his success (there is a fleeting reference to the orator's own
pleasure in his skill at Cic. *Cael.* 46 *tanta uoluptate dicendi*). (For this
passage see M. W. Gleason, *Making men: sophists and self-presentation in
ancient Rome* (Princeton 1995) 159–60; this reference is owed to Dr M.
B. Trapp.)   **oratoriae eloquentiae:** 5.4n.   **non uno aliquo
momento:** the expression prepares the way for Aper's criticism of
the short-lived success of poetry, cf. 9.1 *uoluptatem … breuem*, 4 *intra
unum aut alterum diem*. The repetition of *prope* is pointless in both the
temporal ablative phrases; the first was deleted by Andresen because
it spoils the climax in *horis*; it is also in an unusual position, for T.
regularly places the adverb before the word it modifies (exceptions
only in *Hist.*, 1.2.1 *mota prope*, 4.85.2 *confecto prope bello*).

   6.2 libero et ingenuo: a doublet (*TLL* VII 1.1545.21–2), the first refers to status, the second to birth.   **honestas** is an important qualification.   **plenam** 'full'.   **frequentem** 'packed'; *plena* and *frequens* are not synonymous. The contrast when someone fell from favour (as did Eprius in 79) was the more remarkable, cf. *A.* 13.19.1 describing Agrippina's deserted *limen*.   **non pecuniae, non orbitati** ['childlessness' (*OLD* 3)]: the two nouns are picked up in reverse order by *orbos et locupletes*, and together point to a recognizable type, often the prey of the infamous legacy hunters, *captatores* (Woodman and Martin on *A.* 3.22.1, and cf. *A.* 13.19.2, 52.2 *pecuniosa orbitate*, and esp. 14.40.1 *orbitate et pecunia*).   **non officii ... administrationi:** picked up by *potentes*.   **ad iuuenem et pauperem:** as certainly happened to Eprius.

6.3 -ne introduces a rhetorical question (*OLD* 1c).   **quam** 'as' is correlated with *tantus* (cf. *OLD* 2c) to avoid a pedantically precise use of *quantus* (H–S 592, K–S II 458–9).   **spectare** depends upon *uoluptas* understood; the inf. with this noun is found in poetry and in Seneca's prose (*Ben.* 4.13.2, 7.2.3).   **ueteres** suggests experience (Smith on Tibull. 1.8.50 *ueteres senes*), and should not be emended or deleted.   **in** 'in spite of' has concessive force (*OLD* 40c 'where the action is surprising in the light of circumstances mentioned', Goodyear on *A.* 2.37.1, Duff on Sen. *Dial.* 11.2.3).   **id quod optimum sit** 'the highest good' is in this context oratorical skill.

6.4 togatorum comitatus et egressus: the speaker's clients, who wore the toga when making an official call, usually in the early morning, accompanied him as he set off for the Forum to conduct business (whether legal or not), cf. Juv. 7.142–3 *togati | ante pedes*.   **qui ... quae ... quae ... quod:** anaphora with elegant variation of gender.   **illud gaudium** 'that supreme delight' (Peterson); *illud* marks the climax of the list. *gaudium* governs the defining genitives of the gerunds, *consurgendi assistendique*, but the construction then changes, and *quod gaudium* [sc. *est*] is predicate to the infinitives, *coire, circumfundi*, and *accipere*, with their subject accusative, *populum*; in effect the noun is made to take the same construction as the verb *gaudeo*. This change of construction is not like the ones found in the later historical works, which are generally designed to produce variety. Here the change is necessary, given the switch from an implied subject, the orator (who is understood as rising), to an expressed subject, the people who crowd round him.   **assistendique** 'tak-ing one's stand' (*OLD* 1), but elsewhere the sense refers more gener-ally to the audience in the court (e.g. 19.5).   **in unum:** cf. similar praise of the orator's unique position at Cic. *De orat.* 1.31.   **coire ... induerit** form a tricolon crescendo. *induerit* = 'may assume' (*OLD* 3b), though 'may implant' (*OLD* 6 and G–G) is possible; the perf. subjunc. is potential. For the notion cf. Cic. *De orat.* 1.87 *et uti ei qui audirent sic afficerentur animis ut eos affici uellet orator*, *Brut.* 185 *ei qui audiunt ita afficiantur ut orator uelit*.

6.5 The opening is carefully balanced.   **quoque** 'even' (*OLD* 4).   **accuratam meditatamque** < Cic. *De orat.* 1.257: 'carefully prepared (cf. 14.2n.) and rehearsed' (the past part. of the deponent verb has pass. force here: G–L §163 s.v.).   **profert:** the subject is unstated, but can be easily assumed from *dicentium* and *orantibus*. **dictionis** = *orationis*.   **nouam et recentem:** the synonymous doublet is not uncommon, but Aper's fondness for it – cf. 8.1 – characterizes this champion of the 'modern'. The distinction, if any, may be that *nouus* = 'unprecedented', *recens* = 'freshly conceived in the mind' (*OLD* 5; see H. D. Naylor, *Latin and English idiom* (Cam-bridge 1909) 13).   **recentem curam** < Ovid (*P.* 2.4.16, 4.2.50). Here *cura* means 'literary work' (*OLD* 3b, to which add Stat. *Silu.* 4.6.1 *remittentem curas*; cf. 3.3n.).   **attulerit:** the tense and mood are debated. The perf. subjunc., used as a potential, would hint, as Peterson's translation brings out, that the occurrence is less usual: 'if he happen to produce ...'; or the subjunc. might be frequentative: 'if ever he produce ...' (*NLS* §196). The future perf. indic., on the other hand, seems a pointless variation upon the present indic. of *profert* in the parallel clause (cf. *steterit* at 37.8).   **lenocinatur** 'en-hance', as at *G.* 43.4 *feritati lenocinantur*.

6.6 audaciae: Statius too uses the word to describe the extem-poraneous composition of his *Siluae* (*Silu.* 3 *praef.*), and in the pre-fatory letter to the first book he admits to the special pleasure the exercise afforded him, *quadam festinandi uoluptate* (see M. D. Reeve in Reynolds (1986) 398 n. 12).   **temeritatis:** of the risks of speaking extemporaneously, cf. *OLD* 2, to which add Quint. *Inst.* 10.6.6 (but he also admits the charm of off-the-cuff development of an argu-ment at 4.5.4).   ⟨**in**⟩ was added by *b*²; it was easily omitted be-tween the final *m* and initial *in*.   **quamquam alia ...:** if the text is sound, this is a condensed/abbreviated comparison for *quam-quam alia, quae diu serantur atque elaborentur, grata sint* (so Persson (1927) 10–12). **diu serantur atque elaborentur:** the verbs go so closely together that they form a single idea, hence *diu*, which modifies only *elaborentur*, can be placed before the pair; cf. *Ciris* 290 *tam longe capta atque auecta*, one of Housman's examples of the word order in his note on Manil. 4.534.

7.1 Aper moves unobtrusively to his third topic, *dignitas*, by relating something of his own advancement thanks to his oratorical skill.   **latus clauus:** the 'broad purple stripe' extended from the neck to the seam on the front of the tunic (*OCD* s.v. clavus angustus, latus; illustrations in Daremberg and Saglio's *Dictionnaire des antiquités* I 2.1242–6). (T. usually avoids technical terminology, but a periphrasis here and from this speaker would be precious (cf. Syme (1958) 460 n. 2).) The right to wear it was conferred by the emperor upon equestrians on the way up (Talbert (1984) 12–15; R. P. Saller, *Personal patronage under the early empire* (Cambridge 1982) 50–1), just as magistracies were 'received' from him; Aper might have received his from Claudius (so Syme (1958) 799).   **homo nouus:** none of his ancestors had reached the Senate at Rome (*OCD* s.v. novus homo; *A.* 3.55, 4.15.2).   **eos quibus:** understand *dies ago*.   **mediocritate** 'limited attainment' (*OLD* 4); cf. Cic. *De orat.* 1.117 *in dicendo mediocritatem*.   **aut reum ... datur:** a tricolon crescendo. **centumuiros:** by this time a panel of 180 men, working in four *consilia* to try civil actions, chiefly concerned with inheritance (*OCD* s.v. centumviri, and cf. 38.2). Pliny, among others, made his reputation in this court (*Ep.* 6.12.2 *in harena mea, id est apud centumuiros*), which had gained in importance in the early Principate as *quaestio*-actions were replaced by hearings before the Princeps or the Senate (J. M. Kelly, *Studies in the civil judicature of the Roman Republic* (Oxford 1976) 35–9).   **principem:** the emperor either sat at ordinary hearings (Millar (1977) 228–40) or as a judge of first instance (Millar (1977) 516–26).   **libertos:** a case heard before Trajan on behalf of Eurythmus, *Caesaris libertus et procurator*, accused of forging part of a will, is described by Pliny, *Ep.* 6.31.7–12.   **procuratores** 'financial agents'; these might be charged with maladministration (Brunt (1990) 90–5 provides a list, where seven of those tried were imperial procurators). The trials of two, P. Celer and Lucilius

Capito, are mentioned at *A.* 4.15.2 and *A.* 13.33.1–2 (the former is exceptional in that it was conducted by the Senate, see Martin and Woodman *ad loc.*).   **tueri et defendere** 'protect from possible danger and defend against actual attack' (a common pair, found e.g. at Cic. *De orat.* 1.172, *Fam.* 13.64.1; see Anderson's n. on *G.* 14.1).   **datur:** the construction with inf. is originally poetic in Latin, and borrowed from the Greek syntax of δίδωμι (*TLL* v 1.1689.48–71).

7.2 in animo: Freinsheim's conjecture for the corruptly transmitted *in alio* is here accepted *exempli gratia*; for recent discussion of readings see W. S. Watt in *Eikasmos* 9 (1998) 263. Aper's point of course is that *orator nascitur, non fit.*   **codicillis** 'letter of appointment' to an imperial commission or candidacy of office, or offering some equestrian or senatorial post (Millar (1977) 306 and his index s.v.; *RE* iv 179.37–46). (This is the first reference to the document.)   **gratia:** an instance would be the praetorship Agrippina secured for Seneca from Claudius, *A.* 12.8.3.   **uenit** 'arise' (*OLD* 15).

7.3 Aper now turns to his last and arguably therefore most important theme, the fame an orator can acquire.   **qui illustriores:** Orelli proposed to replace the nonsensical paradosis, *qui non illustres*, which has been variously emended, with *quinam illustriores*. This produces a stylistically attractive parallelism with the next two sentences, both by the anaphora of the interrogative pronouns (*quorum, quos*) and by the comparatives (*prius, saepius*). The only difficulty is that T. uses *quisnam* elsewhere only in indirect questions: hence *qui* is preferred here.   **fama et laus:** the pair forms less a doublet than a hendiadys, since *fama* is a neutral word and needs specification: 'laudatory report'.   **[iuuenes et] adulescentes:** an intolerable doublet (and a false, or perhaps latent, antithesis with what precedes?): T. can hardly have Aper use the pedantic (and not universally accepted) distinction between *adulescens* (16–30 years of age) and *iuuenis* (31–45 years of age); nor does it receive support from *TLL* i 797.29–34. If there were to be a reference to two categories of young person, we should expect rather *pueri* for one or the other term (cf. 35.3 *pueri et adulescentuli* and Sen. *Con.* 3 pr. 15 *pueri et iuuenes*). For *iuuenes* b conjectured *uacuos*, an attempt to remove the doublet and provide an antithesis with the preceding expression; it is not necessarily derogatory (cf. *OLD* 11 'free from distractions or pre-occupations'); for a similar pair cf. Sen. *Ep.* 20.2 *iuuenum et otiosorum*. It seems best to follow Professor Kenney's suggestion and delete *iuuenes et.*   **recta ... indoles:** the phrase is also found at Sen. *Phaed.* 454.

7.4 quorum nomina prius parentes liberis suis ingerunt?: the same sort of thing could be claimed for poets, as Statius avows was the case for his successful father: *natis te monstrauere parentes* (*Silu.* 5.3.137).   **uulgus quoque imperitum et tunicatus hic populus:** the run of the essential words is also found at *Agr.* 43.1 *uulgus quoque et hic aliud agens populus* and *H.* 1.89 *uulgus et magnitudine nimia communium curarum expers populus*. *uulgus imperitum* recurs at *A.* 2.77.3, and is owed to Cic. *De or.* 3.195 *uulgus imperitorum*. **tunicatus ... populus** < Hor. *Epist.* 1.7.65 *tunicato ... popello*; the phrase contrasts with *togatorum*, 6.4.   **hic:** i.e. 'at Rome'.   **digito demonstrat:** cf. Hor. *C.* 4.3.21 *monstror digito praetereuntium*. The point is taken up by Maternus at 13.1 *apud populum Romanum notitia.*   **aduenae ... peregrini:** a common synonymous doublet, as old as Plautus (*Poen.* 1031). An example of their own notoriety among visitors to Rome was relayed by T. to Pliny, and by Pliny (who wished to preserve the flattering details) to Maximus in *Ep.* 9.23.   **auditos:** compressed, in the manner of the style associated more with the historical writings, for 'those they have heard of'; this usage is far more common with the neuter, singular or plural: *audita* 'hearsay' (*OLD* 9; *TLL* 11 1274.32 has no special comment).   **cum ... concupiscunt:** for the notion cf. Plin. *Ep.* 9.23.4: Pliny and a close friend, Fadius Rudinus, were reclining at dinner with a fellow-townsman of the latter, to whom Fadius was making known Pliny's accomplishments. From these he 'as it were' (*uelut*) recognized him.

8 Aper now illustrates the points treated above with examples drawn from the ranks of contemporary orators (whose names have been reversed, see 1.1n.).

8.1 modo locutus sum: at 5.7.   **nouis et recentibus:** 6.5n. **Crispum Vibium:** L. Junius Vibius Crispus; a famous orator, he secured a bad reputation as an accuser (T. himself disapproved: *pecunia potentia ingenio inter claros magis quam inter bonos* (*H.* 2.10.1)). He is again paired with the similarly successful Eprius Marcellus in §3 and at 13.4. Reference to another *delator* somewhat undermines the effectiveness of Aper's argument (Luce (1993) 36). Crispus' full name and career (he was perhaps *ter consul*) are discussed by Courtney on Juv. 4.81; his manner was 'bland, graceful, humorous' (Syme (1958) 4, 101, 594 n. 6), and Quintilian often referred to his *iucunditas*, e.g. *Inst.* 10.1.119: he made a witty remark about Domitian's penchant for killing flies (Suet. *Dom.* 3). ⟨**notos**⟩ is the supplement of Ursinus, and printed here *exempli gratia*; some reference to their renown is required.   **in extremis partibus terrarum:** how they came by this renown is suggested at 20.4.   **Capuae:** Eprius' birthplace; cf. the dedication found near there, *ILS* 992.   **dicuntur:** urbane imprecision on a matter of no significance: 'their birthplaces, I gather'.

8.2 hoc ... sestertium praestat: *hoc* is the object of *praestat*, and *sestertium* 'a hundred thousand sesterces' (commonly treated as a neuter singular noun, see *OLD*) is its subject.   **bis⟩ ... ter milies sestertium:** if written out in full the figures would run: *bis/ter milies ⟨centena milia⟩ sestertium* (really = gen. plural of *sestertius*, see *OLD* s.v.) 'the twice/thrice one thousand times one hundred thousand sesterces' = 200,000,000/300,000,000 (it was Crispus who possessed the two hundred million according to the scholiast to Juv. 4.81). Such wealth was staggering, especially when it is recalled that eight million sesterces is estimated as the appropriate capital for a senator (see R. Duncan-Jones, *The economy of the Roman empire* (Cambridge 1982, edn 2) 18, and for a list of private fortunes under the Principate 343–4).   **opes:** Nero rewarded Eprius handsomely for the attack on Thrasea (*quinquagies sestertium, A.* 16.33.4).   **beneficio** 'thanks to' (*OLD* 4).   **numen et caelestis uis:** a powerful expression, perhaps reflecting the divinization of Πειθώ.   **ad quam** introduces an indir. qu. explanatory of *exempla*, as at *A.* 3.6.3.   **fortunam** 'status' (*OLD* 11b).   **quae ... haberemus** 'for us to ...'; probably a final relative clause, suggesting intent on the part of the divine power of eloquence (*NLS* §148, with note (ii)).   **non auditu ... sed oculis:** Aper has in mind the wellnigh proverbial (Otto §1272) reliance upon sight rather than hearsay for solid evidence (Woodman on Vell. Pat. 2.92.5, p. 277 n. 2, and 121.3).   **cognoscenda ... haberemus:** *habeo* + gerund(ive) is a post-republican prose usage, common in the younger Pliny and T. (and particularly frequent in *D.*) (Martin and Woodman on *A.* 4.40.2, *OLD habeo* 17a).

8.3 sordidius et abiectius: the strong language may mean no more than that the families from which they sprang were not politically notable, and indeed both Vibius and Eprius were *noui homines* (cf. *A.* 4.21.3 on the *sordida origo* of Cassius Severus, and Syme (1979) 1 51 on the *infima fortuna* of the poet Gallus).   **paupertas:** cf. the success of the *delatores* at *A.* 1.74.2 *ex pauperibus diuites*.   **nascentes** 'in their early years' (*OLD* 1c).   **oratoriae eloquentiae:** 5.4n. **sine commendatione natalium** 'without the advantage (*OLD* 5) of good circumstances at their birth' (*OLD natales*[2] 7); this picks up the substance of the first *quo*-clause. The point at issue was also made by Juvenal, 8.47–9 *ima plebe Quiritem | facundum inuenies, solet hic defendere causas | nobilis indocti.* The form of expression may recall *Brut.* 96 *sine ulla commendatione maiorum,* where Cicero was describing another *nouus homo,* who also became a successful orator, Q. Pompeius. Now this Pompeius (for whom see *OCD* s.v. Pompeius, Quintus) had used his oratorical skill to get himself out of some potentially disgraceful situations, and Cicero was to judge him *improbe callidus* at *Fin.* 2.54. So there is an even greater similarity between him and the men to whom Aper refers than meets the eye.   **sine substantia facultatum** 'without the availability [*OLD* 1b] of resources' picks up the second *quo*-clause. *substantia* is a fashionable word in the first century; its meaning was carefully plotted by C. Arpe, *Philol.* 94 (1941) 65–78, esp. 69–70.   **neuter moribus egregius:** a damning point (cf. 12.2), which further undermines Aper's case (for Eprius' character cf. *H.* 2.95.3, where he along with Mucianus (see 37.2n.) is ranged with the moral degenerates of the previous reign: *magis alii homines quam alii mores*). Tradition held that Cato the Elder had defined the ideal orator as *uir bonus dicendi peritus.* Quintilian, *Inst.* 12.1.1, made this concept the backbone of his educational programme (see Winterbottom (1964)). The younger Pliny quotes a friend who parodied the expression in deploring that an orator like Regulus was a bad man: *uir malus dicendi imperitus* (*Ep.* 4.7.5), and he urged Hispulla to ensure that her son had a sound moral training: *trade eum praeceptori, a quo mores primum mox eloquentiam discat, quae male sine moribus discitur* (*Ep.* 3.3.7). Yet it remained the case that Vespasian needed *delatores,* for the property of the condemned (minus a quarter, which went to the successful prosecutor) came into imperial hands (cf. *H.* 2.84.1 *passim delationes,* Suet. *Titus* 8.5); so the bad continued under him to prosper. The slander shows that by the time the *D.* was published both men were dead. **habitu quoque corporis:** physical presence is always desirable in actors, barristers, singers and university lecturers, cf. Quint. *Inst.* 11.3.2. It was also felt in antiquity that physical defects might legitimately be drawn attention to when attacking an enemy (cf. T.'s own reference to Vatinius' *corpore detorto* at *A.* 15.34.2). **donec** in the sense of *quamdiu* appears first in prose in Livy (*OLD* 4); T. used it often (cf. 40.4). **principes fori:** Quintilian so described Domitius Afer at *Inst.* 12.11.3. *principes* is perhaps emphasized here by repetition so as to contrast with the reference to the peculiar deficiency of the sole *princeps* which Aper is about to refer to. **agunt feruntque cuncta** 'carry all before them' (*OLD ago* 1b); Livy introduced the expression to Latin on the model of ἄγειν καὶ φέρειν, but invariably in reverse order. T. to be different restored the original order of the Greek, but at *H.* 1.2.3, describing *delatores*, he preferred a novelty, *agerent uerterent cuncta*. The expressions are hardly flattering; Aper again advances a counter-productive point. **senex:** in 74/5 Vespasian was 64/5 years of age. T.'s audience will have savoured an ironical twist here: about four years after the dramatic date of this conversation Eprius was brought down by Titus for complicity in an assumed conspiracy just before Vespasian's death in 79 (Levick (1999) 192–3). In the end oratory did not save him: *perniciem aliis ac postremum sibi inuenere* (*A.* 1.74.2). **patientissimus ueri:** Vespasian was 'a realist'; for the expression, cf. Sen. *Dial.* 5.36.4. **amicos:** almost a technical term for favourites at court (*OLD* 3b). **sit**, a correction by Halm, normalizes the syntax; the MSS read *est*. There seems no reason why Aper should artificially interject a notion that forms no part of what he reports Vespasian as knowing. **quod** refers to their eloquence, which they put at his disposal (cf. Marcellus' attack on Paetus and Nero's reward). It serves both as object of *acceperint* and subject of *possit*, a not unusual practice with neuter pronouns (Woodman and Martin on *A.* 3.52.3, p. 383).

8.4 imagines ... et statuae: commonly combined (Cic. *Arch.* 30, Apul. *Met.* 2.1, and cf. Hor. *S.* 1.6.17, Plin. *Pan.* 10.3). *imagines* were 'portraits' of famous men, perhaps even of the orators in question (*noui homines* had no ancestral wax portraits to display, but did

not want to have bare walls in their atria). Juvenal at 13.119 *statuam
... Vagelli* – Vagellius was an orator, cf. id. 16.23 – provides evidence
that grateful clients might present their patrons with portrait statues
(see Courtney's n. *ad loc.* for further references to the practice); for a
statue of Crispus see 13.6n.   **tituli:** eulogistic inscriptions under
the portraits or on the statue bases.   **neque ... tamen** 'and yet
... not' (*OLD neque* 9c).   **tam hercule quam:** this lively expression is also found on Aper's lips at 21.5, a piece of verbal characterization.   **diuitiae et opes:** often found together in Cicero (*TLL*
v 1.1633.74–6).   **igitur** is found in second position, the norm in
Cicero and Caesar, also at 10.7 and 20.6; elsewhere in *D.* (3.1, 24.3,
34.4) it is the first word, the norm in the historical works (167 occurrences), where it is perhaps an archaism. It is placed second only
once in each of T.'s other works (*Agr.* 16.3, *Germ.* 45.5, *H.* 4.15., *A.*
1.47.1), so the higher incidence in *D.* suggests a conscious attempt to
recapture the practice of the Ciceronian age. (Quintilian had noted
that the positioning of this word called for nice judgement, *Inst.*
1.5.39.)

9–10.2 Aper opens up a second front of his argument, a *refutatio*
devoted to belittling the practical advantages of poetry. He briskly
rehearses the heads of his previous argument in favour of oratory
(*dignitatem, utilitates, uoluptatem, laudem*), this time to the detriment of
poetry.

9.1 Nam elliptically begins the new section: poetry does not con-
fer similar benefits, for ... (Many examples of T.'s elliptical usage of
nam are collected and elucidated in G–G 835–6.)   **inde enim
omnis fluxit oratio** < Cic. *Brut.* 201 *haec omnis fluxit oratio* (cf. too
33.4n).   **utilitates** 'advantages'.   **uoluptatem autem breuem:** contrast 6.1 *non uno aliquo momento*.   **laudem inanem:** a
Ciceronian phrase (*Fam.* 6.4.4, 15.4.13).   **infructuosam** perhaps picks up the agricultural simile from 6.6, and prepares for the
proverbial expression *in herba* at §4 (an instance of interaction, which
also suggests an agricultural metaphor in *inanis*, cf. Virg. *G.* 3.134
paleae ... inanes).

9.2 cui bono est: a common expression with the predicative dat.
of *bonum* (*OLD bonum* 2c, G–L §356 R1); *cui* is a dat. of advantage (G–
L §350.2).   **apud te** 'in your writings' (*OLD apud* 6). Aper refers
to traditional figures of tragedy, though a *Medea* was mentioned in

3.4, and Jason will have appeared in that.   **diserte:** there is no denying Maternus' skill, but it is thrown away on trifles.   **egregium poetam:** not uncommonly coupled (*TLL* v 2.288.1–3, Juv. 7.53). For the enhancement by *uatem* cf. Virg. *E.* 9.32–4 *et me fecere poetam | Pierides ... me quoque dicunt | uatem pastores* (with Clausen's n.). Aper guys the still fashionable term resuscitated by the self-important poets of Augustan times (for the recovery of the word see N–H on Hor. *C.* 1.1.35, *OLD* 2). Lucan had used it of himself, 1.63.   **deducit aut salutat aut prosequitur:** a Roman's prestige was visible to all when he moved about the city with a crowd of attendants; for the first two verbs see *OCD* s.v. salutatio, and for *deducit* 'escort from home to the Forum or Senate' see Powell on Cic. *Sen.* 63.

   9.3 negotium 'suit' (*OLD* 9).   **non quia poeta es:** the indic. is usual when the repudiated reason none the less states a fact (K–S II 386; cf. 37.6n.).   **domi nascuntur** 'Bassus can get that done in house', a proverbial form of expression (Otto §574, *OLD* 7b; the translation is based upon Shackleton Bailey's of the expression at Cic. *Att.* 1.19.3 and n.).   **pulchri ... et iucundi:** the first adj. suggests artistic quality, the second aesthetic appeal, 'engaging' (cf. *iucunditatem* 10.4, and see Peterson on Quint. *Inst.* 10.1.46 and 119 (referred to at 8.1n.), Brink on Hor. *AP* 99 *non satis est pulchra esse poemata, dulcia sunto*). The latter term does not imply a particular genre of poetry; it is for instance used of the tragedies of Pacuvius by Gellius, 2.26.13.   **magna noctium parte:** the crescendo of a nicely gauged triad (year, day, night) hints at the traditional sleeplessness of the hard-working writer. Callimachus praised the ἀγρυπνίη of Aratus (*Epig.* 27.4 Pfeiffer = *HE* 1297–1301; Cinna echoed him when he called Aratus' work *carmina multum inuigilata* (fr. 11.1)), Horace said the student must turn over Greek books *nocturna manu* (*AP* 269), and Ovid spoke of the *uigilatum carmen* and the *cura uigil* of the poet (*AA* 2.285, 3.412). (The commonplace is somewhat implausibly extended by Statius from writers to sculptors, *Silu.* 4.6.25–6 *multum uigilata ... aera* (he echoes Cinna).)   **excudit:** the metaphorical sense of 'hammering out' a written work is Ciceronian (*Att.* 15.27.2, and cf. Plin. *Ep.* 1.3.4) and underscores the notion of toil.   **elucubrauit:** another Ciceronian verb, referring specifically to work at night.   **rogare ultro ... audire:** Pliny, who liked giving and attending

recitations, complained that many had to be cajoled into agreeing to
come, *Ep.* 1.13.4 *nunc otiosissimus quisque multo ante rogatus et identidem
admonitus aut non uenit aut si uenit queritur se diem ... perdidisse.*   **nam
et domum ... dispergit:** Aper describes 'con brio' the prepara-
tions for a *recitatio*, if the author, like as not, is not grand enough to
have a house suitable for such entertainments; the repeated *et* (polysyndeton) emphasizes the tiresomeness of the business.   **domum
mutuatur:** Mayor amply illustrates the practice in his notes on Juv.
1.12 and 7.40; the orator on the other hand sees *his own* home packed
with clients (6.2 *domum suam*).   **libellos** 'invitations' (it seems: cf.
G–G, Mayor on Juv. 7.84, and esp. on Plin. *Ep.* 3.18.4), but some
think 'programmes' are meant (and anyway that could come to the
same thing).

   9.4 ut 'even granting' (*OLD* 35b).   **unum aut alterum** 'one
or at the most two' (*OLD unus* 1d). The opinion contrasts with *non uno
aliquo momento*, 6.1; Aper develops with similar imagery the critique
with which he began. The comparison turns into a metaphor, a
common feature of similes in Horace's conversational poems (see
Mayer on Hor. *Epist.* 1, pp. 28–30). The epithets contrast with one
another: *certam* with *uagum* ('fickle' *OLD* 8); *solidam* with *inanes*; *mansurum* with *uolucre*.   **in herba** 'in the blade' as we should say, a
proverbial expression (Otto §798); *herba, flore, frugem* – three stages of
plant growth – reactivate the idea of *infructuosa* in §1 above.   **refert:** the subject is now Bassus.

   9.5 The sentence begins in asyndeton, the usual way of introducing a specific example. Suetonius, *Vesp.* 17–18, attests to his generos-
ity: *in omne hominum genus liberalissimus ... ingenia et artes uel maxime fouit.
praestantis poetas ... insigni congiario magnaque mercede donauit* (cf. Levick
(1999) 76). Some of the contemporary poets whose work survives,
Valerius Flaccus and the consular Silius Italicus, flatter the new imperial family in their verses, and it may be supposed that they secured rewards for their services; cf. Val. Fl. 1.7–21, Sil. *Pun.* 3.594–
629.   **quingenta sestertia** (sc. *milia*) is named by Suet., *loc. cit.*,
as the sum he was also prepared to give *annually* to needy consulars,
so it puts the poet in his place, who received that sum once and for
all. Anyway, Nero's gift to Eprius (see *opes* 8.2n.) had been spectacu-
lar, ten times as much.   **donasset:** the subjunc. is used because
the *quod*-clause is part of virtual reported speech.   **indulgentiam:**

by now a technical term for imperial favour (Courtney on Juv. 7.21).   **quanto ... liberalitatem!:** the poet needs a patron, but the orator looks after his own interests.   **si ita res familiaris exigat** 'if domestic circumstances require it'; the phrase is also found in Quint. *Inst.* 12.7.9. The sentence ends on a tricolon crescendo in which the anaphora of the reflexive helps to stress the self-sufficiency of the orator compared with the client-poet.   **ipsum** is the subject of the inf., i.e. the original idea is *ipse se colit.* **colere** 'court' (*OLD* 7).   **suum genium propitiare:** each man is born with his own *genius*, which he and his household honour, usually on his birthday. It was also becoming customary by this time for Romans generally to pay respects to the *genius* of the emperor (see *TLL* vi 2.1831.83–1832 and *OCD* s.v. Genius). This phrase, given the context, glances at that practice, and encourages self-reliance: it is one's own genius one should win over, not another's, however grand.

9.6 conuersatio amicorum et iucunditas Vrbis 'the agreeable association with friends in the City'; on the other hand, Cicero in *Pro Cael.* 46 had stressed the loneliness of the hard-working barrister: *obterendae sunt omnes uoluptates, relinquenda studia delectationis, ludus, iocus, conuiuium, sermo paene est familiarium deserendus.*   **deserenda cetera officia** ('obligations', e.g. visits, greetings) suggests something selfish and reprehensible.   **in nemora et lucos:** cf. Hor. *Epist.* 2.2.77 *scriptorum chorus omnis amat nemus et fugit Vrbem* (Brink in his n. *ad loc.* draws attention to T.'s intelligent use of the symbol here and at 12 below) and Juv. 7.58 *cupidus siluarum.* The expression was recalled flatteringly in a letter to T. from Pliny, *Ep.* 9.10.2 *itaque poemata quiescunt, quae tu inter nemora et lucos commodissime perfici putas* (cf. Intro. 19).   **solitudinem:** see 39.3n.

10.1 opinio ... et fama: the doublet is common in Caesar (*TLL* vi 1.211.71–4), and forms a single idea, hence the number of the verb, *sequitur.*   **soli:** cf. Ov. *AA* 3.403–4 *quid petitur sacris, nisi tantum fama, poetis? | hoc uotum nostri summa laboris habet,* where Ovid insists, as here, that wealth is not their goal. Other poets too had avowed a desire for fame, implying indifference to other benefits: Lucr. 1.923 *laudis spes,* Virg. *G.* 4.6 *at tenuis non gloria.*   **aeque ... quam:** the construction is found in comedy, then apparently goes underground, and is resuscitated by first-century prose writers (*TLL*

1 1044.8–24 for negative sentences).   **sequitur** 'attaches to' (*OLD*
14, Reid on Cic. *Fin.* 1.32).   **mediocres** < Hor. *AP* 372–3 *medi-*
ocribus esse poetis | non homines, non di, non concessere columnae. These
are the only places where the epithet is applied to poets, so the recollection seems deliberate (G. B. A. Fletcher, *Annotations on Tacitus*
(Brussels–Berchem 1964) 104), and indeed the argument is similar to
that of Hor. *AP* 366–78 as a whole, where as here the contrast is
between the humdrum orator, who has some value (*in pretio est*), and
the middling poet, who has none. Pliny on the other hand reckoned
that neither the middling orator nor the poet secured much interest
(*Ep.* 5.8.4), though he had lasting fame in mind, unlike Aper.

10.2 rarissimarum 'very infrequent' (*OLD* 3). Aper has already
pointed out that a poet may only complete a book a year (9.3). The
trouble of organizing a *recitatio* suggests that for any one writer the
event is rare, and Juv. 7.82–6 shows that Statius' recitations were
few and far between. The barrister, on the other hand, pleads often
and in public, so can the more readily secure a following.   **ne-**
dum ut 'to say nothing of'. *nedum* alone would have sufficed, but
Livy treated it as an adverb, and so added *ut* to introduce the subjunc.; this construction was then occasionally followed (*OLD ut* 1 *sub*
fin., K–S 11 67).   **quotus quisque** 'how few' (*OLD quotus* 2a).
Hispania uel Asia form a 'polar' expression, for the provinces
mark the western and eastern limits of the whole empire (but cf.
Hor. *C.* 2.20.19 for the Spaniard as reader at least of his works,
and Ov. *Tr.* 2.5–6 for the desire of his readers to know him). Pliny
tells the story of a man who came all the way from Cadiz just to see
Livy, and having clapped eyes on him, returned to Spain (*Ep.* 2.3.8).
So literary men did in fact command some renown. Aper's point
may be that it would be worth the visitor's time to get to hear the
famous barrister.   **Galliis:** the conjecture of Schultingh is here
preferred to *Gallis*, because it puts the expression on all fours with
the preceding (two regions); it refers to *Gallia Comata*, which Augustus had divided into three districts.   **nostris** might apply only to
Aper, but it might also include all the other speakers in the dialogue
save Messalla, cf. 28.3 (see Courtney's extensive note on Gallic orators *ad* Juv. 7.147 *Gallia*).

10.3–8 Aper in conclusion reiterates that he is not attacking
poetry as such (it will be clear from 20.5 that he admires poets

considerably), but singles out Maternus as a special case (cf. 5.3–4). His argument involves anticipation, *anteoccupatio*, of Maternus' presumed defence at 5 and 7.

10.3 accipi 'to be construed' (*OLD* 20).   **tamquam +** subjunc. (*OLD* 5c 'indicating the contents of a dubious belief, rumour, etc.') introduces the equivalent to an English noun clause of indirect discourse, after *accipi* (cf. §5).   **nomen ... famae:** a bolder expression than the similar *Laus Pisonis* 249 *aeternae nomen committere famae.*   **inserere** suggests the notion of 'to include [in the canon]'; the verb thus represents ἐγκρίνειν (N–H on Hor. *C.* 1.1.35 *quodsi me lyricis uatibus inseres*).

10.4 Aper, though partial to his own calling, has a fundamental admiration for verbal skill in any form, including poetry. He here politely corrects the charge of Maternus at 4.1 *nec tu agitare ... poetas intermittis.*   **eloquentiam** 'the artistic use of language', 'language as an artefact', not specifically 'oratory'.   **sacras** will be picked up by Maternus at 12.1; Aper of course regards oratory as sacred, a not uncommon view (cf. Sen. *Con.* 1 pr. 10 *sacerrimam eloquentiam*, Cornelius Severus fr. 13.9 *sacris exculta quid artibus aetas* (sc. *profuit*; said of Cicero).   **coturnum:** the buskin was a boot on a high platform worn by tragic actors, hence the word comes to serve by metonymy for 'tragedy' (so introduced into Latin by Virgil, *Ecl.* 8.10).   **uestrum** 'of you tragedians'. The order of genres listed by Aper presents a hierarchy similar to those found in Hor. *Epist.* 1.3.6–14, Mart. 12.94, and the canonical list of Greek and Latin authors in Quintilian's tenth book. Tragedy in deference to Maternus comes first, with epic (elsewhere invariably first) as its partner. Then lyric, and then elegy (so too Martial, who, however, puts satire between them); then invective, and finally epigram (which also closes Martial's list). The second characteristic feature of the list is the attempt to provide a one-word description of each genre (or author, cf. 25.4, 31.6).   **sonum:** applied to epic in Quint. *Inst.* 10.1.68 (*OLD* 3b).   **iucunditatem:** not confined to lyric, cf. 31.6, *OLD iucundus* 1b and Quint. *Inst.* 10.1.101 on Livy's narrative.   **lasciuias:** of elegiac writing, Ov. *Tr.* 2.313, Mart. 3.20.6 (but contrast the use of the word to describe an unrestrained style, 26.2).   **iamborum amaritudinem:** of any form of invective (not necessarily in iambic rhythm); cf. Plin. *NH* 36.12 of Hipponax; *epigrammatum* *lusus*, and Mart. 4.49.2.   **quamcumque ... habeat:** subjunc. in an indefinite relative clause, cf. Woodman and Martin on *A.* 3.74.2 *quoquo inclinarent.*   **speciem** 'genre', 'kind' of the genus *eloquentia*, as at Cic. *Top.* 30. Aper leaves out the traditionally sub-poetic forms of comedy and satire.   **ceteris aliarum artium studiis:** Aper means music, painting, and sculpture. Cic. *De orat.* 1.12 *ceterarum artium studia* provides the springboard for the unusual phraseology.

10.5 arcem eloquentiae: Quintilian used the same metaphor of Cicero: *arcem tenente eloquentiae* (*Inst.* 12.11.28).   **ferat** 'is making for'; *fero* is here intransitive, as at *A.* 2.23.4 *quo uentus ferebat* (cf. *OLD* 6).   **errare** 'go off course' (*OLD* 4) sustains the metaphor. **adept⟨ur⟩us:** the fut. part., Acidalius' generally accepted correction of the reading of the MSS, suggests potential.   **leuioribus:** Roman men of affairs, however cultured, tended to regard poetry and the arts generally as 'slight' activities; even Cicero used this term of poetry when contrasted with oratory or jurisprudence, e.g. at *Brut.* 3 *in leuiorum artium studio* (with Douglas's n.).   **Graecia** 'the Greek world'; Goodyear on *A.* 2.10.5 n. 1 takes this to be the sense here, for generally T. uses *Graecia* to mean 'Greece of old' (the Roman province of Greece was called *Achaia*, 30.3). **ludicras ... artes** 'sports' (not 'acting').   **quoque** 'even' (*OLD* 4).   **honestum est:** the Romans noted that Greeks esteemed success in the less serious pursuits of life; e.g. Nepos, *praef.* 5 *magnis in laudibus tota fere fuit Graecia uictorem Olympiae citari.* That it was not respectable in Roman eyes is vividly demonstrated by their contempt for Nero's charioteering and wrestling.   **Nicostrati:** Nicostratus, an Olympic victor in 37, had been seen by Quintilian in his youth (*Inst.* 2.8.14 – T. may even owe the reference to him; see *RE* s.v. §11, XVII 543).   **robur ac uires:** the synonymous doublet is common (see Heubner on *H.* 1.87.1); cf. 26.5 *uirium robore.*   **di dedissent:** the alliterative phrase seems to be traditional, cf. Hor. *Epist.* 1.4.7 *di ... dederunt.*   **pugnam** 'boxing' (*OLD* 1b). Aper goes on to refer to the two contests in the pentathlon which required strength of arm.   **et theatris:** there has been no suggestion that Maternus' plays were performed by actors; this phrase may have been added to identify the kind of poetry he recited in the auditoria as dramatic. **uera proelia:** for the military metaphor see *armatus* 5.5n.   **uoco** 'summon' (in parody of the legal sense).   **tamquam:** see §3n.

obnoxium 'liable' + inf. is a unique construction (*TLL* IX 2.128.69).
offendere recalls the purpose of the visit of Maternus' friends: he
has given offence. The notion will provide the keynote of Aper's
concluding remarks, for it is repeated frequently (*offendis* and *offensa*
§6, *offendere* §8) and so forms a sort of ring-composition with the
opening remark of Secundus at 3.2.

10.6 nec 'and yet not'.   **periculosius:** because, as he goes on
to explain, gratuitous.   **fide aduocationis** 'an advocate's responsibility [*OLD* 6]' (Winterbottom).   **fortuitae et subitae** <
Cic. *De orat.* 1.150 (but T. has reversed the order).   **impetu:** oratorical 'dash'; cf. 2.1, 26.1, and *A.* 4.61 for part of the judgement on
the orator Q. Haterius: *impetu magis quam cura uigebat*; and on extempore inspiration see M. Winterbottom 'On impulse' in (edd.) D.
Innes, H. Hine, C. Pelling, *Ethics and rhetoric. Classical essays for Donald
Russell on his seventy-fifth birthday* (Oxford 1995) 321, n. 33.   **meditatus:** adversative asyndeton.

10.7 †ex his† has been regarded as a gloss on *hinc*, and Gesner
deleted the words. But the absence of a verb to parallel the infinitives in the second clause seems unsatisfactory, so some follow
Muretus in reading *existere*. For lack of a convincing solution, the
words are here marked as corrupt.   **tolle igitur . . . :** the connection of thought is brought out by Goelzer's translation: '⟨Soit⟩, mais
alors . . .', 'Fair enough, but in that case, away with . . .'   **quietis
et securitatis:** the pair reappear in Maternus' reply as adjectives at
13.1, and the second noun at 11.4. That Maternus sought a quiet life
was implicit in the reference to 'groves and woods', 9.6.

10.8 Aper concludes as Secundus had begun their plea, with the
dangers Maternus runs, not the waste of his time on poetry. His
concern for his friend's well-being lies at the bottom of his attack
upon his poetry.   **priuatas:** Aper's point is oblique: he has just
referred to a 'stronger opponent' (probably the emperor himself),
which suggests a political (*publicus*) dispute (*res est publica Caesar*, as
Ovid neatly put it at *Tr.* 4.4.15). A subject like Cato is political (as
well as old-fashioned), so Aper here implies that they have no business meddling in politics.   **[expressis]:** the word was deleted by
Heumann, since it makes no sense. Most editors now follow him.
Some however have tried to emend it, whilst some commentators
seek to defend it, both unsuccessfully. Nevertheless, as Winterbottom

(1975) makes clear in his apparatus, it is hard to account for the presence of the word in the tradition, since it does not seem to be a gloss that has crept into the text.   **libertas** 'candour', 'frank-ness', as usual (cf. *H.* 1.1.1 (quoted at 27.3n.), 85.3, 4.44.1, *A.* 1.74.6). C. Wirszubski, *Libertas as a political idea at Rome during the late Repub-lic and early Principate* (Cambridge 1950) 160–7, discusses the concept in T.

11–13 The reply of Maternus

Maternus makes it clear that his reply will have to be off-the-cuff; he must abandon his prepared answer in order to deal with the unex-pected turn his friend's admonition has taken. (The bantering obser-vation that Aper has forestalled him somewhat replicates a similar scene in Cic. *De orat.* 1.74.) Maternus will avoid the issue of *utilitas*, following Aper's hint that this was not a point which he could try to controvert, but addresses himself to the other topics, viz. *uoluptas* (12.1–6), *gloria* (12.4–6), *fortuna* (13.1–4).

The tone of Maternus' reply is markedly elevated: he picks up Aper's word *sacer*, and applies it to poetry, three times, stressing too the purity, innocence, and divinity of the poet's activity. All this is in contrast with the tarnished occupation of the public speaker. In sub-stance too this reply imports a fresh dimension into the debate: Aper had stuck professedly to contemporary oratory and poetry. Maternus on the other hand appeals back to the past, first with reference to the Golden Age (12.2–3), but then more relevantly to the distinguished pleaders and poets of Greece and Rome (12.5). He also introduces the notion of the book of the published oration (12.6 *liber*), the vehi-cle of posthumous fame, which also provided the standard of com-parison and generated a sort of 'anxiety of influence' among the more thoughtful. At 13 Maternus introduces the Augustan Age, and even when he speaks of their contemporaries, the tragedian Pom-ponius Secundus and the orator Domitius Afer, it is significant that they are both dead by the dramatic date of the conversation. Maternus dwells upon the past, and so he gives a turn of the screw to the issue of fame, by introducing the notion of its *perpetuitas* at 13.3 (not mentioned by Aper as something to be bothered about). Again, this prepares us for comparison between past and present, which will inform the discussion between Aper and Messalla, and form the basis of Maternus' own summing-up. In a word, this speech lays the historical foundation of the dialogue.

11.1 Aper acrius ['rather passionately' *OLD* 7]: a play upon his name, as Woodman and Martin observe on *A.* 3.75.1, p. 492, cf. Virg. *Ecl.* 10.56 *acres ... apros* and Hor. *Epod.* 2.31–2. *acrius* contrasts with *remissus*; *intento ore* with *subridens*. At the end of his speech, however, Maternus too will be strongly moved, as might be expected of an inspired poet (14.1 *concitatus et uelut instinctus*). We sense his warming to the theme in the course of his argument.   **subridens:** T. is here indebted to Cic. *De orat.* 1.74, where Scaevola, described as *ridens*, replies to Crassus, who he says has *artificio quodam* (= here *arte quadam* 'ingeniously'; cf. *OLD* 3) granted a point (*concedo* appears in both passages). Therefore Scaevola will not contend (*non luctabor*), an idea here represented by *me ... mitigauit*.   **facerent:** cf. 5.3, 10.3.

11.2 The interpretation of this section was by and large cleared up by J. Stroux, 'Vier Zeugnisse zur römischen Literaturgeschichte der Kaiserzeit I. Maternus, Redner und Dichter', *Philol.* 86 (1931) 338–49; his punctuation (a full stop after *tragoediarum*, undeniably somewhat abrupt) and explanations are here adopted.   **efficere aliquid et eniti:** a Ciceronian pair, but here (as often) reversed, for which cf. Cic. *Phil.* 2.23 *quantum facere enitique possum.*   **ingredi ... auspicatus:** pleonasm is particularly common in phrases conveying the notion of beginning (Austin on Virg. *A.* 1.372 *prima origine*, Kraus on Livy 6.12.10, H–S 796, cf. 3.3n.).   **quidem** 'namely' (cf. *OLD* 1e; the usage is discussed more fully by Güngerich *ad loc.*).   **im⟨perante⟩ Nerone:** this conjecture, made independently by Haupt and Müller, is here accepted *exempli gratia*, following Stroux, who noted that it provides a contrast with *hodie*.   **studiorum quoque sacra profanantem:** the activity referred to is unknown. Vatinius was a *scurra*, dear to Nero (*A.* 15.34.2, Dio 62.15; *RE* VIIIA 520.17–56); Maternus either attacked him in a speech in someone else's defence, or prosecuted him at some time late in Nero's reign.   **notitiae ac nominis:** 36.4.

11.3 Maternus is now determined to abandon the lawcourts (*forensis labor*); he is not however retiring altogether from public life, since he goes on (§4) to make it clear that he will continue to attend the Senate, and will even be prepared to speak up on another's be-

half. He thus remains an active citizen.   **deiungere:** the metaphorical use of this verb is far less common than that of its synonym,
di(s)iungo, so it preserves some of its radical sense of unyoking a draft
animal, the impression Maternus wishes to convey. For the senti-
ment cf. Hor. *Epist.* 1.1.8 *solue senescentem ... equum*, of releasing the
poet from lyric chores.   **comitatus istos et egressus** pick up
6.4, as *istos* 'that you go on about' shows.   **frequentiam salutationum** picks up 6.2 *frequentem domum*. For the metonymy *salutatio* = 'stream of visitors' cf. Cic. *Fam.* 9.20.3 *ubi salutatio defluxit, Ad
Brut.* 2.4.1 *hoc paululum exaraui ipsa in turba matutinae salutationis*. Editors
print Schele's easy correction *salutantium*; but, in the light of the the
Ciceronian metonymy, it is hard to see why the same sense is inapplicable here.   **aera** ['statues' *OLD* 7] **et imagines** picks up
8.4.

11.4 securitatem picks up 10.7.   **innocentia** appears to remove the grounds of his friends' complaint altogether: he believes he
has harmed no one in his plays. The close proximity of the adjective
at 12.1 underscores his conviction.

12.1 Nemora uero et luci: 9.6; for *secretum* cf. Hor. *AP* 298
secreta petit loca.   **increpabat:** he did so by calling them a desert,
solitudo, 9.6 (a notion Maternus has just corrected).   **strepitu:** cf.
Hor. *C.* 3.29.12 *strepitumque Romae*; *Epist.* 2.2.79 *inter strepitus nocturnos
atque diurnos* (with reference to poetic composition). Maternus is
gently correcting Aper's reference to the *iucunditas Vrbis* (9.6).
sedente ... litigatore: cf. Hor. *Epist.* 1.5.31 *atria seruantem ...
clientem.*   **inter ... reorum:** the defendant in a Roman court
might dress in a stained toga (*OLD sordes* 2b), and even resort
to weeping to elicit pity from the jury (the paired words occur in
Cicero: *TLL* VII 2.837.66–7). Cf. Quint. *Inst.* 10.3.22–30.   **innocentia** recalls 11.4.   **sedibus sacris:** perhaps tragic phraseology; cf. Cic. *De orat.* 3.102 *sed quid uideo? ferro saeptus possidet sedes
sacras* (a citation from an unknown play by an unknown author). The
cretic + spondee clausula is impressive.

12.2 eloquentiae: 10.4n.   **haec ... haec ... hoc:** anaphora
emphasizes the claim.   **primordia ... primum:** Maternus here
deploys a venerable argument, found earlier in the Latin literary tradition, for instance, in Horace, *AP* 391–407; he reminds his
hearers that poets were the first to civilize mankind, which in that

primitive age still lived in the woods (*siluestres homines* is how Horace
begins his paragraph).   **penetralia** sustains the exalted tone of
the previous sentence (Quintilian uses the word of philosophy, *Inst.*
12 pr. 3); cf. *sacrario* 20.5.   **habitu cultuque:** the expression
refers to the verse-form of poetry, but may also hint that primitive
eloquence did not metaphorically wear *sordes*.   **commoda:** with
active nuance, 'making herself agreeable to' (*OLD* 5).   **mortalibus** seems deliberately chosen to enhance the suggestion of the
quasi-divine origins of *eloquentia* (which now becomes personified and
the subject word).   **et nullis contacta uitiis pectora:** for the
not very intricate word-order cf. 31.5 (where the pattern is the same,
an abl. phrase with perf. part.); Goodyear on *A.* 1.10.1 *simulatam* and
67.1 collects some more complex examples of interlacing. *et nullis*
emphasizes the negative (contrast the more regular *nec ullis* at §4); T.
affects this sort of expression, cf. *Ger.* 10.4 *et nullo mortali opere contacti*
[*equi*] (Nipperdey collected instances on *A.* 1.38.2 *et nihil*). *contacta*
'polluted', as in the passage from *Ger.* just quoted (*OLD* 6, *TLL* IV
717.20–2). The belief that primitive man lived *sine probro, scelere* is reiterated at *A.* 3.26.1, a digression on the history of law (see Woodman and Martin *ad loc.*).   **sic oracula loquebantur** picks up
Aper's ironic *uates* at 9.2, and emphasizes the verse-form of oracular
utterances (cf. §3 *uatibus*, §4 *proferre responsa* and Horace's *sacer inter-
presque deorum … Orpheus, AP* 391–2). The tense of the verb is important: prophets at Delphi were believed to have used verse in days of
yore, and Olen, a mythical seer, was even credited with the invention of the dactylic hexameter (Pausanias 10.5.7–8). But in T.'s day
prose was the medium, a point that elicited a dialogue from his contemporary Plutarch, *De Pythiae oraculis* (= *Moralia* 394d–409d). For
further discussion see J. Fontenrose, *The Delphic oracle* (Berkeley, etc.
1978) 194, 213–14, 223–4.   **lucrosae huius et sanguinantis:**
powerful disapproval is expressed; *huius* contrasts with *illud* in §3 (see
Intro. 34). Maternus has an eye on the motives of *delatores*. If successful, they secured a portion of the property of the condemned;
lucrosae looks back to Aper's reference to the wealth of Eprius and
Vibius (8.2), but of course fortunes had always been made by successful pleaders. In 204 BC the *lex Cincia* had, among other measures,
sought to forbid payment of barristers for their services, but many
eluded its provisions (see Furneaux on *A.* 11.5.3). There were dread-

ful instances of greed and treachery by barristers: Suillius 'threw' a
case he was defending (*praeuaricatio*), and his client, Samius, committed suicide in Suillius' house (*A.* 11.5.3, in AD 47). Maternus thus
repudiates the *whole* of Roman forensic oratory (not just that of his
own day) for its blood-stained greed.   **recens:** if Aper wants 'recent' history (cf. 8.1), then Maternus will supply it, but for him it
is only 'recent' in contrast with the fabled Golden Age. The predicate forms a tricolon crescendo.   **ex** ['as a result of', *OLD* 18]
malis moribus natus draws out the implication of *neuter moribus
egregius* at 8.3. Contrast 41.3 *inter bonos mores*, where again Maternus is
speaking.   **ut tu dicebas:** cf. 5.6. Maternus views the expression
in a new light, since one characteristic of the Golden Age, to which
he is about to turn, is that it had no weapons (cf. Ov. *Met.* 1.99 *non
galeae, non ensis erat: sine militis usu* ...); these appeared only later, in
the 'bronze' or 'iron' ages (cf. Ov. *Met.* 1.126 *ad horrida promptior arma*,
Cic. *De nat. deor.* 2.159 *ferrea ... proles ... ausa ... prima est fabricarier
ensem*).

   12.3 nostro: i.e. of us poets.   **aureum saeculum** < Virgil,
esp. *A.* 6.792–3; cf. *OCD* s.v. golden age. The concept is further discussed by W. Heilmann, ' "Goldene Zeit" und geschichtliche Zeit im
Dialogus de oratoribus', *Gymnasium* 96 (1989) 385–405.   **criminum
inops** 'deficient in [*OLD* 6] crimes'; *inops* suggests ironically a bene-
ficial aspect of the innocence of the Golden Age; tradition maintained that it had no laws, no judges and no protectors (cf. Ov. *Met.*
1.89–93). Maternus will develop this point in his concluding remarks, 41.3–4.   **poetis et uatibus abundabat** recalls 9.2.
qui ... canerent, non qui ... defenderent: probably final subjunctives in relative clauses to express the purpose of their existence. Cf. of the early poets Arist. *Poet.* §4.1448b 24–7 and Hor.
Epist. 2.1.130 *recte facta refert*. This need not refer to epos, but to *laudes*
generally.

   12.4 ullis: the use of this adjective as a substantive is rare (*OLD*
1b).   **gloria maior aut augustior honor** form a reply to
Aper's charge at 10.1. There is no main verb expressed; understand
erat.   **quorum proferre responsa:** cf. §2 *sic oracula loquebantur*.
There were a number of mythical Greek poets whose prophecies
had been collected and circulated (Musaeus' were gathered by Ono-
macritus in about 500 BC).   **interesse epulis** < Hor. *C.* 4.8.29–

30 *sic Iouis interest | optatis epulis impiger Hercules* (but the phrase also appears at Cic. *Sest.* 111); no evidence of this claim has been uncovered, but heroes did dine with gods, and Aeolus at Virg. *A.* 1.79 *tu das epulis accumbere diuum* refers to the privilege conferred on him by Juno.   **dis genitos** 'heroes' < Virg. *A.* 6.131, 9.642; cf. Ov. *AA* 3.405.   **neminem causidicum ... accepimus:** sc. *fuisse* (so *TLL* 1 308.15). The humorous point is not idle, since it was held by historians of culture that laws came late into societies, when their misdoings were beyond endurance; cf. Columel. 1 *pr.* 6, and *A.* 3.26. For the infrequent adjectival use of *nemo* see *OLD* 5.   **Orphea:** he accompanied the Argonauts as minstrel.   **Linum:** a mythical singer, mentioned by Virgil in the *Eclogues* (see *OCD* s.v.).   **altius** 'further back' (*OLD alte* 11).   **Apollinem:** Apollo was credited with singing as he pastured the herds of Admetus, and he sang at the wedding of Peleus and Thetis (*Il.* 24.62, Plato, *Rep.* 2.383b referring to a now lost play of Aeschylus').

12.5 fabulosa ... et composita 'mythical and made-up [i.e. fictional]' (*OLD compono* 10).   **nimis** goes ἀπὸ κοινοῦ with both. **Demostheni:** Demosthenes (384–322 BC) was by common consent held to be the greatest of the Greek orators, comparable therefore in distinction to Greece's greatest poet, Homer (Kennedy (1963) 206–36).   **apud posteros:** used of the fame of Pomponius Secundus at *A.* 12.28.2, quoted at 13.3. But Aper the realist may not have been all that interested in posterity's opinion (though cf. 23.6).   **Lysiae aut Hyperidis:** the two were linked as models of the purest Attic prose style at Cic. *Brut.* 67, and Hyperides was reckoned to have acquired many of his graces from Lysias (Longinus, *Subl.* 34–5). Lysias (*c.* 459 – *c.* 380 BC), as a non-Athenian, delivered almost none of the speeches attributed to him, but wrote many for others to speak on their own behalf (*OCD* s.v.). Hyperides (389–322 BC) was also a professional speech-writer, who on some estimates ranked second in esteem only to Demosthenes (Longinus, *ibid.*; *OCD* s.v.). Naturally Maternus sets tragic poets, his own literary models, in comparison with them.

12.6 Maternus closes a section of his argument with elaborate chiasmus, achieved by placing the names of the orators and poets immediately either side of their respective *aut*.   **Ciceronis gloriam:** the complaints of his own contemporaries are more fully set out at 18.4 (cf. Quint. *Inst.* 12.10.12–14). Later Pollio's son, C. Asinius Gallus, wrote damningly of him and was answered by the emperor Claudius (Suet. *Claud.* 42, Aul. Gell. *NA* 17.1; Schanz–Hosius §178, 1 545; Kennedy (1972) 282 n. 162). That rhetoricians still belittled him is hinted at 26.8.   **Vergili:** Virgil had always found critics (Schanz–Hosius §246, 11 97); Q. Asconius Pedianus (9 BC – AD 76) wrote an essay *contra obtrectatores Vergilii*, which perhaps put a stop to cavilling, and the result is noted here.   **detrectent:** potential subjunc. in a consecutive relative clause.   **Asini:** Asinius Pollio (76 BC – AD 5, *cos.* 40 BC; *OCD* s.v. Asinius Pollio, Gaius) was one of the most distinguished figures in the political and literary world of the late Republic, but he is a somewhat odd choice here because he was also a tragic poet (see 21.7).   **Messallae:** Messalla was born in 64 BC and died in AD 8 or 13 (a disputed date: see R. Jeffreys, 'The date of Messalla's death', *CQ* 35 (1985) 140–8 and Syme (1986) 217–26). He was *cos.* 31 BC; see *OCD* s.v. Valerius Messalla Corvinus, Marcus. Like Asinius Pollio, he was a distinguished politician. Not much of a poet himself, he was none the less the patron of great poets, Tibullus and Ovid. For his oratory see 18.2n.   **liber** 'a published speech' (*TLL* VII 2.1274.82–3); by the same token it is used of a play-book at 3.1, etc.   **Medea Ouidi aut Vari Thyestes:** the fame of these, the only successful tragedies of the Augustan age (and, significantly, the only dramatic works by their respective authors) is also attested by Quintilian, *Inst.* 10.1.98 *Vari Thyestes cuilibet Graecarum comparari potest* and by Philargirius on Virg. *E.* 8.10. L. Varius Rufus' tragedy was produced in 29 BC at the triumph of Augustus, who gave the poet a million sesterces (Schanz–Hosius §267, 11 162–4). Both his *Thyestes* and Ovid's *Medea* are lost.

13.1 ne ... quidem 'not ... either' (*OLD ne* 6b, so too at §3 below).   **fortunam** 'rank' is the theme word, cf. §4, and picks up Aper's discussion at 8.2.   **illud felix** picks up *felix illud* from 12.3.   **contubernium** corrects Aper's charge of solitariness at 9.6, but Maternus is unspecific about the poet's associates: some think the Muses, others that a small band of like-minded writers is intended; *caeli* is to be understood, suggests *TLL* IV 793.60, perhaps recalling Ovid's *nobis ... sunt commercia caeli*, *AA* 3.549. Alternatively, it is argued that the text needs a supplement: Gronovius added *secum*, Shackleton Bailey *sui* (*CJ* 77 (1981–2) 255).   **timuerim:**

potential perf. subjunc. **inquieta et anxia** contrast with *securum et quietum* (in chiastic order); for *inquieta* cf. 40.2 *non de quieta*, for the latter pair see 10.7; Maternus is clearly replying to the point made there. **Vergili secessum:** the Suetonian *Vita* 48–9 Rostagni records the poet's preference for a quiet life in Campania or Sicily. *secessum* recalls *secedit*, 12.1. **populum** is dignified by the addition of *Romanum*, contrast 7.4 *uulgus .... imperitum et tunicatus hic populus*. Maternus will again have recourse to this elevated tone, 37.4. There may be yet more to the form of the expression, since, as Maternus has hinted before now, the modern public speaker has very restricted access to the people of Rome (4.2n. *angustiis*); the poet however may retain a link with the mass of his fellow citizens. Virgil was by this time seen to be the mouthpiece of the Roman people: he is styled by Petronius (118.5) *Romanus ... Vergilius*.

13.2 testes ... testis: a highly emphatic anaphora appeals to historical evidence (*OLD* 4). **Augusti epistulae:** some of these are quoted in the Suetonian *Vita* 120–4 Rostagni (= E. Malcovati (ed.), *Imperatoris Caesaris Augusti operum fragmenta* (Turin 1962, edn 4) 21–2), and by Macrobius, *Sat.* 1.24. It would be interesting to know when they became generally available. **auditis in theatro Vergili uersibus:** the Suetonian *Vita* 103–4 Rostagni and Servius on *E.* 6.11 both refer to recitations of the *Eclogues* in the theatre. **Vergilium** was deleted by Ernesti as not strictly necessary, but the name is repeated to complete a chiasmus: *Augusti*: *Vergili*:: *Vergilium*: *Augustum*. (For repetition of a proper name where a pronoun would have been sufficient see Goodyear on *A.* 2.28.3.)

13.3 Secundus Pomponius: for the reversal of the names see 1.1n., and for a short account of his career see *OCD* s.v. Pomponius Secundus. P. [?Calu]isius Sabinus Pomponius Secundus was an illustrious tragic poet of the first half of the century (cf. *A.* 5.8.2 *multa morum elegantia et ingenio illustri*, 11.13.1 *is carmina scaenae dabat*, and Quint. *Inst.* 10.1.98 *quem senes parum tragicum putabant, eruditione ac nitore praestare confitebantur*; modern admirers of Senecan drama conveniently forget his rival's unchallenged pre-eminence in contemporary opinion). He was also a successful public servant, suffect consul in 44 and governor of Upper Germany. At *A.* 12.28.2 T. uses the notice of his defeat of the Cherusci to make clear once again his view that the life of the imaginative artist is of more account in the long run than that of the high achiever in contemporary public life: *decretusque Pomponio triumphalis honos, modica pars famae eius apud posteros in quis carminum gloria praecellit.* This judgement overthrows traditional Roman values (Syme (1958) 338–9).   **Afro Domitio:** Cn. Domitius Afer (again, for the reversal of the names see 1.1n., and for a brief account *OCD* s.v.) began his career discreditably as a prosecutor under Tiberius (*A.* 4.52.4); his obituary at *A.* 14.19 damns him by contrast with M. Servilius, but he may have tried to put his bad start behind him (for an appreciation see Kennedy (1972) 442–6). His performance at any rate was distinguished, and Quintilian, Afer's pupil and admirer, regarded him as supreme in his field, among those known personally to him (*Inst.* 12.10.11, 11.3). Quintilian was equally impressed by Secundus, so juxtaposition of the two here must have carried great weight with contemporary readers.   **dignitate uitae:** the lives of poets are more creditable than orators' (9.1; cf. Winterbottom (1964) 92). Syme (1958) 538 n. 5 observed that *dignitas uitae* was something T. admired along with *elegantia* in the nobility. **perpetuitate famae:** the phrase seems to glance at 10.1–2, where Aper was more concerned with the extent of fame, rather than its endurance.   **cesserit:** potential perf. subjunc.

13.4 Crispus iste et Marcellus: 8.1n.   **concupiscendum** agrees with *quid*, 'what that is to be desired', so the syntax is not the same as that described at 8.2n.   **quod timent, an quod timentur:** they fear failure and are feared by their fellow citizens, the lot of *delatores*, whose job was not plain sailing (Eprius Marcellus is reported at *H.* 4.8.3 as pleading that his friendship with Nero had caused him anxiety): their prosecution might be deemed malicious, or, if it seemed to be failing, the defendant might turn the tables on them (see *DNP* (1997) III 387 s.v. delator). The word-play is favoured (see Durry on Plin. *Pan.* 35.3 *timeantque quantum timebantur* (said of *delatores*) to which Professor Winterbottom adds Sen. *Ep.* 105.4 *qui timetur timet*). It may also be noted that T. used words for 'fear' far more often than any other writer (see the table in *TLL* s.v. *metus*); this says something about the society he described. The three *quod*-clauses form a tricolon crescendo.   **cotidie aliquid:** picked up (?accidentally) below, §5.   **ii quibus praestant indignantur:** those who are obliged to us may resent our help, even though it was sought, cf. Sen. *Ep.* 19.11 *quidam quo plus debent magis oderint.*

omni: Walther's conjecture for *cum* of the paradosis is printed here *exempli gratia*; another suggestion is that some words have dropped out, e.g. *metu tum*, between *cum* and *adulatione* (so M. Winterbottom, *CQ* 49 (1999) 338).   **tantum posse liberti solent:** the imperial freedmen had great personal power (*potentia*); for exx., particularly under Claudius and Nero, see *OCD* s.v. freedmen, freedwomen. The point here prepares the way for the attack on oratory in the contemporary world, where the free Roman citizen is of less account than the Greek ex-slave. The whole foundation of contemporary oratory's prestige is thus undermined. This pithy (but non-gnomic) *sententia* concludes the argument to this point with great force; the economy of the four words is characteristic, especially of Lucan (cf. Mayer on Lucan 8.85), and Reitzenstein (1915) 185 n. 3 drew attention to it as an instance of Tacitean σεμνότης. We may compare Boudicca's taunt at *A.* 14.35.2: *uiuerent uiri et seruirent.*

13.5 Me uero dulces ... Musae is quoted from Virg. *G.* 2.475. There is a special appropriateness to the citation since Virgil is contrasting the pursuit of poetry with other, perhaps more esteemed, activities.   **illa sacra** 'those hallowed places' (*OLD* 2); *fontes* perhaps recalls the rivers mentioned by Virgil in the same context at *G.* 485–6.   **sollicitudinibus et curis:** a common doublet (*TLL* iv 1470.42–8).   **insanum ... forum** < Virg. *G.* 2.500, where the farmer's life in the country is being praised. Propertius picked up this expression, 4.1.133–4, where there is a contrast between the orator and poet.   **lubricum:** cf. Sil. 7.542 *lubrica rostra*.   **fallacem** is Bötticher's conjecture, here accepted only *exempli gratia*, for *palantem* (vel sim.) of the tradition (*TLL* vi 1.224.78–9 seems to give the passage up).   **trepidus** 'excited' (*OLD* 3), not 'fearful'.

13.6 non emphatically negates *me*, which picks up *me* in §5: 'let it not be *me* the clamour awakes'. For *non* + jussive subjunc. see G–L §270 R1, K–S I 191–2, and for T.'s usage Nipperdey and Andresen on *A.* 1.11.1 and 13.40.2; for the continuation with *nec* (rather than *neue*) see G–L §270 R2, K–S I 194 A.2, and for T. Nipperdey and Andresen on *A.* 1.43.3.   **fremitus salutantium:** cf. 6.2, Virg. (again) *G.* 2.462 *salutantum ... undam*, and Sen. *Ep.* 84.12 *illa tumultuosa rixa salutantium limina*.   **libertus:** presumably an imperial freedman, come to summon him to a meeting (or perhaps give him some commission as at Stat. *Silu.* 5.2.168–71).   **incertus** 'uncertain

about' (*OLD* 9).   **pro pignore** 'as a guarantee' (*OLD* 3). Maternus
refers to the practice of including the emperor among the benefi-
ciaries to ensure the will's execution. For the grasping emperor cf.
H. 1.48.4 *testamentum Titi Vinii magnitudine opum irritum; Pisonis supremam
uoluntatem paupertas firmauit.*   **quandoque [enim] fatalis et
meus dies ueniat:** a difficult and much discussed clause. The
interpretation of Güngerich *ad loc.* is here accepted. *quandoque* is
relative 'at whatever time', and *enim* has to be deleted following
Nipperdey. *fatalis ... dies* refers to a natural death (*OLD fatalis* 3b);
meus is also not uncommonly used with *dies* to express one's last day
of life (cf. *TLL* v 1.1056.30–2, quoting *CIL* vi 22355a *hic tuus fatalis
dies*; *ibid.* 1032.38), but the combination with *et* gives the whole expression an unusual cast (so unusual indeed that Zwierlein (1997) 89
would delete *enim fatalis et* as an intrusive gloss). One view can be
dismissed immediately. Some suppose, following Heller, that the
sentence contains part of an iambic line, perhaps even from one of
Maternus' own tragedies. But unless he was a bungler, he will have
conformed to the metrical practice of Seneca, and eschewed an
iambic word in the fifth foot (here *meus*) before an iambic word in the
sixth (here *dies*); this is nowadays known as the Bentley–Luchs law
(for which see Tarrant's edition of Sen. *Thy.* p. 29, or H. Drexler,
Einführung in die römische Metrik (Darmstadt 1967) 36, 137). Once it is
seen that this cannot be verse, the road lies open to other strategies
of interpretation, including emendation.   **statuarque** 'may I be
set up', a somewhat poetical usage, cf. Ov. *Her.* 2.67 *media statuaris in
urbe,* cited in *OLD* 4.   **tumulo:** the simple abl. of place is again
poetic (Furneaux (1896) 1 section v §25; *NLS* §51 (iv)).   **non
maestus et atrox:** Reitzenstein (1915) 219–20 suggested that T.'s
hearers would recall the famous statue erected by the Athenians in
honour of Demosthenes, in which he is indeed depicted as grimly
pondering. It strengthens this suggestion to note that the statue was
often reproduced – we still possess some fifty copies, of which there
is a head in the Ashmolean Museum in Oxford (*EAA* iii 76–7), and
Brutus, according to Cic. *Orat.* 110, had erected one in his gardens in
Tusculum. As much in point, however, is the statue erected in Rome
in the basilica Iulia to commemorate C. Sallustius Crispus Passienus
(*RE* xviii 2.2097–8; Schol. Juv. 4.81); T., his readers and the interlocutors in the dialogue would all have seen it.   **hilaris et**

coronatus: like a poet (so Orelli).   **pro memoria mei:** the objective gen. is preferred to the possessive adj. for emphasis, cf. *A.* 1.43.3 *tui memoria* and *TLL* VIII 684.54–5 (where by an oversight the present example, found on 672.10, is omitted).   **nec consulat quisquam nec roget:** Maternus does not want his friends to seek a resolution of the Senate or petition the emperor for a more public recognition of his services, e.g. a portrait medallion in the Palatine library (cf. *A.* 2.83.3 for Germanicus). He may still have Virgil in mind, for he had averred that he would be content to be *inglorius* at *G.* 2.486. (Many commentators however take the reference to be to an appeal for posthumous clemency towards the memory of one who died under a cloud; but Maternus is not out to alarm his friends.) **nec ... nec:** with jussive subjunc. (K–S I 194).

14–16.3 Interlude

The dramatically striking introduction of a new character was not uncommon in the course of dialogues. Alcibiades' arrival at Agathon's symposium was famous (Intro. 37 n. 93, and cf. Cic. *De orat.* 2.12), but the formal model here is Cic. *Rep.* 1.17, describing the arrival of L. Furius, who asks if he has interrupted a conversation (*num sermonem uestrum aliquem diremit noster interuentus?*; cf. *De orat.* 2.14), but he is assured by Scipio that he has not (*minime uero*). A new character is essential if the argument is to be developed, and it is clear from Messalla's failure to explain why he has come that his presence is only dramatically motivated. (H. Wagenvoort in *Mnem.* 54 (1926) 428 acutely suggested that his entrance was delayed by T. out of tact, so that he did not have to hear Maternus' attack upon contemporary forensic oratory, which by implication would incriminate his step-brother, Regulus.) At this point we have reached a stalemate: Aper cannot convince Maternus that he should abandon poetry and resume oratory, Maternus, despite some hinted criticisms, has shown no desire to mount a full-scale attack upon the contemporary role of the orator. What is more, his own view must be saved for the last word, since it gives the truest account of the failure of modern conditions to sustain the oratorical tradition. What we need before that is an alternative hypothesis, attractive at first sight – the sort of analysis offered by the elder Seneca at *Con.* I pr. 6–9 or per-

haps by Quintilian in the now lost *De causis corruptae eloquentiae* – but
on closer inspection one-sided. No one of the available interlocutors
is in a position to propound such an hypothesis (Secundus sticks to
his role as mediator). Thus Messalla provides an essential ingredient
in the debate; it will fall to him to take on Aper, as we move closer to
the theme enunciated at the opening of the dialogue.

14.1 Vixdum finierat appropriately parodies epical style with
the opening half of an hexameter line, cf. Ov. *Met.* 2.47 *uix bene de-*
sierat, Petr. *Sat.* 122.122 *uixdum finierat* (in the Civil War poem).
concitatus: contrast *remissus* 11.1; used of Lucan by Quint. *Inst.*
10.1.90 *ardens et concitatus*. Maternus is described in the character of a
poet possessed by enthusiasm for his topic.   **uelut instinctus:**
the term is highfalutin (cf. Sen. *Dial.* 10.9.2 *uelut diuino furore instinctus*,
Quint. *Inst.* 12.10.24 *instinctis diuino spiritu uatibus*) and so qualified by
uelut.   **cum:** *cum 'inversum'* after *uixdum* introduces the leading
idea, an unexpected event (*OLD uixdum* b, G–L §581, H–S 623).
Vipstanus Messalla: for him and his speech see Syme (1958) 104–
8. He was a Roman of Rome, related to the great family of Republican times (*H.* 3.9.3 *claris maioribus*; Syme (1986) 242; cf. 27.1n. *maiores*
tuos). T. himself expressed approval of his character and his eloquence at *H.* 3.9.3 *egregius ipse et qui solus ad id bellum artis bonas attu-*
lisset, all the more because he spoke in defence of his step-brother,
Regulus (15.1n., *H.* 4.42); but, after seeing military service, he seems
not to have had much of a career (*tr. pl.* in 69), and perhaps died
young. This may account for Aper's somewhat abbreviated praise of
his eloquence below (23.6).   **tempestiuus:** used as a secondary
predicate with adverbial force; *OLD* 3d notice only Stat. *Theb.* 9.825
for *tempestiuus*, but other adjectives, especially those denoting time,
are commoner in prose of the first century after the liberal example
of the Augustan poets (Roby §1069, K–S I 234–6, H–S 172, Löfstedt
II 368–72). Draeger §8 lists examples in T., and remarks that his
usage is wider than in earlier prose authors.   **meditationem**
'preparation' (*OLD* 3). Messalla assumes they are discussing a case
(as in a way they are).

14.2 Minime, minime: a colloquial denial, colloquially repeated.   **atque adeo** 'and what is more' (*OLD adeo²* 6b).
uellem 'would that' indicates an unfulfilled wish, hence *interuenisses*
(see *OLD uolo¹* II *uellem*).   **accuratissimus:** Secundus is aware

that Aper had his speech more or less ready (6.5n.).   **sermo ...
oratio:** the two are contrasted, and the choice of words seems deliberate, as Orelli urged: Aper 'spoke' very carefully, and Secundus
gives Messalla the gist of his argument. Maternus clearly secures
Secundus' implicit approval from the range of descriptive terms, all
favourable, which he lavishes upon the inspired 'oratory' of the
poet. A similar distinction between the words is found at Quint. *Inst.*
12.10.43, and at *H.* 1.19.1 (Heubner *ad loc.*).   **cum ... exhortatus est:** the *cum*-clause explains *sermo* (we could regard it
as = *in quo*; cf. 15.1), so the verb is in the indicative.   **ingenium
ac studium** 'talent and application': the pair are a variant on
the notion of 'talent and training', cf. 24.1n.   **laeta** 'brilliant'
(Winterbottom), a stylistic term (*OLD* 2), cf. *laetitia* 20.3n., 21.9n.
audentior: terms for 'daring' were often used to characterize literary undertakings, especially ventures of style (Brink on Hor. *AP* 10),
and Aper himself had applauded the *audacia* of extempore speaking
(to which he has driven Maternus), 6.6. Poets particularly referred to
their boldness in tackling certain themes, so again his word has been
carefully chosen.

   14.3 [et] is difficult to account for; if it is correlative with *atque*
'both ... and' it forms a most unusual combination (*TLL* II 1055.14
and J. H. Schmalz in *Glotta* 6 (1915) 179–80 are referred to by
Hofmann in *TLL* v 2.888.59–64), perhaps inappropriate to a conversation. Its deletion by Halm is the simplest course, though other
alterations are proposed by various editors.   **infinita** reappears
at 15.2 and 30.2, always on the lips of Messalla (cf. Aper's use of
natus ad, 5.4n.).   **uiri optimi** strikes the moral note again (cf. the
description of Saleius Bassus at 5.2).   **⟨optimi⟩ temporum
nostrorum** places a restriction upon *oratores*; Aper will of course
catch the note, cf. 14.3 *hoc tempore*. *optimi* was added by Muretus, and
is here accepted *exempli gratia* (other supplements have been proposed), since even if in calling his friends *oratores* Messalla means that
they are the only ones deserving of the name, the noun all on its own
makes no sense with the gen.   **declamatorio studio:** Bonner
(1949) offers the fundamental study of this aspect of rhetorical training, which had profound effects on all literary forms of the day.
alunt: for the common metaphor see Brink on Hor. *AP* 307.
eruditionis ac litterarum 'literary culture': hendiadys.   **iis**

... peruenerint: we the readers of *D.* are thus implicated in the discussion 'recorded' by one of those present; cf. 32.7. There is a similar self-reflexive suggestion that the fictional 'conversation' may be leaked to the outside world in Cic. *Brut.* 231. The tense and mood of the verb (fut. perf. indic. or perf. subjunc.) are in doubt; an iterative subjunc. (19.2n.) seems likely. The perf. is rare but not unexampled in this period (K–S II 207–8).

14.4 Iuli Africani: Julius Africanus was, alongside Secundus himself and Domitius Afer, the best of the orators whom Quintilian personally had heard (*Inst.* 10.1.118, 12.10.11); for more on him see *OCD.*   **uitam componendo spem ... fecisti:** Reitzenstein (1915) 230 drew attention to the peculiarity of the expression: it was the biography which secured approval, not the hope men entertained of further such works.   **quam in Apro quod ... :** the interpretation and text here are problematic. If we accept the tradition, then Messalla says, not without irony, that Aper too finds favour (*probari*), with those who approve modern methods of training the orator. Some editors regard this explanation as unacceptable, and reckon that Messalla more openly reproaches Aper for his modernism; they follow Andresen, *exempli gratia*, in adding *improbari* before *in Apro*. Alternatively, an ellipse of the verb of opposite sense to *probari* might be argued for, with support from the examples collected by Kenney on Lucr. 3.614; Livy 45.20.9 ... *orantes ne noua falsaque crimina plus obesse Rhodiis aequum censerent quam antiqua merita* [sc. *prodesse*] provides the closest parallel, for it too is a comparison. But such an ellipse seems too artificial for a conversation, and irony among friends is surely politer than an open reproof.   **scholasticis** imports a tone of disapproval, as at 15.3, cf. Sen. *Con.* 1 pr. 12, Plin. *Ep.* 2.3.5.   **ueterum** 'of old' harks back as usual to the pre-imperial republic (G–G 1762 a–b; 33.4; cf. 1.1n. *priora*). Messalla is contrasting not only periods of time, but also approaches to the discipline of public speaking, for he implicitly indicts contemporary reliance upon the professional teacher of oratory, the rhetor. It is this jibe which opens the way to the main topic of discussion, the decline of modern oratory.

15.1 uetera ... et antiqua: a colloquial synonymous doublet (16.7, 17.6; *TLL* II 180.54, 181.22 lists seven examples in Plautus), which can be differentiated, as by Mayor or Courtney on Juv. 15.33, thus: '*vetus* because it has lasted a long time, *antiqua* because it started long ago'. But the pairing is too common in conversational style to justify this distinction in all cases (so Lorenz on Pl. *Most.* 476; Sonnenschein *ad loc.* appears to agree).   **fratris tui:** really step-brother (they will have had the same mother), a reference, the only one in the conversation and suitably veiled, to the dreaded *delator* M. Aquilius Regulus, who was himself one of the age's most impressive speakers, often mentioned by Pliny in his letters (*OCD* s.v. Aquilius Regulus). Aper is highly complimentary to Messalla; debate will be courteous.   **hoc tempore:** cf. 14.3n. *temporum nostrorum.*   **oratorem:** in the strong sense, 'a true orator' (cf. 20.4, 26.4); the noun forms the complement with *esse* to *neminem.*   **contenderes:** the subjunc. indicates indefinite repetition (*NLS* §196).   **[antiquis]** was deleted by Acidalius. Alternative measures are to add *parem* with Lipsius before *antiquis*, or to delete *esse*, and take *contenderes* in the sense 'compare' (*OLD* 9); *antiquis* will then be dat., and *neminem* used adjectivally with *oratorem* (*OLD* 5).   **cum** 'in that ...' explains why he does not fear the *malignitatis opinionem.*

15.2 in contrarium disputes: cf. 16.3. This was a valid philosophical tactic, particularly in the New Academy (cf. Quint. *Inst.* 12.1.35 with Austin's note, and the reference at 31.6 to the *pugnacitas* to be learnt in that school), which maintained that the truth could be reached by arguing the opposing sides of an issue. We find this strategy in Cicero's dialogues, esp. *Rep.* 3.8, where Philus is reassured that so long as he does not give an impression of believing his counter-arguments against justice, the exercise may readily lead to the truth. Messalla's dig at Aper here recalls what Crassus said of Antonius in Cic. *De orat.* 1.263 *haud scio an aliter sentias*. In fact, Aper will not deny the charge; rather, like a good barrister, he will maintain that the opposite argument must be aired (cf. his opening remark at 16.4).   **aliter sentire:** cf. 24.2 *ne ipse quidem ita sentit.*   **uelim impetratum:** this construction, common in Cicero (G–L §280.2(c)), emphasizes the speaker's impatience for his wish to be realized (for more examples see *OLD uolo* 6b (with predicate adjective or part.), and cf. 23.4 *fortem ... uolo*).   **causas:** the key word recalls the opening of the work, 1.3. Messalla thus proposes the topic of discussion.   **plerumque** 'often' (*OLD* 2), a sense favoured by T. (see Furneaux on *A.* 14.53.5, where the context is similar to this).

15.3 solacio: this predicative dat. is common (Roby p. liv *a*). The sentence is composed chiastically.   **quaestionem** again echoes a key word from 1.2.   **uideo:** logically parenthetic, since it is the fact that the Greeks have degenerated, not his seeing it, which soothes others but increases the difficulty of the point at issue for him.   **etiam Graiis accidisse ut longius:** two ideas are blended here, first, that decline has befallen the Greeks too, and secondly, that it is greater among them than among us.   **Graiis:** Puteolanus' conjecture is accepted by many editors, and it is closer to the MSS variants than Dronke's *Graecis*. The distinction of connotation is carefully set out by Austin on Virg. *A.* 2.148: though *Graius* was normal in elevated poetry, in prose it served to contrast the Greeks with other nations, here, the Romans.   **absit** 'is inferior to' (*OLD* 7b).   **Aeschine:** Aeschines was a contemporary and rival of Demosthenes (Kennedy (1963) 236–45).   **Sacerdos iste Nicetes:** Nicetes Sacerdos, from Smyrna, was a teacher of Pliny's (*Ep.* 6.6.3, see Sherwin-White's n.). It may be that he is the Nicetes referred to by Philostratus (*VS* 1.19–21) as the first orator of note since Aeschines (who has just been named) (Crook (1995) 186 n. 80). T. himself does not approve of 'Asian' oratory (of which Ephesus or Mytilene may be taken as centres), whereas Pliny embraced it and enthused about one contemporary exponent, the declaimer Isaeus (*Ep.* 2.3.1).   **scholasticorum:** 14.4n.   **quatit** 'shakes [with noise]' (*OLD* 2b); cf. what Philostratus says of a young *aduocatus fisci*, Quirinus of Nicomedia, that he was adept at 'shaking' (κατασεῖσαι) the ears of his audience (*VS* II 29.621).   **Afer:** 13.3n.   **Africanus:** 14.4n.   **Asinio:** 12.6n.   **recessistis:** Messalla does not count himself among the true orators of the day (14.3), validating Aper's judgement (15.1). The verb is picked up again at 32.5 by Messalla himself.

16.1 Magnam ... quaestionem deliberately recalls 1.2 and endorses the fresh initiative, to account for the decline in oratorical skill. Fine manners are here to the fore, as in the possible model, Cic. *Rep.* 1.71 *quis enim te potius* ... where Laelius encourages Scipio to speak.   **eruditionem ... ingenium cura ... meditatio:** the ideal combination of talent and application. For these concepts see 2.1n. and for the combination of *ingenium* and *cura TLL* IV 1463.22–5. Messalla plainly scores on both counts.

16.2 The exchange parodies Cic. *De orat.* 2.27 *nisi prius a uobis impetraro*, where Crassus begs others to be on hand at the debate and Julius agrees, *pro utroque respondeo*. Messalla's request for support prepares us for Maternus' return to the fray.

16.3 Maternus here implies that Secundus is not acting as an impartial arbiter (cf. 5.4). It may be that in the lacuna between 35 and 36 Secundus declined to take further part in the conversation. This polite undertaking to make good a gap in another interlocutor's exposition is perhaps derived from Cic. *De orat.* 2.126.   **paulo ante:** at 15.2.   **manifestus est ... accingi:** the construction *manifestus* + inf., not found earlier, recurs at *A.* 2.57.3 *dissentire manifestus* (see Goodyear *ad loc.*). Like Virgil's use of *certus* + inf., it replaces an impersonal construction and may be indebted to a Greek model, δῆλός ἐστι + part. (so Persson (1927) 23–4); Latin had no pres. pass. part.   **iam dudum in contrarium accingi:** this is suggested by his reply at 15.1. He will indeed leap to the defence of contemporary oratory, perhaps a trifle rudely, for Messalla had indicated at §2 that he was now prepared to speak; Aper seems to be jumping the queue.

16.4–23 Aper's second speech

Aper launches into a defence of modern eloquence (discussed by D'Alton (1931) 340–3). He focuses first upon the concept of an era, *aetas*; though his argument is somewhat playful, it has its serious side, and above all he is prepared to confront the issue historically. He was by no means alone in his regard for contemporary achievement (see Intro. 14–15).

16.4 inauditum et indefensum: the former is legal terminology, the latter is first used in a judicial context by T. (Goodyear on *A.* 2.77.3); the words are paired frequently by T. (*H.* 1.6.1, 2.10.2). **hac uestra conspiratione** ironically reformulates *hanc nostram ... concordiam.*   **interrogabo:** judicial (*TLL* VII 1.2268.83) and so slightly hectoring (though the fut. is milder than the pres.); contrast the more urbane *scire uelim* of Horace. Aper's argument is like Horace's in *Ep.* 2.1.34–49 and Quintilian's at *Inst.* 8.5.33: where does the contemporary world start? Aper is as satirical as Horace, but both have a substantial point, viz. that our historical consciousness is highly arbitrary. (There is a similar discussion of the relative concepts of periods at Cic. *Brut.* 39.)

16.5 audio 'meet with the word' (*OLD* 4).   **Vlixes et Nestor:** Homer, *Il.* 3.222 and 1.249, praised their oratorical powers; cf. Cic. *Brut.* 40 (where too they represent the oldest masters of eloquence) and Ov. *Met.* 13.92. The point Aper makes is not perhaps entirely a joke. Literary historians of Greece used the term νεωτερικός to describe any writer after Homer, and the term was copied by Latin commentators to describe post-Virgilian poets. (For Quintilian see Peterson on *Inst.* 10.1.40.)   **mille fere et trecentis annis:** abl. of measure. The computation is owed to the critical chronology of Eratosthenes, for whom see R. Pfeiffer, *History of classical scholarship from the beginnings to the end of the Hellenistic age* (Oxford 1968) 163–4. *fere* was the current form of the adverb, and so it alone is found on the lips of the speakers in *D*. But in his historical works T. used almost exclusively the archaic form *ferme*, a stricter practice than that of his predecessors (see *TLL* VI 1.492.62).   **uos autem** picks up Messalla's reference to Demosthenes at 15.3.   **Demosthenen:** 12.5n.   **Hyperiden:** 12.5n.   **Philippi:** 382–336 BC.   **Alexandri:** 356–323 BC. It was a tradition of Greek literary criticism, or more particularly of the criticism of oratory, that the death of Alexander marked the end of the 'classical' period, because Greek liberty perished under him (E. L. Bowie, 'Greeks and their past in the Second Sophistic', *Past and Present* 46 (1970) 3–41, revised in M. I. Finley, ed. *Studies in ancient society* (London and Boston 1974) 166–209). This prepares the ground for Maternus' concluding argument that the natural field of eloquence in Rome has disappeared under the Principate.   **ita tamen ut** 'albeit', a restrictive consecutive clause (*NLS* §167). They survived Alexander by only a year each!

16.6 trecentos annos: T. may have in mind the argument advanced by Scipio in Cic. *Rep.* 1.58 that the four hundred years or so which separated the last king of Rome from his own time was no great span in the life of the city; Laelius assented to that proposition.   **referas** 'assess by reference to' (*OLD* 10); with *respectum* 'regard' it produces a slight pleonasm, but the words are neither in the same clause, nor close together.   **si** is used in the sense of *sin*.   **in proximo:** here = *proximum*, *OLD* 2; this type of adjectival or adverbial expression – *in* + a neuter adjective used substantively (*OLD in* 38) – becomes widespread after Livy (cf. *in confesso* 25.2n., and Goodyear on *A.* 2.44.2 *in aequo*). Variety is clearly in part the motive for its use, as for instance at *A.* 4.32.3 *in arto et inglorius labor.* **est:** the change to indicative emphasizes the truth of Aper's contention. For the general sense of Aper's argument – the slightness of the purely human reckoning of time, Professor Winterbottom compares Sen. *Ep.* 99.31.

16.7 in Hortensio: *Hortensius* was one of Cicero's most influential dialogues, a protreptic ('encouragement'; *Div.* 2.1.1) to the study of philosophy (Schanz–Hosius §171.2, 1 523–5, and cf. L. Alfonsi, 'Dall'Hortensius al Dialogus de oratoribus', *Lat.* 24 (1965) 40–4). Its title derived from its dedication to the famous rival orator. It had a profound effect upon Augustine (*Conf.* 3.7), but is now unfortunately lost. The relevant passage is fr. 80 Grilli = 35 Mueller, preserved by Servius, *horum annorum ... magnus* $\overline{\text{XII}}$ *DCCCCLIV* [12, 954] *amplectitur.* Thus a month in such a year comprised 1,071 solar years. For the fascination exerted by Plato's Great Year see G. de Callataÿ, *Annus Platonicus: a study of world cycles in Greek, Latin and Arabic sources* (Publications de l'Institut Orientaliste de Louvain 47; Louvain 1996).

The context within the dialogue in which Cicero deployed the notion of the Great Year is uncertain. But at *Hort.* fr. 52 Grilli = 32 Müller an argument is put forward by Hortensius himself to show that *sapientia* is older than *philosophia*, which he calls *recens*, since it dates only from Thales. Now, he ought at some point (though there is no room in the context of the transmitted fragment) to have justified the odd claim that Thales, who lived five centuries before him, was 'recent'. Did Hortensius slyly insinuate the reckoning by the Great Year to support his unusual assertion? If that were so, Aper's reference to the eponymous dialogue would have more point. He is not just reminding his hearers that Cicero had happened to refer to that calculation in the work, but might even be employing a strategy similar to that of one of its interlocutors, and for a similar purpose, to weaken an opponent's position in advance. **magnus et uerus annus:** the 'great year, properly so called' (*OLD annus* 1b) was the 'total period between two times when the sun, moon, and the five known planets would all be in the same positions relative to the constellations or fixed stars' (Cic. *ND* 2.51, and cf. Zetzel's n. on

Cic. *Rep.* 6.24.2, where the use of *uere* is similar to Aper's *uerus* here); it also occurred when all the heavenly bodies were in the same position as at the beginning of time.   **caeli siderumque** 'of the stars in heaven', hendiadys.   **quae cum maxime est** 'which exists at this very moment' (*OLD maxime* 6b).   **nongentos:** Ernesti's correction brings the text into line with Servius' citation from Cicero; the MSS say 800.   **incipit** 'begins to seem' (further examples, chiefly from Seneca, are collected by J. B. Hofmann in *TLL* VII 1.919.14–32); *uidetur* must be regarded as a gloss upon this unusual sense, according to Zwierlein (1997) 89 n. 16.   **ueterem et antiquum:** 15.1n.   **quo nos:** understand *existimus*.   **etiam** is the emendation of Michaelis for the transmitted *fama* (Murgia (1978) 175–6 explains the origin of the error). Zwierlein (1997) 91 has proposed instead *plane*, and W. S. Watt (*Eikasmos* 9 (1998) 263) *paene.*

17.1 Menenium ... Agrippam: M. Menenius Agrippa, *cos.* 503 BC. His was the type of untutored yet effective oratory; Livy at 2.32.9 described his speech to the people as *prisco illo dicendi et horrido modo* (see Ogilvie's commentary *ad loc.*). If he really was preferred, he would serve as an example of archaism, but genuine speeches of his can hardly have been extant, otherwise he would not have been omitted from Cicero's *Brutus.* Aper may be insinuating an important historical point, namely that the admirers of 'the ancients' fail to take account of the long process of the development of formal prose. By starting their discussion with the imagined Golden Age, they can quite unfairly paint a picture of steady decline.   **puto** 'I daresay' (*OLD* 8 'sts. iron.'; but cf. 21.1). The placement of the phrase within the name enhances its irony.   **Caesarem:** C. Julius Caesar (100–44 BC); for his oratory see Kennedy (1972) 283–92; T. records his own opinion at *A.* 13.3.2: *dictator Caesar summis oratoribus aemulus.* The list is presented in chronological order. All appear in Quintilian's 'canon': Caesar at *Inst.* 10.1.114, Caelius *ibid.* 115, along with Calvus, Brutus *ibid.* 123 (NB), Pollio and Messalla together *ibid.* 113; Quintilian again lumps together Caesar, Calvus, Caelius and Pollio at 10.3.25.   **Caelium:** M. Caelius Rufus (82–48 BC); for his oratory see Schanz–Hosius §139.4, 1 398–9. His published speeches were clearly still known to Pliny and Quintilian.   **Caluum:** C. Licinius Calvus (82–47 BC; *OCD* s.v. Licinius Caluus); for his oratory see Kennedy (1972) 244–6, and 18.1, 21.2–4. He was also esteemed for his poetry.   **Brutum:** M. Junius Brutus (85–42 BC; *OCD* s.v. Brutus (5)), an assassin of Caesar's, left writings in poetry and philosophy as well as speeches. Some admired his style, and Quintilian noted its *grauitas* (*Inst.* 12.10.11, cf. 25.4 *grauior Brutus*), but there were also carpers (Kennedy (1972) 246), e.g. a near contemporary slur in Statius, *Siluae* 4.9.20 *Bruti senis oscitationes* ('yawnings'; see Coleman *ad loc.*)

17.2 Hirtio nempe et Pansa consulibus: in 43 BC. The expression here is conversational in tone: no *praenomina* are given, and the addition of *et* avoids the asyndeton of the official formula. The two died at Mutina (mod. Modena) on 14 March 43.   **Tiro:** M. Tullius Tiro, Cicero's freedman, wrote his biography, presumably the source of the date given here (Schanz–Hosius §178, 1 548; *OCD*).   **VII idus ⟨Decembres⟩** = 7 December (the name of the month was supplied by Lipsius).   **Q. Pedium:** a nephew of Julius Caesar; he died of shock at having to announce the proscriptions in the year of his suffect consulship (Appian, *BC* 4.6.26).

17.3 The whole sentence forms in effect a paratactic conditional, where imperatives constitute the protasis. The sentence also displays careful variety of terminology.   **sex et quinquaginta annos:** i.e. from Octavian's first consulship, which began 19 August 43 BC to his death on 19 August AD 14 (see Intro., §7 Authenticity). *sex*, the emendation of Lipsius for the transmitted *nouem*, is accepted by all editors. But as H. Furneaux pointed out in his review of Peterson's edition in *CR* 8 (1894) 108, T. does occasionally err in his chronological calculations (see 34.7n.); Syme (1958) 746 provides a convenient list of these mistakes, some of which are emended away (e.g. at *A.* 3.31.1, 12.25.2, and 14.64.1), but others seem genuine. It is unlikely that T. here miscalculated the length of Augustus' reign, but the other calculations in this section should perhaps be taken liberally. **rexit:** the verb is not uncommonly used of the Princeps (G–G s.v. 2(1)).   **illum** 'that notorious'.   **longum et unum annum:** 9 June 68 to 20 December 69, 'reckoning from the calendar years of Vitellius's effective rule at Rome' (Syme (1970) 117). For the expression cf. 41.4 *sapientissimus et unus*.   **stationem** 'post' as applied to the role of the Princeps became almost a technical term; Woodman on Vell. Pat. 1.124.2 *stationi paternae succederet* traces and illustrates fully the usage; to his examples may now be added the *Senatus con-*

sultum de Pisone Patre of Dec. AD 20, line 130: *spem futuram paternae pro r. p. stationis*. It here refers unusually, however, to the individual years of a reign (*OLD* 5a), a sense perhaps derived from a notion that the annual military oath of loyalty (*sacramentum*) confirmed the emperor in his position (so John; cf. Goodyear on *A.* 1.8.4).   **centum et uiginti anni:** Cicero was executed 117 years before the dramatic date of the dialogue (AD 75), so the number is a round one, as are the 820 years at *H.* 1.1.1 or the 200 at *A.* 14.21.1; the urbane speaker would apologize for the pedantry of exactitude (cf. 32.6, 37.2). **colliguntur** 'are computed' (*OLD colligo*[1] 12).   **unius hominis aetas:** according to the (variously recorded) span of Arganthonius of Tartessus (Cic. *Cato* 69 with Powell's n.).

17.4 nam 'for example' (*OLD* 3c).   **qui ... fateretur:** the verb of speaking in the consecutive relative clause is attracted idiomatically into the subjunc., 'he was so old that, as he said, he ...' (G–L §630 N3, *NLS* §242 n. ii).   **aggressi sunt:** the indic. is usual in a subordinate clause in indirect discourse when it is not a part of the reported thought or statement but adds a comment or elucidation by the one reporting (*NLS* §§286–8; for T. see Nipperdey and Andresen and Goodyear on *A.* 1.10.2 *abstulerat*, 1.53.6 *sperauerat*). The old man will simply have said that he was present at the battle; Aper must clarify for his hearers which was meant.   **ipsum** 'that' Caesar, not one of his descendants.   **audire potuit** 'could have heard'; 'the indic. is the regular construction in the Apodosis with verbs which signify Possibility or Power': G–L §597 R3. Caesar first attacked Britain in 55 BC. Aper's military service here should fall in 43 under Claudius, so his public career as a barrister may have begun in 44/5. Pseudo-Plutarch, *Plac.* 5.30.6, refers to Britons of 120 years of age; the one Aper saw was born about 70 BC.   **actionibus** 'trial speeches' (*OLD* 5).

17.5 congiario: originally gifts of foodstuffs from magistrates, electoral candidates, or generals to the people, the *congiaria* become special forms of imperial largess (*OCD* s.v. congiarium); there had been one in AD 71/2 (Levick (1999) 125).   **plerosque:** 2.1n. **diuo ... Augusto:** see 3n., about sixty years before the imagined date of the dialogue. His last 'doles' were in 5 and 2 BC (*RG* 15).

17.6 colligi 'be deduced' (*OLD colligo*[1] 11b).   **Coruinum:** 12.6n. The text hesitantly printed adopts an exchange of the

proper names proposed by the great numismatist and epigrapher
B. Borghesi (cf. *Encyc. Italiana* VII 470). This makes Aper's statement
only somewhat more accurate than it would be if we kept the order
of names in the MSS, especially if we agree with Güngerich that
medium does not so much refer to the exact middle of the Principate
(however its duration might be calculated), but simply means
that Pollio survived into the middle period of Augustus' reign (he
died about ten years before the emperor). Alternatively, we might
agree with Syme (1986) 220 n. 13 that 'error and confusion about
Messalla's death had an early origin', where he refers without comment to the text of this passage as transmitted.   **ab illis ...
audiri:** take ἀπὸ κοινοῦ.   **ne ...:** 'I say this to stop you from
...' (a common sort of elliptical purpose clause: *OLD* 13, G–L §545
R3).   **antiquos ac ueteres:** 15.1n.   **uocitetis:** this, the reading of the Γ tradition, is here a true frequentative (so Heubner on *H.*
1.13.1 *uocitabant*, who offers a general account of the word's usage);
the other part of the tradition has *uocetis*, but for the confusion cf.
22.5 *fugitet*, which is undoubtedly correct as against *fugiet*.   **uelut:**
Aper needs to soften his metaphorical use of *aures* to mean 'the
hearers'.

    18.1 praedixi: Aper has merely been warming up, and at §2
turns to his main argument, that there has been, not decline, but
variety, change, and development in oratorical taste and style, not
least because the audience itself is more exigent (19–20), and demands something different to hold its attention. In conclusion, he
attacks older models of oratory (21–3). His inspiration will have been
the *Brutus* of Cicero, especially in this regard: neither Cicero nor
Aper accounts for change of taste and style as a product of altered
social and political institutions. Messalla had desiderated an account
of the causes of change (15.2), and the insights into them will be reserved for Maternus.   **fama gloriaque:** a common synonymous
doublet.   **eam:** Halm's correction seems right. It is unlikely that
eandem, the reading of the MSS, has attenuated sense, = *eam* (cf.
21.6n. *eorundem*), where it picks up a relative clause.   **in medio
sitam:** 'common property' (*OLD medium* 4a), i.e. neither period can
claim it.   **Seruio Galbae:** Servius Sulpicius Galba (*cos.* 144);
Cicero found his speeches *redolentes antiquitatem* (*Brut.* 82) and he
was still listed among the great by Velleius Paterculus (1.17.2), hence

the notice of him here (Kennedy (1972) 72–3).   **C. Carboni:** C.
Papirius Carbo (*cos.* 120); Cicero praised him highly at *Brut.* 105
(Kennedy (1972) 73); cf. 34.7.   **uocauerimus:** potential perf.
subjunc.   **horridi** [*OLD* 4b] **et impoliti** [*OLD* 2] **et rudes**
[*OLD* 2b] **et informes** [*OLD* 4b]**:** the first three are common terms
of disparagement in literary criticism; only the last seems to be novel
and refers to the lack of overall design. The last two form a pair at
20.7 and *A.* 12.35.2. The repeated *et* (polysyndeton) emphasizes
Aper's disgust.   **Caluus:** see 17.1n.   **uester** shows he was still
much admired in certain quarters; Pliny had taken him for a model
(*Ep.* 1.2.2, where *nuper* indicates a fresh departure), and T. might
have had this in mind, esp. when he has Aper deliver a fuller critique
of Calvus' style in 23.

    18.2 agere 'proceed' (*OLD* 36).   **si ... praedixero** 'after this
observation'. *si* here, at 28.3 and *H.* 4.48.1 *ea de caede quam uerissime
expediam si pauca supra repetiero* has virtual temporal force in conven-
tional expressions of diffidence, e.g. 'when, with your permission'; it
always seems to follow the main clause. This usage is not discussed
in *OLD*, but is explained and well illustrated from Cicero by Fordyce
on Catull. 14.17 *si luxerit*. The sense at 16.2 is clearly related, though
there *si* can be a true condition; yet we see from that passage how
the senses overlap.   **mutari cum temporibus:** cf. *A.* 3.55.5 *nisi
forte rebus cunctis inest quidam uelut orbis, ut quem ad modum temporum uices,
ita morum uertantur; nec omnia apud priores meliora, sed nostra quoque aetas
multa laudis et artium imitanda posteris tulit.* This is T.'s own opinion and
shows that he will have had some sympathy for the purely stylistic
argument he put into Aper's mouth. (Proof that he holds this view is
shown by his way of praising Seneca's style at *A.* 13.3.1, quoted
at 21.2n.) But Aper is using the argument to distance himself from
the common educational practice of modelling one's style upon the
classic writers of the past (so Fantham (1978) 114–15); he does not,
as noted above, enquire deeply into the cause of the changes.
formas quoque et genera 'types and styles' (Winterbottom); cf.
formam quoque ac speciem 19.2.   **Catoni:** Cato (234–149, *cos.* 195;
OCD s.v. Porcius Cato (1), M.) was in some ways the archetypal
Roman, shrewd, practical, versatile. Portions of his oratory he preserved by transcribing speeches into his historical work, the *Origines*,
but other speeches must have circulated independently. They came

to be much more admired once the archaist movement gathered force (Kennedy (1972) 38–60). Aper's list follows chronological order, as he claims steady stylistic improvement along with change. **seni** 'of old' (*OLD* 1c) indicates that he was a figure of the venerable past; it is not a reference to his having lived into old age.   **C. Gracchus:** 154–121; *OCD* s.v. Sempronius Gracchus, Gaius. During his notorious tribunates (123 and 122) he passed many laws to further the programme of his assassinated elder brother, Tiberius. His oratory was remarkable and much praised by Cicero; the vigour of his delivery (cf. 26.1) deeply affected his hearers (Kennedy (1972) 76–9).   **plenior et uberior** picks up the opinion of Cicero (who is not comparing him to Cato), *Brut.* 125 *noli enim putare quemquam pleniorem aut uberiorem ad dicendum fuisse.*   **Crassus** (140–91, *cos.* 95; *OCD* s.v. Licinius Crassus, L.; Kennedy (1972) 84–90) was Cicero's ideal orator in the *De oratore*, because his style was correct, rhythmical, dignified.   **distinctior** 'more methodical' (*OLD* 3) refers to skills of organization of the subject matter, *dispositio*: *De orat.* 3.53, cf. Quint. *Inst.* 11.3.35.   **urbanior:** Quintilian lists the constitutive qualities of *urbanitas, Inst.* 6.3.107: *illa est urbanitas in qua nihil absonum, nihil agreste, nihil inconditum, nihil peregrinum,* but he also insists that it characterizes the whole of a man's utterance, not particular details. **altior:** Cicero was reckoned a model of sublimity (*OLD* 13c). His superiority to Gracchus in particular is argued for by Aulus Gellius (10.3, a reference owed to Professor Winterbottom).   **mitior** 'more placid' (*OLD* 3c).   **dulcior** 'more charming', Quint. *Inst.* 1.7.35, *OLD* 7c.   **in uerbis magis elaboratus:** Messalla Corvinus was a precisian, cf. Sen. *Con.* 2.4.8 *Latini … sermonis obseruator diligentissimus.* These praises (12.6n.) flatter his descendant, but Messalla was in fact generally held to be second in eminence only to Pollio, with whom he was commonly paired, the Augustan duumvirate in oratory (Kennedy (1972) 308; cf. *A.* 11.6.7; Quint. *Inst.* 10.1.113; Rudd on Hor. *AP* 370, where he is cited as a pre-eminent barrister; he and Horace had studied in Athens at the same time). Aper however will be mildly critical of him at 21.9.

18.3 nec quaero quis disertissimus: in fact, this is what he has implicitly done, and Cicero appears to come out on top; he uses this expression simply as a transitional device. The verb in the indirect question, *sit*, is in ellipse.   **probasse contentus:** elsewhere too in *D. contentus* takes the perf. inf. (23.2, 26.7), and this is the norm (*TLL* IV 680.41–56). The tense may be aoristic.   **non esse unum eloquentiae uultum:** the point had been made already by Cicero at *De orat.* 3.34; cf. Quint. *Inst.* 12.10.69.   **plures** 'a number', 'more than one' = *complures*, a sense common in T. (G–G 882b); *OLD* seems not to notice the usage.   **statim** 'automatically' (*OLD* 6).   **uetera semper in laude, praesentia in fastidio esse:** a commonplace thought, cf. Vell. Pat. 2.92.5 (with Woodman's n.) *praesentia inuidia, praeterita ueneratione prosequimur.* The form of the sentence deserves note, just because its careful balance, with the distribution of the common elements, *semper* and *esse*, between the two halves, is the sort of thing T. avoids in his historical prose.

18.4 pro 'rather than' (*OLD* 7) is illogical combined with *magis*, but reckoned not unidiomatic (*TLL* X 2.1426.18–21).   **Appium Caecum:** Appius Claudius Caecus, *cos.* 307, 296; he spoke in the Senate against making terms with king Pyrrhus *c.* 280 BC. That speech may still have been extant in Cicero's day (he certainly thought it was, *Sen.* 16 and *Brut.* 61), and there was a poetic version of it in Ennius (*Ann.* 199–200 with Skutsch's comm.; Kennedy (1972) 26–9). Aper for the first time glances at a tendency, increasingly important in Rome, to prefer the oldest writers (cf. 23.2n.).   **obtrectatores:** cf. 12.6n.   **inflatus** 'bombastic' (*OLD* 2b); used by Quint. *Inst.*12.10.16 of the Asian style.   **tumens:** Quint. *Inst.* 12.10.12 *tumidiorem* (a criticism of Cicero).   **pressus:** 2.2, Cic. *Brut.* 51.   **exsultans** 'prancing'; the word describes excessive rhythmic variety at Quint. *Inst.* 12.10.12 (with Austin's n.), but at Cic. *De orat.* 3.36 it is used of verbal luxuriance (and perhaps so here). **superfluens** 'overflowing' is not found elsewhere as a critical term (but cf. Cic. *Brut.* 316 *supra fluentis*); perhaps it is used to avoid the more commonplace *redundans.*   **Atticus** in effect sums up the preceding criticisms, which are redolent of the Atticist fashion of the late 50s BC (for which see Kennedy (1972) 241–6).

18.5 epistulas: these have not survived, but were clearly referred to by Quintilian at *Inst.* 12.10.12 as well; for their views of each other's style, and the physiological metaphors applied to criticism, see Kennedy (1972) 244–6.   **exsanguem** 'lacking vitality'; *uerum sanguinem deperdebat*, says Cicero of Calvus at *Brut.* 283 (cf. Quint. *Inst.* 12.10.14); metaphorically blood was seen as a source of vigour in literary style (*OLD* 5b, Douglas on Cic. *Brut.* 36.10; cf. 21.8, 26.4).   **attritum** 'threadbare' is nowhere else attested in a metaphorical sense of literary style, but was presumably drawn from the letter of Cicero's.   **otiosum atque diiunctum:** cf. 22.3, where Aper turns the tables on Cicero. The criticism points to lack of interest in periodic structure, which gave an impression of sluggishness.   **tamquam:** see 2.1n.   **solutum et eneruem:** the first term refers to lack of rhythm (see Sandys's intro. to Cic. *Or.*, LVIII), for the second see Cic. *Or.* 229 (cf. Petr. *Sat.* 2.2 *corpus orationis eneruaretur*).   **fractum atque elumbem** 'mincing and dislocated'; the metaphor in *elumbis* is remarkable (as is the word itself, but cf. Cic. *Or.* 231 *delumbet* 'lame' in reference to rhythm). Calvus and Brutus appear to be saying the same thing. The chiasmus of *et* and *atque*, connecting the varied stylistic criticisms, betrays the careful composition of the sentence.

18.6 negotium est: the expression is found in Cicero's letters, and so is presumably colloquial (*OLD negotium* 10).

19.1 Nam: 2.1n. It seems that despite the query at 16.4, Aper has had all along a clear idea of the terminal date set to 'ancient' oratory. The text at this point is hopelessly corrupt, and editors have offered a variety of solutions. Here it is assumed that after *qui* there is a lacuna in the tradition, in which there was some clear definition of the terminal date, viz. those who were active up to the time of Cassius Severus (whose name ought to appear in full at first mention). After another gap in the text, Aper goes on to designate him as the pivotal figure.   **uelut** apologizes (5.5n.) for the use of *terminus* in a metaphorical sense (but no such apologies are found in the examples of the usage in *OLD* 3).   **Cassium:** Cassius Severus (44 BC – *c.* AD 35; *OCD* s.v.; Kennedy (1972) 310–12) reappears at 26.4 in a reference to this section. T.'s own view of him is found at *A.* 4.21.3: *sordidae originis, maleficae uitae, sed orandi ualidus* (see Martin and Woodman's n. *ad loc.*). Aper, who respects his oratorical achievement, treats him as the Roman equivalent of Demetrius of Phaleron in the history of Greek oratory, indeed he even borrows Cicero's own description of Demetrius, *primus inflexit orationem* (*Brut.* 38, cf. Quint. *Inst.* 10.1.80); his scheme of Latin oratorical history was thus shaped upon a Greek last. (Heldmann (1982) 163–98 stresses that the atti-

tude here adopted to Severus is unique, for nowhere else is he regarded as a turning point.)

19.2 Aper takes the charge against Severus as proof that men
recognize historical development in oratorical style, which they call
decline; he sees it rather as change, and arguably for the good (cf.
Winterbottom (1964) 91).   **namque** is postponed to the second
position by poets, and the practice first enters prose with Varro *apud*
Gell. 3.10.1, then Livy (cf. Müller, Anhang to Liv. 2.36.4). T. has it
thrice in *A.*, where it contributes to the elevated style (see Martin
and Woodman on 4.21.1).   **paulo ante:** namely, at 18.2.   **condicione temporum et diuersitate aurium:** the latter phrase
adds a new notion, change of taste (Quintilian makes similar observations in similar terms at *Inst.* 12.10.2 and 45). *aures* is here used
figuratively of a discriminating 'ear' for oratory (cf. 20.6, *OLD*
4).   **formam ... ac speciem orationis** 'the ideal type of oratory'; the expression is Ciceronian and *forma* is used as the equivalent
of ἰδέα (Sandys on Cic. *Or.* 2 collects examples).   **imperitus:** but
see Quint. *Inst.* 10.1.43 on contemporary audiences. Of course all
who succeed believe in the discrimination of their audience.   **si**
'if ever'; here and in the following sentence (*uideretur, insereret*) the
subjunc. is iterative (15.1n.).   **dicendo** is emphasized by a slight
hyperbaton, the unusual separation of *si* from *quis* (found nowhere
else in T.).   **eximeret** 'use up' (*OLD* 4).

19.3 longa principiorum praeparatio: Quintilian indeed
warns against this at *Inst.* 4.1.62.   **Hermagorae et Apollodori:**
Hermagoras of Temnos and Apollodorus of Pergamum, the teacher
of Octavian, were noted Greek rhetoricians; their careers and contributions to the subject are treated by Kennedy (1963) 303–21 and
(1972) 338–41. It seems likely that T. here uses Aper to undermine
the educational programme of Quintilian, who regularly appealed
to these Greek rhetoricians in his recently published *Institutio oratoria*,
esp. book 3 (see M. Winterbottom, 'Quintilian and rhetoric', in
T. A. Dorey, ed., *Empire and aftermath. Silver Latin* (London 1975) ii
83–4).   **odoratus** 'got a whiff of' (cf. *OLD* 2b); the sense of
having acquired a superficial knowledge of some subject (cf. *degustare*)
is an unusual extension of the verb's figurative use.   **philosophiam:** Cicero, at any rate, despite his interest in philosophy, was

pretty careful to avoid displaying it in his forensic oratory.
uideretur ... insereret: iterative subjunc.   **locum** 'general
reflection', not peculiar to the case in hand (*OLD* 23c). Aper may be
referring to *loci philosophoumenoi*, commonplaces of philosophical discussion, favoured by the declaimers (Summers (1910) xxxix, n. 3).

19.4 haec noua et incognita: cf. Suet. *Rhet.* 25.1. But it is
hardly true of Cicero's generation: Aper is opportunist in his argument.   **quoque** 'even' (*OLD* 4).

19.5 peruulgatis iam omnibus sounds like an echo of Virg.
G. 3.4 *omnia iam uulgata.*   **corona** is the correction of Ursinus
(approved by J. Delz, *MH* 27 (1970) 239–40) for the MS *cortina*,
which makes no sense, even taken figuratively.   **assistat** 'attends
court', but not necessarily only as a spectator (*OLD* 3b; cf. 39.3).
imbutus: 2.2n.   **exquisitis ... itineribus:** contrast 19.1 *derecta
... uia.*   **orator:** Aper is not shy of the word.   **effugiat:** final
subjunc. in a relative clause.   **ui et potestate** 'the power of his
authority' **... iure et legibus** 'the specific laws within the legal
code': both common doublets, here used in hendiadys. The point is
that the president of the court, as was his privilege, interpreted the
law in his own way. This point will be glanced at again, 38.2 *legibus.*   **cognoscunt** 'hear the case' (*OLD* 4).   **exspectandum
habent oratorem:** the syntax is like that described on 8.2n. with
this difference, that this is the only example in all T. of the verb
habeo with a substantive as direct object (cf. Sen. *Ira* 2.6.2 [*uirtus*] *iram
ipsam castigandam habet,* the first such example apparently).   **ultro
admonent:** restrictions upon a speaker's time were often noticed
and complained of, cf. Sen. *Con.* 7 pr. 8 with Winterbottom's n.,
Quint. *Inst.* 4.5.10 *festinat enim iudex: ... si ... in aliqua potestate, ... cum
conuicio efflagitat,* and Plin. *Ep.* 6.2.5. Maternus will pick this up at
39.3. The issue here is brevity (cf. that of *D.* itself), see Plin. *Ep.* 7.20,
Cic. *Brut.* 50.

20.1 ualetudinis: Quintilian had referred with approval to
Messalla's prefatory references to his frailty (*infirmus*) or lack of preparation or general inadequacy (*Inst.* 4.1.8). Aper's remark is designedly a mocking exaggeration of this practice (cf. R. Güngerich,
'Der *Dialogus* des Tacitus und Quintilians *Institutio Oratoria*', *CP* 46
(1951) 159–60, whose argument concerns the priority of Quintilian).
That Aper is made to exaggerate has been questioned by R. L.

Jeffreys, 'The *infirmitas* of Messalla Corvinus, *Latomus* 46 (1987) 196–8; Zwierlein (1997) ejects *ualetudinis* and proposes to read *infirmitate sua*. But that Messalla used ill-health as a plea for sympathy may lie behind Varro's logistoricon entitled 'Messalla de ualetudine'. **quinque:** Aper again exaggerates: Verres on the advice of his counsel, Hortensius, took himself off into exile before Cicero had finished with him (37.6n.), so the five books (all extant) of the second *actio* to which Aper refers were published, not delivered.   **exspectabit** 'sit through'; i.e. wait for something to end, as at Petr. *Sat.* 17.2 *nos ... exspectauimus lacrimas ad ostentationem doloris paratas* (*TLL* VIII 2.1892.23).   ⟨de⟩ **exceptione** 'a counterplea on behalf of the defendant' (*OLD* 3).   **et formula** 'a summary, agreed by both parties, of the points at issue, with directions for judgement' (*OLD* 6b); the term refers to the plea of Caecina.   **pro M. Tullio:** Cicero delivered two speeches on his behalf, in 73 and 71 BC. One has come down to us in a tattered state (OCT vol. II).   **Aulo Caecina:** delivered in 69 BC; Cicero was pleased with it: *tota mihi causa pro Caecina de uerbis interdicti fuit: res inuolutas definiendo explicauimus, ius ciuile laudauimus, uerba ambigua distinximus* (*Or.* 102, with Sandys's careful n.).

20.2 Three virtues of the modern style are recorded: pace (*cursu*, cf. Quint. *Inst.* 9.4.138), brilliance (*colore*; *OLD* 2c), and polish (*nitore*; *OLD* 4b). Aper specially prizes this last quality (he alone refers to it: cf. 21.3 and 9, 23.6 and the use of the verb at 20.7), but the pair *nitore et cultu* are found in Quintilian too, e.g. *Inst.* 10.1.124 of Cornelius Celsus, 11.1.48, 12.10.79.   **sententiarum** 'epigrams' (*OLD* 6b); these were much admired by the Romans (see Merrill on Plin. *Ep.* 1.16.2; cf. Sen. *Con.* 2.6.12, Quint. *Inst.* 8.5.1, 12.10.48).   **descriptionum** 'descriptive narrative'.   **corruptus** 'allured' (*OLD* 5c).   **[dicentem]:** Schele's deletion is here accepted, since we may either supply *dicentem* ἀπὸ κοινοῦ from earlier in the sentence as object, or take *auersatur* absolutely.

20.3 assistentium: 19.5n.   **affluens et uagus auditor:** courts were held in the open air (though the centumviral court met in a basilica), and so idlers in the Forum could come and go as the whim took them.   **laetitiam** 'brilliance' (the only other example before Macrobius of the noun so used as descriptive of style is at 21.9, but cf. *laeta* 14.2n.).   **tristem** 'sour' (*OLD* 4c).

impexam: the striking metaphorical sense appears to be unique to
T. here (but cf. *incomptus, horridus*), but κτενίζω 'comb' was so used
by Dionysius of Halicarnassus of Plato's refined style, *Comp.* 25; cf.
calamistros 26.1n.   **Rosci:** Q. Roscius Gallus, Cicero's favourite
actor, mentioned at *De orat.* 1.251 for the grace of his movements,
which an orator would do well to acquire. He died in 62 BC (*OCD*
3).   **[aut]:** deleted by Lipsius, the word must have been added by
someone who did not know that L. Ambivius Turpio was one person, an actor and the producer of the plays of Terence and Caecilius Statius. Here the names are reversed (1.1n.).   **exprimere**
'imitate' (*OLD* 6).   **gestus:** orators might indeed study the movements of actors for tips, since management of the body was an important part of delivery (*actio*): Cic. *De orat.* 3.220, *Orat.* 59; Quint.
Inst. 10.3.65–136. But styles of acting are as much subject to fashion
as oratory, and an outdated manner damaged credibility. Cf. *histrionales, histriones* 26.2n.

   20.4 et is epexegetic (explanatory), as in the similar phrase at 33.2
iuuenes iam et Forum ingressuri. Still, the metaphor which follows is
bold, indeed unique in the classical period (unless this boldness
characterizes Aper's speech). It would seem to require apology and
uelut might have fallen out after *et* (or have been replaced by it); for
this sort of phrase see 5.5, 14.1, 26.5 (where *uelut* has become *uult* in
most MSS), 33.1.   **incude:** the metaphor, a rare one (*TLL* VII
1098.16), is related to *acuo*, used of sharpening the tongue; cf. Pindar,
P. 1.86 πρὸς ἄκμονι χάλκευε γλῶσσαν ('forge your tongue upon the
anvil').   **oratores:** again Aper does not hesitate to see true orators in his own day (cf. 15.1n.).   **referre domum aliquid illustre et dignum memoria:** this is precisely what the elder Seneca
did (at any rate from the declamation schools), and he later produced a memorial of his excerpts from particularly clever declamations for the use of his sons; it is still extant.   **in uicem** = *inter se.*
in colonias . . . : cf. 5.4.   **sensus** 'conceit' (*OLD* 9c).   **aliquis:**
take ἀπὸ κοινοῦ with *locus* (for which see 19.3n.).   **arguta et
breui:** for the pair cf. Plin. *Ep.* 7.9.9 (the letter was referred to in
2.2n., where again T. has the same pairing of epithets as Pliny).
sententia: 2n. above.

   20.5 poeticus decor: the increasing use of poetic language and
even syntax in the prose of the early Principate is indeed remarkable

(see Summers (1910) li–lii, liv); from Aper's remark we learn that it was a deliberate choice. **ueterno** 'filth'; the sense is rare (*OLD* 3), and the metaphorical use is not found elsewhere as a term of literary criticism (but cf. *sordes* 21.4n. and *OLD situs*³ 2b). **inquinatus:** for its use in reference to style see *OLD inquino* 2. L. Accius (170 – *c.* 86 BC) and M. Pacuvius (220 – *c.* 130 BC), the nephew of Ennius, were stage poets (chiefly of tragedy; see *OCD* for their careers) still much admired as literary classics, but Aper regarded them as poor sources of poetic diction for use in forensic oratory (Quintilian's censure of their styles at *Inst.* 10.1.97 is more politely expressed: defects belong to their age rather than to them personally). He had a point: orators at this time, e.g. Pliny's friend Pompeius Saturninus (*Ep.* 1.16.2), were looking out for *uerba . . . antiqua*, an instance of literary archaism. On the other hand, Aper's bracketing of the epic poet M. Annaeus Lucanus (AD 39–65; again, see *OCD* for his career) with Horace (cf. 23.2 infra) and Virgil is evidence of his rapid inclusion in the ranks of literary classics (a status confirmed by Quintilian's high praise at *Inst.* 10.1.90: he is a good model for orators). Aper subtly exploits the notion that what we call the canon of poets was felt to be still growing; if modern poets could enter the ranks of the classics, why not modern orators, he implies. (The openness of the so-called canon was taken for granted by Quintilian too, cf. *Inst.* 10.1.94 (unnamed satirists), 104 (an unnamed historian), 122 (contemporary orators)). T.'s own admiration of these poets is clear from his borrowings from them in his historical work (see B. Walker, *The Annals of Tacitus. A study in the writing of history* (Manchester 1952) 71–4). On the other hand the omission of Ovid's name is very odd, since no poet had greater influence upon the prose of the generations after him. **sacrario** 'shrine'; for the metaphorical use cf. *penetralia* used of *eloquentia* at 12.2 by Maternus. Aper is made to forget himself momentarily, and to concede to poetry its claim to holy status; cf. Florus *Verg.* 3.8 *sacrarum studia litterarum*.

20.6 auribus: 19.2n. **nostrorum oratorum aetas:** cf. 1.1 *nostra aetas*. It is as if Aper were answering the criticism voiced there, but his expression also reminds us that he is once again making an historical point: time and taste change. **efficaces** is telling, since oratory is after all practical. Aper's opponents are arguably overwhelmed by their sense of the past; nourished upon books of speeches, they want oratory to be more of a literary form. **iudicantium** = *iudicum*.

20.7 quid ... si ... credas 'what [would you say] if someone believed ...?'; the expression is always elliptical (*OLD quis*[1] 13), and the idea in ellipse depends on the tone of the context, here mocking. **templa:** the argument is suggested by *sacrario*. Cf. 22.3. **rudi ... informibus:** cf. 18.1. **tegulis** 'facing-tiles' (*lateres cocti*) for walls (*OLD* b; odd, that this unusual sense is only found in T., once again at *G*. 16.2). **marmore nitent et auro radiantur:** marble was usually used as a veneer on the brick rind of temples; Augustus notoriously took pride in having found Rome brick and left it marble (Suet. *Aug*. 28.3), presumably a reference to his campaign of refurbishing the temples in 28 BC. In 142 BC the ceiling of the temple of Iuppiter Optimus Maximus was gilded, and its exterior roof was later covered in gilded brass tiles by Q. Lutatius Catulus between 79 and 60 BC (Plin. *NH*. 33.57; see P. Gros, *Aurea templa. Recherches sur l'architecture religieuse de Rome à l'époque d'Auguste* (Rome 1976) 41–2); its restoration and gilding by Domitian is mentioned by Silius Italicus, *Pun*. 3.623 *aurea ... Capitolia* (Richardson (1992) 222–3). Aper assumes that such sumptuous decorations do not call for comment, but it is significant that Velleius Paterculus, who provides notice that Q. Metellus Macedonicus first built a temple of marble in Rome after 146 BC (1.11.3–5), qualifies his praise by noting that the splendour could be styled luxury (a loaded term), and Pliny, like many a moralist, records contemporary disapproval of Catulus' gilded decoration: such display and expense were somehow un-Roman; cf. Sen. *Con*. 2.1.1 *bella ciuilia aurato Capitolio gessimus*. **auro radiantur** < Ov. *Pont*. 3.4.103 *scuta sed et galeae gemmis radientur et auro* (is 'Aper' unconsciously illustrating his point about the debt prose owes to poets?).

21.1 At 17.1 Aper had listed the seven orators of old who he reckoned were probably preferred to any of the moderns; here he deals at greater or lesser length with all of them again to point up their deficiencies, leaving pride of place to Cicero (22–3). **Equidem ... in quibusdam ... uix risum ... uix somnum tenere:** a neat fusion of two passages in Cic. *Brut*., viz. 278 *somnum uix tenebamus* (where Cicero upbraided M. Calidius, a proto-Atticist), and 293 *equidem in quibusdam risum uix tenebam* (so Atticus, when he hears Cato compared to Lysias).   **tenere** 'restrain' (*OLD* 19b).   **unum de populo** 'a commonplace figure', cf. Cic. *Brut.* 320 *unus ex populo* and Kroll's n. on 186 *de populo*.   **†ganuti aut atti de furnio et coranio†:** the text is hopelessly corrupt, and the chance of successful emendation is diminished by the very nature of what Aper is saying: he is not going to denigrate small fry (*unum de populo*), of whom he gives representative examples. Not surprisingly we have never heard of them. Some known names are however discernible amid the wreckage: P. Cannutius was referred to by Cicero, *Brut.* 205, and his name may lurk in *ganuti* here, as J. F. Gronovius thought. By the same token he referred *atti* to the Q. Arrius at Cic. *Brut.* 242. Cicero also knew and respected C. Furnius (see *RE* VII 377.19–33 for his activity as a pleader).   **in eodem ualetudinario** 'in the same sanatorium' attaches closely to *quique alii*; the metaphor is proverbial (Otto §1845). *ualetudinarium* is vivid and dismissive; Aper here betrays his real contempt for Atticists, a contempt the more biting since they claimed 'health' as their stylistic keynote (cf. *sanitas* 23.3, 4).   **ossa ... maciem:** for the metaphorical usage, esp. as applied to the Atticists, cf. Cic. *Brut.* 68, then Quint. *Inst.* proem 24, 2.4.9 (*OLD os²* 1 (NB not always pejorative), *macies* 3). Aper prepares for the developed comparison at §8 below. For Calvus see 17.1n.   **ut puto:** only pedants flaunt their learning in polite conversation (cf. Cic. *Brut.* 58 (with Douglas's n.), where Brutus' *ut opinor* apologizes for precisely locating a quotation from the ninth book of Ennius' *Annales*). Similarly *ut opinor* is used with a numeral at 37.2 (cf. 32.6 in a quotation).   **libros:** 12.6n.   **oratiuncula:** the tone of the diminutive is slighting.

  21.2 quotus ... quisque: 10.2n.   **Calui in Asicium:** understand *librum* or *orationem*. The case is assumed to be the one referred to by Cicero in *Pro Caelio* 23–4, in which P. Asicius was acquitted of complicity in the death of the Alexandrian ambassador Dio (see Austin *ad loc.*).   **in Drusum:** he was acquitted of *praeuaricatio* 'collusion', Cicero defending (Shackleton Bailey on Cic. *Att.* 4.16.5). **studiosorum:** almost a technical term by now for students of rhetoric (*OLD* 2); the elder Pliny indeed wrote a treatise entitled *Studiosus* in three books (and six volumes), *quibus oratorem ab incunabulis instituit et perficit* (Plin. *Ep.* 3.5.5).   **in Vatinium:** Calvus composed apparently three speeches against him, and they were still the object of admiration (see 34.7); for the second see L. G. Pocock, ed., *Cicero in Vatinium* (London 1926) 191–4. Catullus, Calvus' close friend, commemorated the admiration of a bystander at one of the trials (see Fordyce's introduction to poem 53).   **sententiis** 'ideas' (*OLD* 6). **auribus iudicum accommodata:** cf. *A.* 13.3.1 *fuit illi uiro* [Seneca] *ingenium amoenum et temporis eius auribus accommodatum*, and Cic. *De orat.* 2.159 *nostra oratio multitudinis est auribus accommodanda*. The problem is the same for Messalla at §9 below.   **quo ⟨minus⟩** (the necessary supplement is owed to Halm) may follow any verb into which can be read an idea of hindering or preventing, here *defuisse* (cf. *A.* 14.39.2 with Woodcock's note, and the examples in K–S II 260, *TLL* v 786.27–31).   **sublimius:** here a stylistic term (*OLD* 7c); for the word see Brink on Hor. *AP* 165.   **ingenium ac uires:** hendiadys (Lucr. 5.1111).

21.3 For Caelius see 17.1n.   **nitorem ... horum temporum:** cf. §9 *nitoremque nostrorum temporum*; Aper harps on the historical change of style and taste.   **altitudinem** 'sublimity of style' (31.6, *OLD* 9) was a crucial contemporary issue. Pliny, along with Quintilian, favoured the grand style (Sherwin-White (1966) 87–8, following Guillemin; M. Armisen-Marchetti, 'Pline le jeune et le sublime', *REL* 68 (1990) 88–98), and tried to defend his attempts at it (*Ep.* 9.26). What he did not there consider was that this style got little airing in contemporary Rome (see the important essay by J. Perret, 'La formation du style de Tacite', *REA* 56 (1954) 90–120, esp. 115 on the impossibility of sublime style). He set up Demosthenes as his model (cf. *Ep.* 1.2 *temptaui enim imitari Demosthenen*, but he goes on to observe that the *materia* 'subject matter' did on this occasion give due scope to that style), and referred to passages from the *De corona*, the *Olynthiacs* and first *Philippic*. But what had such speeches to do with the centumviral court? (Isaeus would have been a better model, or if Demosthenes, then his 'private orations'.) Demosthenes was pleading before his fellow citizens for his career and dignity, or for the liberty of Athens. What had that to do with inheritance and property? Pliny is faintly aware of the problem at *Ep.* 2.19.6, but does not give it much time. He was caught in a tradition which encouraged imitation and praised sublimity of manner; that the arena had contracted was a nuisance to be ignored.

T., on the other hand, cannot ignore it, for two reasons. First, he is naturally a master of the grand style, as Pliny observed at *Ep.* 2.11.17 *respondit Cornelius Tacitus eloquentissime et, quod eximium orationi eius inest,* σεμνῶς, and will want opportunity to employ it. Secondly, as an observer of the past, he is alive to changes in society, their causes, and the subsequent restrictions upon the very opportunities for grand speaking that he requires. Hence his dissatisfaction with contemporary oratory, his refusal to publish his speeches and at last his devotion to history, a form which allowed him to cast his imagination into a mould that gave scope to his own taste for sublimity. In history, as in tragedy, one could dwell upon and write up occasions that appropriately employ the grand style. The speech, for instance, of C. Cassius at *A.* 14.43–4 recommending the Senate to punish with death all the slaves of their murdered master, may give a hint of what the grand Tacitean oratorical style was like (so Norden (1909) 1 330 n. 1).

21.4 sordes 'filth'; the metaphorical use in literary criticism (which has nothing to do with obscenity) is also to be found at Sen. *Ep.* 114.13 (correct *OLD* 6), but cf. *sordida uerba*; cf. *ueternus* 20.5n. Contrast the favourable use of πίνος 'patina' by Dion. Halicarn. **illae:** the reading of ζ*, is approved by Murgia (1977) 337, who explained the variant *regulae* in the rest of the tradition as based upon a mistranscription of a contracted form of the word. **uerborum ... compositio ... sensus:** these three terms form a logical progression from the choice of words to their arrangement so as to form periods; cf. 22.2. **hians compositio** 'disjointed writing' (*OLD* 4b); *compositio* here seems to mean no more than arrangement of the words (= σύνθεσις), without specific regard to rhythm (so *TLL* III 2141.43; cf. 22.2, 23.6 and contrast 22.1, 26.2 where rhythmical arrangement is plainly intended). **inconditi** 'shapeless' (*OLD* 1). **sensus** 'periods' (*OLD* 10). **redolent antiquitatem** < Cic. *Brut.* 82 (quoted on 25.7). **antiquarium** 'an admirer of the distant past'; first found in *D.* (37.2, 42), clearly used of literary students (Suet. *Aug.* 86.2, Juv. 6.454 of a bluestocking).

21.5 For Caesar see 17.1n. **magnitudinem cogitationum** 'grandeur of his intentions'; the phrase is also used of him by Velleius Paterculus, 2.41.1, whom T. may have recalled here (but it is also found at Sen. *Dial.* 9.1.14). **occupationes** < Cic. *Brut.* 253 *in maximis occupationibus*, again of Caesar. **ingenium:** 2.1n.

diuinum characterizes it as 'superhuman' (*OLD* 3b; cf. Cic. *Orator* 109 *sed quid poetas diuino ingenio profero*). Quintilian agrees with this judgement at *Inst.* 10.1.114.   **tam hercule quam:** cf. 8.4n.   **Brutum:** cf. Quint. *Inst.* 10.1.123 *egregius uero multoque quam in orationibus praestantior.*

21.6 nisi forte quisquam 'unless anyone perchance reads ...' (*OLD nisi* 2b, putting forward a far-fetched idea); in sense this amounts to saying, 'there is no-one who reads ...', so that an exception can be made by the addition of *nisi qui*; for the somewhat negligent construction of the sentence cf. *A.* 3.57.1 *nisi ut ... nisi quod.*   **pro Deci⟨di⟩o:** Cn. Decidius – the name is restored from Cic. *Clu.* 161 – was a Samnite proscribed under Sulla at an unknown date; the defence speech of Caesar (possibly delivered in the late 70s BC) may have had political significance, as the vindication of a victim of the established order (so Syme (1979) 156).   **pro Deiotaro:** for Deiotarus, king of western Galatia, see *OCD.* Cicero liked the speech (*Brut.* 21, though that may be mere compliment), and Caesar was reported to have admired Brutus' energy and outspokenness (Cic. *Att.* 14.1.2). The adverse judgement recorded here was doubtless based upon the published text: delivery made all the difference.   **lentitudinis ac teporis:** cf. *otiosus* 18.5; *teporis*, a conjecture of Lipsius' for the MS *temporis*, is found only here applied metaphorically to 'lukewarm' composition. Brutus was something of an Atticist (Cic. *Att.* 15.1a.2).   **libros:** 12.6n.   **et** 'even' (*OLD* 6).   **carmina:** Suetonius, *Iul.* 56, discusses Caesar's poetic compositions, and draws attention to the letter of Augustus forbidding their publication; hence they were indeed not well known. **eorundem** has attenuated sense = *eorum* (Kraus on Livy 6.1.2; J. B. Hofmann in *TLL* VII 1.205.28–40 refers also to *H.* 1.25.1 and *A.* 6.46.4).   **et carmina** 'poems as well' (*OLD et* 5).   **et in bibliothecas rettulerunt:** this clause contains a sort of subordinate idea, since the following adverbs clearly modify only *fecerunt*. The authors may have hoped thus to preserve, if not exactly publish, their poems, since the libraries referred to would have belonged to their friends (the first public library in Rome was founded by Pollio in the *Atrium Libertatis* as late as 38 BC (see *OCD* s.v. libraries)). Cicero's poetry was by the time of the Augustans generally derided; Cassius Severus said, *Ciceronem eloquentia sua in carminibus destituit (apud*

Sen. *Con.* 3 pr. 8), but Plutarch more judiciously observed that in his own day he was ranked highly (*Cic.* 2). Indeed, he was a master of technique, and later poets owed a debt to him on that score. W. W. Ewbank, *The poems of Cicero* (London 1933) 27–39 offers still useful discussion.

21.7 Asinius: 12.6n. Aper's dim view of Pollio's style was by no means unique to him. The tragedies – of which we do not have a single title – do not appear in Quintilian's list, and the speeches struck him as antiquated compared with Cicero's (*Inst.* 10.1.113 *a nitore et iucunditate Ciceronis ita longe abest ut uideri possit saeculo prior*; for his tragedies see N–H on Hor. *C.* 2.1.9, and Kennedy (1972) 304–8 for his oratory).   **Menenios:** 17.1n.   **Appios:** 18.4n. For the generalizing plural see K–S I 92; the tone seems sarcastic here (cf. Catull. 14.18 *Caesios, Aquinos*).   **Pacuuium ... et Accium:** 20.5n.   **certe** 'at any rate'.   **expressit:** 20.3n.   **adeo** 'so completely' introduces an explanation of the preceding statement (*OLD* 5).   **durus** 'harsh', perhaps with particular reference to its unrhythmical quality (Quint. *Inst.* 9.4.76; Brink on Hor. *AP* 446 – used there of archaic writers; *OLD* 7b).   **siccus** 'unadorned', Cic. *Brut.* 285 (*OLD* 9, not necessarily derogatory, but so here).

21.8 This elaborate physiological metaphor, anticipated by *ossa* and *macies* at §1, develops a notion originally found in Plato, *Phaedrus* 264c, that a good speech has a structure like that of living organisms, in which the parts contribute to the whole, without drawing undue attention to themselves individually. The metaphor is common, but the precise reference of the individual body-parts often depends upon the context. Here bones (cf. Cic. *Brut.* 68) presumably suggest the structure of the argument, sinews or muscles commonly refer to force and energy of style (Sandys on Cic. *Or.* 91), whilst blood or flesh denote fullness, richness, and warmth of expression (so Mayor on Quint. *Inst.* 10.1.60, and Colson on Quint. *Inst.* proem 24 *ossa detegunt*).   **eminent uenae:** this may mean only that no part should be unduly prominent, but Petr. *Sat.* 118.5 *curandum est ne sententiae emineant extra corpus orationis* may suggest that here too an idea of overly prominent *sententiae* may be in mind (though in fact Aper likes them to shine out, cf. 20.4).   **sanguis:** 18.5n.   **exsurgit toris** 'rises over the muscles'; the verb is also used of oratory (but less metaphorically) at Petr. *Sat.* 2.6 *grandis ... oratio ... naturali*

pulchritudine exsurgit.   **tingit:** Schultingh's conjecture for the transmitted *tegit* seems right. Peterson's translation of *rubor* as 'ruddy
complexion', and Winterbottom's (1982) 'fine red flesh' show up the
difficulty with *tegit*, which must refer to some covering of the sinews;
rubor, however, does not usually refer to flesh but to the redness of
blood, cf. Sen. *Phaed.* 376 *non ora tinguens . . . rubor.* The conjecture
secures that sense.

21.9 nolo Coruinum insequi: not in Messalla's presence! Aper
is polite, and so only glances at this orator's defects.   **non per
ipsum stetit** 'it wasn't his fault' (*OLD sto* 22); the idea of prevention inherent in the context accounts for *quo minus* (*NLS* §184, K–S II
260).   **laetitiam nitoremque:** cf. Cic. *De orat.* 1.81 *nitidum quoddam orationis genus est uerborum et laetum.* Cicero's interlocutor at that
point, Antonius, is in fact urging that the florid and polished style of
the philosophers favoured by Crassus is *un*suitable for forensic oratory. T. seems to be subtly undermining the modernist position. For
laetitiam see 20.3n. and cf. *laeta* 14.2.   **exprimeret:** 20.3n.
quam 'to what an extent', i.e. 'how little'.   **uis . . . animi** 'will-
power', 'self-confidence', as in Sen. *Con.* 2.10.12 of Ovid (*OLD*
8).   **uis . . . ingenii** 'creative power'. Cf. 1.3n. and for *ingenium*
and *animus* combined with *uis*, Cic. *Brut.* 93 *quem fortasse uis non ingeni
solum sed etiam animi . . . dicentem incendebat.*   **suffecerit** 'met the
demands of' (*OLD* 6). Quintilian admits as much, *Inst.* 10.1.113 *uiribus
minor.* Messalla had the same problem as Calvus, 21.2 *uires defuisse*:
they lacked the stamina to achieve their aspirations.

22.1 Aper interprets the literary history of the period to suit himself (we do not in fact know that Cicero had to contend with admirers of an earlier age), but handsomely acknowledges Cicero's
pre-eminence, and the many reasons for it, not least his improvement with age and experience. It is his suitablity as a model which
Aper doubts.   **iudicio:** 1.2n.

22.2 primus . . . primus: the anaphora enhances his achievement; the second member elucidates the first.   **delectum** =
ἐκλογή, cf. Cic. *De orat.* 3.150.   **compositioni:** 21.4n.   **locos
. . . laetiores** 'florid passages', cf. Quint. *Inst.* 4.3.1 *plerisque moris est
prolato rerum ordine protinus utique in aliquem laetum ac plausibilem locum . . .
excurrere* (a practice he rather deprecates); for *laetus* see 14.2n.
sententias: 20.2n.   **orationibus quas senior iam et iuxta**

finem uitae: the speeches of the mid-40s on behalf of Marcellus, Ligarius, and Deiotarus, as well as the *Philippics*, are presumably in mind. Aper follows Cicero's own lead in condemning his earliest style (cf. *Orat.* 107, with Sandys's n. on *deferuisse*).   **postquam ... profecerat ... didicerat:** T. and Livy are especially fond of the pluperf. indic. after *postquam* (K–S II 355–6).   **usuque:** epexegetic.   **genus** 'style' (*OLD* 10).

22.3 lentus est in principiis: Aper has in mind Antonius' advice at Cic. *De orat.* 2.213 *et principia tarda et exitus spissi ... esse debent* (he means that one should not rush into an emotional passage); cf. 19.3 (also for *narrationibus*).   **otiosus:** so of Brutus at 18.5, but Cicero too had a well-established reputation for this fault, cf. Quint. *Inst.* 10.2.17 *otiosi ... iurant ita Ciceronem locuturum fuisse.*   **excessus** 'digressions' (the word had just come into fashion, Quint. *Inst.* 3.9.4 *egressio uero uel quod usitatius esse coepit excessus*); Cicero piqued himself on them (*Brut.* 322).   **tarde commouetur, raro incalescit:** an odd criticism, since Cicero was renowned for pathos and often spoke last to rouse the passions of his audience. Aper ends each colon with a double-trochee clausula.   **sensus:** here 'sentences' (*OLD* 10; but cf. 21.4n.).   **apte** 'harmoniously', cf. Cic. *Orat.* 149, 219.   **lumine** 'highlight' of thought or style (*OLD* 11b); for modern taste in these see Quint. *Inst.* 8.5.13 *sed nunc aliud uolunt, ut omnis locus, omnis sensus in fine sermonis feriat aurem.*   **referre:** sc. *domum*, cf. 20.4.   **uelut ... :** an abbreviated comparison. For the building imagery see 20.7.

22.4 A digression, marked by another impressive comparison, which sustains the building metaphor.   **quod ... arceat ... quod ... delectet ... quae ... sufficiat:** consecutive relative clauses.   **uisum et oculos:** a common pair. Aper presumably refers not to the exterior roof (which was generally plain on private residences), but to the interior ceiling (*OLD tectum* 1b), which the wealthy had coffered and gilded (for further details see N–H on Hor. *C.* 2.16.11 *laqueata ... tecta*, and 2.18.1 *aureum ... lacunar*).   **supellectile:** an orator's 'stock in trade' (*OLD supellex* c notes that at Sen. *Ep.* 88.36 there is, as here, an allusion to the main sense 'furniture').   **sit:** the singular is owed to the nearer subject.   **gemmae** is also used metaphorically of literary ornament at Mart. 5.11.3.

22.5 oblitterata et olentia: unique terms in a literary critical context, the latter is especially strong. Aper had used *oblitteratus* of out-of-date orators at 8.1. The order of topics touched upon – *uerbum, sensus, structura, modus* – is replicated in the remark of Messalla at 26.2. **nullum ... infectum:** a warning against the rising tide of archaism (see 20.5 *ueterno inquinatus*, 23.2n., and 23.3 for the practical consequences of ill-timed verbal antiquarianism). Caesar had long before urged the orator to avoid unusual language like a rock in the sea, but this is a more specific warning. **rubigine** 'rust', used figuratively to imply antiquity (*OLD* 1b), seems to be found only here applied to language, hence perhaps the apology for the metaphor in *uelut* (5.5n.). **in morem annalium:** the native Roman historical form was the year-by-year chronicle; its inartistic shapelessness was notorious (and vilified by Catullus when transferred into a poetic genre, 36 *Annales Volusi* ...). Cicero discusses the form at *De orat.* 2.51–3. **fugitet ... scurrilitatem:** Cicero gives his view at *De orat.* 2.239 *ne quid insulse ... ne aut scurrilis iocus sit aut mimicus*, and 244 *scurrilis oratori dicacitas magno opere fugienda est. fugito* is colloquial, chiefly found in comedy and in Lucretius, and it seems to have been avoided in higher styles. **compositionem** here has regard to rhythmical arrangement of words, see 21.4n. (*TLL* III 2141.71). **nec** instead of *neue*: see 13.6n. **clausulas:** for Cicero's view see *De orat.* 3.192, *Brut.* 274; passages are collected in H. Bornecque, *Les clausules métriques latines* (Paris 1907) 188–9.

23.1 Aper turns to consider aspects of Cicero's style which illustrate the faults of low-bred humour and repetitive clausulae just mentioned; hence the asyndetic continuation. **Nolo irridere:** that of course is just what he means to do, and *irridere* picks up the prefatory *irrisa* at 1.4 (cf. 24.1 *uexauit* n.). This is an instance of the rhetorical figure called *paraleipsis*, whereby a matter is bypassed so as to call attention to it (cf. 30.1 *transeo*). Aper is referring to *In Pis.* 22 *rotam Fortunae* and, unfairly, to *Verr.* II 1.121 *ius uerrinum* (Quintilian, *Inst.* 6.3.4, was aware that Cicero referred to the poor witticisms current at the time). In the former case Nisbet in his n. *ad loc.* suggests that the expression was criticized for its comparison with the *orbis saltatorius* (a dancer's hoop?). The latter expression involves a double pun: taken one way, the phrase meant 'Verrine justice', taken another 'boar gravy'. (This pun on *ius* was as old as Plautus, and Cicero clearly liked it, for he recycled it in *Fam.* 9.18.3 (*TLL* VII

2.705.66–79). The pun was not unanimously decried: the late rhetorical writer, Rufinus, offered it as an example of *asteismos* 'urbanity', *RLM* 39.21–3.)   **quoque** < *quisque*.   **sensu:** 21.4n.   **in omnibus orationibus pro sententia** 'in place of an epigram'; 20.2n.   **positum "esse uideatur":** a wild exaggeration (so Kinsey on Cic. *Quinct.* 68, where the actual usage is discussed), but the clausula was notorious: see Quint. *Inst.* 10.2.18 (9.4.73), Sacerdos, *GLK* vi 494.27–8 *chorius et paeon tertius facient illam structuram Tullio peculiarem esse uideatur*, and Rufinus, *GLK* vi 566.2–4 *Tullius hunc laudat cui sit paenultima longa:* | *esse trochaeus adest, uideatur tertius ille* | *quem paeana uocat Musis deuota uetustas.* Aper's point is also that the expression is sometimes a redundant periphrasis for *sit*.   **tamen** 'anyway'.   **exprimunt:** 20.3n.

23.2 Aper winds up with a grandly constructed sentence, articulated in three cola, each introduced by the relative pronoun; the last colon is the most elaborate. He observes in three literary forms – poetry, history, oratory – a preference for early Latin style, called archaism (see Courtney on Juv. 6.454, citing Mart. 8.69, 11.90). The movement was noted by Seneca in the early 60s, *Ep.* 114.13 (cited on 21.4), and Quintilian too drew attention to the fashion: *quidam solos ueteres legendos putant, neque in ullis aliis esse naturalem eloquentiam et robur uiris dignum arbitrantur* (*Inst.* 10.1.43). It is important to appreciate, however, that the authors favoured by archaists were generally deemed classics of the language; it was their usefulness to the contemporary orator that was debated or even denied.   **significasse contentus:** 18.3n.   **Lucilium pro Horatio:** Aper starts with poetry. C. Lucilius (180–103 BC) was the father of Roman verse satire (see *OCD*, *HRL* 241–66). Horace followed in his footsteps up to a point, but reckoned to have surpassed him in point of stylistic finish (*Serm.* 1.4 and 10). Quintilian appreciated that it was hard to decide between them, but personally preferred the Augustan (*Inst.* 10.1.93).   **Lucretium pro Vergilio:** the style of Lucretius is markedly more rugged than Virgil's, but it should not be forgotten that perhaps only fifteen years separate his *De rerum natura* from the *Eclogues*.   **Aufidi Bassi ... Seruili Noniani:** Aufidius Bassus and M. Servilius Nonianus wrote histories, probably of the reign of Tiberius (see *OCD*). Aufidius was too sickly to take part in public life; as an historian he was esteemed (Quint. *Inst.* 10.1.103). Servilius, on

the other hand, had been consul in 35, and that in T.'s view will
have equipped him better for his task, though Quintilian (*ibid.*) is not
uncritical of his style. T. accords him an obituary notice at *A.* 14.19
(cf. Syme (1970) 91–109, esp. 104). As historians they too needed
eloquentia 'formal prose style', as Cicero had urged. T. of course concurred, and makes it clear that he finds the quality in some practitioners: *Liuius ueterum, Fabius Rusticus recentium eloquentissimi auctores*
(*Agr.* 10.3).   **Sisennae:** L. Cornelius Sisenna, praetor in 78 BC,
had considerable repute as an historian (*OCD*; T. refers to him at
H. 3.51.2), but was 'eccentric and innovatory' as a stylist (so E. D.
Rawson, *Roman culture and society* (Oxford 1991) 385), which may
account for his omission from Quintilian's list of approved models;
none the less Quintilian does refer to him for examples of usage, and
Cicero too acknowledged his merit as a writer, with qualifications
(*Brut.* 228 *huius omnis facultas ex historia ipsius perspici potest, quae cum
facile omnis uincat superiores, tum indicat tamen quantum absit a summo
quamque genus hoc scriptionis nondum sit satis Latinis litteris illustratum*, 259,
261; *Leg.* 1.7).   **Varronis:** M. Terentius Varro was a polymath
(*OCD*), but as a stylist he brought little to the language; cf. Quint.
Inst. 10.1.95 *plus . . . scientiae collaturus quam eloquentiae*, and Aug. *Ciu. D.*
6.2 *minus est suauis eloquio*.   **commentarios** 'model speeches' (so
Winterbottom (1989), following Reitzenstein (1915) 216n.) conveys
the sense here, since Aper is referring to the work of professional
rhetoricians, cf. Quint. *Inst.* 3.8.67. Originally the *commentarius* (or
-ium) was a written summary of the lines of argument the orator
meant to pursue; he would keep it by him to put him 'in mind' of
what he had to say. But *commentarii* became ever more elaborate, and
Cassius Severus wrote out whole speeches in his (Sen. *Con.* 3 pr. 6);
others adopted this practice and the 'notebook' was hardly different from the *liber* (Quint. *Inst.* 10.7.30, cf. *TLL* III 1858.1–25).
fastidiunt oderunt < Hor. *Epist.* 2.1.22 *fastidit et odit*; the Horatian
context is similar, for he is referring to those who disdain contemporary literature in favour of the classics of the past. Vahlen (1907)
56n. drew attention to the borrowing in a discussion of the use of
asyndeton *bimembre* (K–S II 151–2, H–S 828, Jocelyn on Enn. *scen.* 9
pugnant proeliant, Goodyear on *A.* 1.33.2 *sermone uultu*). Since, however,
such asyndeton, though found in *G.* and the historical works, is ab-

sent from *Agr.* and the rest of *D.* some editors delete *oderunt* with Heumann.

23.3 fabulantes implies an undignified style (cf. 39.1, where Maternus turns the tables on Aper, and uses the word of contemporary pleaders); Quintilian too used the word with this connotation (*Inst.* 11.2.131). **sequuntur** 'follow by listening' (*OLD* 18c cites Plin. *Ep.* 8.1.2 for the sense). **adeo:** 21.7n. **sanitatem:** this term of self-approval went back to the time of Calvus (see Douglas's intro. to Cic. *Brut.*, xlii–xliii; cf. Quint. *Inst.* 12.10.15, Plin. *Ep.* 9.26 (*OLD* 3)). **ieiunio:** Quint. *Inst.* 10.2.17 used *ieiunus* of the followers of Pollio (the metaphor starts in Latin with Cicero, *De orat.* 1.218, *OLD ieiunus* 2c and cf. *ieiunitas*).

23.4 porro develops the argument (5.2n.). **ne ... quidem** 'not ... either', 'neither' (*OLD ne* 6b). **in corpore:** Aper reverts to his similitude of speech to a human frame, 21.8. **aegrum** is contrasted with *fortem* 'hale': cf. Juv. 4.3–4 *aegrae solaque libidine fortes | deliciae.* For the construction with *uolo* see 15.2n. *uelim impetratum.* **prope est ab** 'he as good as' (*OLD prope* 6); for the idiom cf. *H.* 1.10.1, 2.76.2.

23.5 Aper concludes with a rousing call to his friends (who are clearly not archaists: *uero* (*OLD* 7)) to excel, in terms which recall Crassus' encouragement to Sulpicius and Cotta in Cic. *De orat.* 1.34 (esp. *ut facitis*). Here begins his peroration. **⟨uiri⟩:** Acidalius' addition is necessary. It was presumably omitted through its similarity to *-imi.* **ut** 'as indeed ...' (*OLD* 13).

23.6 laetissima: 14.2n. **grauitati** 'solemnity' (of a speaker, *OLD* 6c); *sensuum* 20.4n. **nitorem et cultum:** cf. 20.2; Aper desiderates these virtues of style and finds them in his friends. Cf. 21.3n. **electio inuentionis:** the most difficult part of a lawyer's task was *inuentio* 'the discovery' of arguments for his case; he had then to choose from among the possibilities, hence *electio.* Once the arguments were found they had to be marshalled (*ordo*). **ea quotiens permittitur breuitas:** this expression seems to recall a letter of Pliny to T. on the question of the desirability of brief speeches in court. Pliny says that a friend of his prefers it, whilst he would allow it only *si causa permittat* (*Ep.* 1.20.2). T. himself arguably would have sided with Pliny's friend, for *breuitas* could be a mark of

the grand and stately style (Dion. Halic. *Comp.* 274, Norden (1909)
I 334–5), which characterized T.'s own public speaking (so Plin. *Ep.*
2.11.17 cited in 21.3n.). He also embraced it for his historical works
because it distinguished his models, Thucydides (Sen. *Con.* 9.1.13 *cum
sit praecipua in Thucydide uirtus breuitas*) and Sallust (Quint. *Inst.* 4.2.45
*quare uitanda est etiam illa Sallustiana (quamquam in ipso uirtutis optinet
locum) breuitas* [cf. *Inst.* 10.1.32]). Here *quotiens permittitur* suggests that
in general there is not much opportunity to exploit this manner,
though, as Pliny makes clear in his letter to T. on the subject, Regulus had favoured it, and so perhaps it was somewhat discredited.   **compositionis decor:** 21.4n. (though here Winterbottom
translates 'agreeable rhythm'); the phrase is also found at Quint.
Inst. 8.6.62 and 9.4.44 (rhythm is discussed in the following section,
45).   **planitas** 'straightforwardness' (not found elsewhere in
classical Latin).   **sententiarum:** 21.2n. Aper means that their
epigrams were not far-fetched.   **libertatem temperatis:** mode-
rating 'outspokenness' is a virtue of the age; see 10.8n., 40.2.
malignitas et inuidia: not infrequently found together, as at 25.6
(cf. *TLL* VIII 181, 38, 46–7, 62). That hostility and envy are the lot of
living greatness, which posterity will recognize at its true worth, is a
commonplace (Otto §871). Aper ties his sentence together with a
contrastive echo: *nostra ... nostri*: we may fail, our progeny will not.
For the clausulae in this peroration see Intro. 30–1.

24 Interlude: Maternus' reply

24.1 agnoscitisne: this seems to recall Cic. *De orat.* 2.362 *human-
itatem et facilitatem agnoscimus tuam*, where Catulus praised Antonius'
disquisition on memory (Professor Winterbottom also compares Cic.
Rep. 3.47 *agnosco*, where Scipio acknowledges Spurius' feelings). *-ne*
here = *nonne*, a colloquial usage that strengthens the emphasis by
only seeming to ask an open question, when really the affirmative
answer is expected (Mayer on Hor. *Epist.* 1.16.31).   **impetu** 'enthusiasm' could be double-edged. Some relied on it too much
(Quint. *Inst.* 2.11. 3 *impetu dicere se ... gloriantur*), and Messalla will use
the term of the demagogic C. Gracchus, 26.1.   **copiose ac
uarie:** an oratorical ideal, often stated by Cic., but most explicitly
at *De orat.* 1.59 *oratorem plenum atque perfectum esse eum qui de omnibus*

rebus possit copiose uarieque dicere.   **uexauit** recalls 1.4 *uexata.*
ingenio ac spiritu: contrasted with *eruditione et arte* (2.1n.); for *eru-ditione* cf. 2.2 *omni eruditione imbutus*; this combination of qualities
marks Aper's pre-eminence, cf. 16.1. Maternus urbanely rallies him
for owing quite a bit after all to the orators of old, with whose works
he had indeed shown himself well acquainted.   **mutuatus est**
is the proper predicate only within its own clause, and some other
verb must be understood zeugmatically with the first clause, e.g. *egit*
(Peterson translates, 'what … ability [etc.] did he display, borrowing
…', which demonstrates the point neatly). The construction perhaps
mirrors the imbalance common in actual conversation.   **per**
'by means of' (*OLD* 14).   **incesseret:** final subjunc. in a relative
clause.

24.2 Maternus seems to anticipate that Messalla, goaded by
Aper's attack upon the classics (*incesseret*), may change his mind and
set about defending them; he seeks to reassure him that in spite of
what Aper said, he none the less (*tamen*) need not be deflected from
his purpose.   **promissum:** given at 16.2.   **immutasse:** the
perf. inf. here lacks perfective force, as commonly in prohibitions (or
an implied one, as here; see LHS 351–2, and cf. 18.3n.).   **quos
insectatus est Aper:** at 18.2.   **ne ipse quidem ita sentit:** cf.
15.2 *aliter sentire.* At Cic. *De orat.* 2.40 Antonius admitted that his
speech of the previous day had been purely eristic, and that he
had now to speak his mind, *quid ipse sentiam.*   **more uetere …
celebrato:** cf. 15.2n. on *in contrarium disputes.* The form of the abl.
singular of *uetus* was here corrected from *ueteri* by Ritter (cf. Goodyear on *A.* 1.60.1).

24.3 in tantum 'to such an extent'; the expression originates
in the Latin of the Principate (*OLD tantum* 6; cf. *in quantum* 2.2n.).
Messalla picks up the phrase to conclude his answer at 32.5.
cum praesertim 'and that although' (*OLD praesertim* 2b, Roby
§1732).   **centum et uiginti:** English must express 'only', which
Latin commonly omits, esp. with numerals (Kenney on Lucr. 3.144
with addenda, Mayer on Hor. *Epist.* 1.14.2 *quinque*). For the calculation see 17.3n.   **effici … collegerit** 'chronological calculation
has reckoned [*OLD colligo* 11b] that only one hundred and twenty
years is made in total' (*OLD efficio* 7, but *TLL* v 2.166.62 is better).
Either verb on its own would give satisfactory sense, but T. prefers a

pleonasm to avoid repeating exactly the same form of words as at
17.3.

25–6 The 'first' speech of Messalla

Messalla makes it clear that before he can follow Maternus' programme (*sequar* is future), he needs to deal briefly with Aper's attack.
He has thus to be reminded of his promise at 27. For an account of
his views see D'Alton (1931) 343–5.

25.1 ut opinor politely qualifies what he is about to say.
nominis controuersiam 'a mere verbal quibble'.   **tamquam:**
similar to the use discussed at 10.3 and 5nn., here it introduces the
substance of Aper's charge, a common usage in first-century Latin
(K–S II 456).

25.2 siue introduces alternatives in cases of uncertain description
(*OLD* 8).   **appellet** 'let him call', an independent jussive subjunc.   **in** [*OLD* 38, cf. 16.6n.] **confesso sit** 'it be generally
admitted' (*OLD confessum* 1); this particular expression, which got
round the lack of a pass. for *confiteor*, was modish in first-century
Latin, though used by T. only in *D*. (again at 27.1).   **Ne ...
quidem:** 23.4n.   **illi ... parti:** namely 18.2–3.   **qua fatetur** is read here *exempli gratia*; the MSS transmit a variety of readings, no one of which makes sense of itself. This, the correction of
Acidalius, seems the most economical of the many options canvassed
by editors.   **plures formas** picks up Aper's *plures species* from
18.3.

25.3 Messalla has in view Aper's refusal to discuss which orator is
best (i.e. which should serve as one's model, 18.3). The best has, in
his view, been identified, but more to the point the period in which
that best is found was itself remarkable for the number of individuals who excelled. This observation ranges with some others
that seek to identify periods of artistic achievement (not always literary; cf. Quintilian's periodization of the masters of Greek painting,
Inst. 12.10.3–6 (it is of course borrowed: see Austin's n., 135–6));
these are distinct from the atemporal 'canons'. We may compare
Velleius Paterculus 1.16.5 for the notion that there was a single great
age of oratory in Athens, centring on Isocrates (not named here).
Certainly he too endorses the view of a 'Ciceronian Age' of oratory

at 1.17.3.   **quo modo ... sic:** for the coordination see *OLD quo-modo* 4b.   **primae:** sc. *partes*, = 'supremacy', a common theatrical metaphor (*OLD* 15b), cf. *A.* 14.21.4 *eloquentiae primas nemo tulit.* **haec:** attracted as usual from the gen. to the case of the leading noun (*TLL* VI 2741.52, cf. 2.1n. *eo*). The choice of Demosthenes and of Cicero as the highest representatives of oratory in their societies is endorsed by the verdicts of Caecilius of Calacte, Plutarch (who juxtaposed their lives), and Longinus. The other Greek orators have been mentioned above; for Lycurgus (*c.* 390 – *c.* 325/4), whose prosecution of Leocrates has survived, see Kennedy (1963) 249–52.

25.4 Messalla's point is that behind the variety of individual styles lay a single criterion of excellence, *eandem sanctitatem eloquentiae ... quandam iudicii ac uoluntatis similitudinem et cognationem.* His list of leading traits in the individual speakers may strike us as glib – style reduced to the ingredients of a recipe. But the ancient critic looked for a distinguishing mark, in Latin *forma* (cf. 26.1), in Greek χαρακτήρ (character), which typified the style of each classic writer (cf. the qualities identified for individual orators in Apuleius' list, *Apol.* 95). As usual the consummate master can never be so easily pigeonholed, and Cicero requires three qualifiers. (Messalla tactfully says nothing of his own distinguished ancestor, to preserve an air of impartiality.)   **specie:** contrasted with *genere*, as at Quint. *Inst.* 2.17.42, 12.10.22.   **astrictior** 'terser' (*OLD astrictus* 4), cf. *pressus* 2.2. **neruosior:** cf. *neruos* 21.8. Cicero so describes the style of Aristotle at *Brut.* 121.   **splendidior** recalls the opinion of 'Atticus' *apud* Cic. *Brut.* 261 *splendidam quandam ... rationem dicendi tenet*, a passage clearly deemed authoritative, for it is quoted by Suet. *Iul.* 55.1. **amarior:** Caelius' *asperitas* was also noted by Quintilian, *Inst.* 10.2.25; we catch echoes of it in later quotations from the speech he delivered in his own defence (see R. Austin's edn of Cic. *Pro Caelio* (Oxford 1960) vii). He was also rather given to prosecutions, which may have enhanced a reputation for pungency.   **grauior:** Quintilian ascribed to Brutus *grauitas*, *Inst.* 12.10.11.   **ualentior:** the term is used of Cassius Severus by Sen. *Con.* 3 pr. 2.   **sanctita-tem** 'integrity' (*OLD* 3b) is the reading of the tradition, but many editors prefer the emendation of Rhenanus, *sanitatem*. The latter is certainly a common enough term of praise (23.3n.), and for that very reason it is hard to see why the altogether rarer term would supplant

it. Moreover, as A. D. Leeman pointed out (*Mnem.* 10 (1957) 231), the
term was used slightingly by Aper at 23.3, and would hardly be appropriate on Messalla's lips without some vindication. For *sanctitatem*
cf. *sanctiorem* 4.2n., and Quint. *Inst.* 1.8.9 with Colson's n., 12.10.11
with Austin's n.   **seruant** 'observe', 'maintain'; the tradition is
here faulty and Baehrens's conjecture, economical and close to
serunt, the reading of *BC*Qζ*, seems preferable to other proposals,
not least for the clausula (cretic + spondee).   **libros:** 12.6n.

25.5 Nam answers Aper's point at 18.4 and his reference to the
carping in their letters at 18.5.   **in uicem se:** where *in uicem*
means 'each other' (cf. 20.4n.) the reflexive is not usually added, but
cf. *Agr.* 6.1 *in uicem se anteponendo* (*TLL* vii 2.179.76–180.4).   **et**
introduces a parenthetical remark (cf. G–G 397a). Messalla refers to
Aper's use of these letters at 18.5.

25.6 [et inuidere] et liuere: the doublet is unexampled and
clumsy; Nipperdey, reckoning that *inuidere* might be a gloss upon
liuere, bracketed it. *liueo* was an unusual verb. It was originally used
(and perhaps coined) by the Augustan poets to refer to colour; the
metaphorical sense only developed during the following century and
was never common. T. uses the word (inf. again) at *A.* 13.42.3 (the
speech of Suillius), where it is securely transmitted in the Medicean
MS; but the fifteenth-century Leiden MS reads *inuidere*. The MSS of
D. too are fifteenth-century, and we seem here to have a similar case
of the gloss entering the text, without this time dislodging the correct reading.   **malignitate nec inuidia:** 23.6n.   **iudicium
animi** 'sincere conviction'; for the phrase cf. 27.2, Cic. *De orat.*
2.363.   **an:** *OLD* 1b.   **inuideret:** the subjunc. is used in questions repudiating a notion that is felt to be inconsistent with what
one knows or believes to be true (the imperf. refers to past time):
'could that man envy Cicero' (*LS* §85).

25.7 Seruium Galbam et C. Laelium: the two are combined
by Cicero, *De orat.* 1.58, and Galba's orations (cf. 18.1n.) were also
referred to, but somewhat more critically, at *Brut.* 82: *exiliores ... sunt
et redolentes ... antiquitatem.* Laelius was the great friend of Scipio
Africanus (*OCD* Laelius (2)); his style was a marked advance upon
that of his contemporaries, and Cicero records that on account of his
elegant Latin it was thought that he had written the plays ascribed to
Terence (*Att.* 7.3.10). In fact Aper had spoken of Carbo (at 18.1);

Messalla's substitution of Laelius gives the impression of spon-
taneous recollection.   ⟨Aper⟩ was added by P. Voss, who also
emended *antiqu⟨i⟩orum*, to supply a subject word; editors who omit it
assume that it is clear from the context who is meant. From the *quod*-
clause supply the idea of Aper's attack upon these speakers as subject of *exigit*.

26.1 Messalla now turns to his main interest. He does not answer
Aper's position but presents his view that oratory has undergone a
decline (this is not what he undertook to do).   **forma** 'style' (*OLD*
10c; cf. 25.4n.)   **C. Gracchi:** 18.2n.   **impetum:** 10.6n. This
'dashing' quality in Gracchus is also noted by Apuleius, *Apol.* 95.5
(which may therefore be one of the few classical reminiscences of *D.*
after Pliny's).   **L. Crassi maturitatem:** for Crassus see 18.2n.;
the reference to his 'ripeness' may be an allusion to Cicero's view,
expressed at *Brut.* 161, that Roman eloquence reached maturity
with him.   **calamistros Maecenatis:** the metaphor from hair-
dressing is not uncommon; 'combing' was felt to be reasonable
(20.3n.), but 'crimping' was an excess of refinement, cf. Cic. *Orat.* 78,
Brut. 262 *calamistris*, *De orat.* 3.100; Dion. Halic. *Comp.* 25; Austin on
Quint. *Inst.* 12.10.47, p. 191. This particular charge was made against
Maecenas by Augustus (he spoke of *cincinnos* 'ringlets', Suet. *Aug.* 86).
The style of Maecenas, in life as in letters, was highly artificial, and
dazzled (or revolted) succeeding ages; he remained an equestrian
priuatus and published no speeches (Sen. *Epp.* 19.9, 92.35, 101.10–14,
114.4–8; Quint. *Inst.* 9.4.28; Schanz–Hosius §214, II 20–1 gives
further references to his writing).   **Gallionis:** L. Junius Gallio
(*RE* x 1035–9 – this interesting figure is virtually unknown to *OCD*;
Schanz–Hosius §336.5, II 349–50) was an outstanding declaimer, and
a friend both of Ovid's (he addressed *Pont.* 4.11 to him on the death
of his wife) and of the elder Seneca's, whose son he adopted.
adeo: 21.7n.   **orationem:** Andresen's emendation is universally
read by editors for the transmitted *oratorem*, who would have to be
literally clothed as described. Our speech should be 'clothed' metaphorically (*TLL* VII 1.1266.7, no further examples).   **uel** 'even'
(*OLD* 5).   **hirta toga:** for the expression cf. Quint. *Inst.* 12.10.47.
There is a suggestion of the Roman of old, dressed in national garb
and performing a citizen's duties – like Lucan's Cato (2.386–7).
fucatis et meretriciis uestibus: the style of Demetrius of

Phaleron had been faulted for indulging in 'colour', which characterized the dress of prostitutes (Quint. *Inst.* 10.1.33 *uersicolorem illam qua Demetrius Phalareus dicebatur uti uestem*). *fucatus* 'dyed red' is commonly used metaphorically of styles that were disapproved of (Douglas on Cic. *Brut.* 36).

26.2 hercule: Messalla is excited; he has just used this exclamation.   **actores** usually has an objective gen., e.g. *causarum* (*OLD* 4), but cf. Quint. *Inst.* 6.1.45.   **plerique:** 2.3n.   **ut:** the train of topics in this clause – *uerba, sententiae, compositio, modi* – follows that of Aper in 22.5.   **lasciuia uerborum** 'exuberant language' (i.e. a stylistic, rather than exclusively moral quality (*OLD* 3b), but cf. 10.4). This is picked up by *omissa modestia ac pudore uerborum* at §4. Quintilian criticized Ovid's elegiacs as *lasciuior* than those of Tibullus or Propertius; it is clear from the context, in which theirs are called *tersus*, that Ovid was not so much 'saucier' as 'wordier' than they (*Inst.* 10.1.93; see Peterson on *ibid.* 88). His charge is emphasized by alliteration of *l* in the three phrases.   **sententiarum:** 21.2n.   **compositionis:** 22.5n.   **histrionales:** a Tacitean word, found also at 29.3, and *A.* 1.16.3 (with Goodyear's n.), always depreciatory, because of T.'s 'almost morbid fear of ostentation' (Syme (1958) 540). *histrio* (used in §3) had come by now to refer more to performers of mime and pantomime than of the regular drama (Furneaux on *A.* 1.54.3; cf. *OLD* b).   **modos** 'rhythms'; Messalla has in mind the extremes of the Asianist style. **exprimant:** 20.3n.

26.3 quod ... debeat: the subjunc. in such parenthetic relative clauses is not always easy to categorize (cf. K–S II 307–9), but is best regarded as generic, 'the sort of thing that ...'   **loco** 'by way of' (*OLD* 18c).   **plerique:** 2.3n.   **cantari:** Pliny similarly complained that modern delivery of speeches in the centumviral court was sing-song at *Ep.* 2.14.13 *illis canticis*.   **commentarios:** 23.2n. **†sicut his clam et†:** all attempts at convincing emendation of this gibberish have failed; Murgia (1979) 238 n.15 regards the words as a conflated doublet of *exclamatio*, and thus with some other editors removes them from the text.   **exclamatio** 'saying' (*OLD* 2).   **ut:** 3.4n.   **histriones:** cf. *histrionales* 26.2n.; clearly mime artistes are envisaged; for the study of the *gestus* of legitimate actors, however, see 20.3n.

26.4 negauerim: potential perf. subjunc. **Cassium Seue-rum:** 19.1n. **oratorem:** cf. 15.1n. **librorum:** 12.6n. **bilis:** something he himself admitted: *non continui bilem* (Sen. *Con.* 3 pr. 16); cf. Quint. *Inst.* 10.1.116–17 for a description of his manner, esp. *stomacho.* **sanguinis:** 18.5n. **primus:** cf. *primum* 19.1; Messalla is clearly among those referred to by Aper, who date decline with Severus. **contempto ordine rerum:** he scorned careful *dispositio*, in Messalla's opinion. Seneca the Elder records that he surpassed himself when he spoke extempore (*Con.* 3 pr. 6), and, if those speeches were published as delivered, a lack of structure may well have been apparent. **omissa modestia ac pudore uerborum:** this does not square with what Seneca the Elder says of him at *Con.* 3 pr. 7: *phrasin non uulgarem nec sordidam, sed electam. modestia ac pudore* form a common doublet (Woodman and Martin on *A.* 3.26.2). **studio feriendi plerumque deiectus ... rixatur:** oratory is here seen as gladiatorial combat (cf. 5.5n.). Quintilian makes the same comparison (adding the wrestler), *Inst.* 2.12.2 *nam et gladiator qui armorum inscius in <u>rixam</u> ruit et luctator qui totius corporis <u>nisu</u> in <u>id quod semel inuasit</u> incumbit ... frequenter suis uiribus ipse <u>prosterni-tur</u>.* **deiectus** 'unbalanced' (<u>*OLD*</u> 6b); Macrobius confirms the result in non-metaphorical terms: *multi Seuero Cassio accusante absoluer-entur* (*Sat.* 2.4.9).

26.5 urbanitatis: Quintilian concurs, *Inst.* 10.1.117. **uirium** 'mental powers' (*OLD uis* 27); for its combination with *robur* cf. Livy 28.35.7 *in medio uirium robore*, and 10.5n. **in aciem:** Messalla plays throughout with the common military metaphor.

26.6 Asinio: 21.7n. **Caelio:** 21.3–4n. **Caluo:** 21.1–2n.

26.7 nunc 'as it is' (*OLD* 11). **neminem sequentium lau-dare ausus est:** Messalla resumes a point made at §4. It is strange that Aper did not refer to, say, the glamorous style of the younger Seneca; indeed, all the stranger, since he recommended the orator to borrow language from Seneca's nephew, Lucan (20.5). **in pub-licum** 'as a body' (*OLD* 7; the only other passage cited for this meaning is *A.* 13.56.1). **in commune** 'in general terms' (*OLD* 5a). **credo:** here the tone is ironic (*OLD* 8c). **offenderet:** a leitmotiv of the whole discourse, cf. 2.1, 10.6nn.

26.8 quotus ... quisque: 10.2n. **scholasticorum** 'teachers of rhetoric' here. **ante Ciceronem:** a similar point is reported to have been made by Cassius Severus in criticism of declaimers, who, he maintained, were convinced that a declaimer like Cestius was superior to real orators like Pollio or Messalla, and even Cicero, if they dared admit it (Sen. *Con.* 3 pr. 15).   **ut:** 3.4n.   **numeret** 'rate' (*OLD* 8).   **plane:** ironic.   **Gabinianum:** Sextus Julius Gabinianus, a famous contemporary declaimer from Gaul; his name and works were still known to Jerome (Kennedy (1972) 482).   **uerebor** 'scruple' (*OLD* 4, with inf.).

27 Interlude

Messalla has allowed himself to be side-tracked into tracing the stages of decline in oratory, and has to be recalled by Maternus to the point at issue, the causes of that decline, rather than its agents. Formally considered, this break in his discourse is essential for the design of *D.*: his 'first' speech is an answer to Aper's, his 'second' is a fresh departure and paves the way to Maternus' answer.

27.1 Parce 'Forbear!' (*OLD* 2d); Maternus now takes full control of the proceedings.   **promissum:** given at 16.2 (cf. 24.2).   **colligi:** 17.6n.   **in confesso est:** 25.2n.   **causas** repeats 24.3, to remind Messalla of the central issue.   **paulo ante:** at 15.2.   **⟨dixisti⟩:** Lipsius' supplement is accepted here *exempli gratia*; clearly some verb of speaking is required.   **antequam ... offenderet:** the subjunc. may be generated by *dixisti*, even though the *antequam*-clause is not directly dependent upon the verb of speaking. But the subjunc. becomes common in temporal clauses even without apparent motivation during the first century (Wackernagel (1926) 246–7; *NLS* §228(b)).   **maiores tuos:** the addition of the possessive (rather than of *istos*, 'those of whom you speak') indicates a reference to his blood-ancestors (cf. 14.1n.).

27.2 mei: the warmth of the possessive adjective validates his assurances (cf. 26.4 *Aper noster*). Plain talk among friends occasions no ill feeling.   **aures ... perstringet:** the same phrase is found in Hor. *C.* 2.1.18, but in a different sense. The present tense of the MSS was corrected by Lipsius.   **iudicium animi:** 25.6n.   **citra** 'stopping short of' (*OLD* 5), a favoured sense in the first century, virtually = *sine*.   **affectus** 'feeling of affection' (*OLD* 7).

27.3 libertate: 10.8n. There is perhaps a hint of the opinion

Maternus will advance at 40.2 that true *eloquentia* goes hand in hand
with freedom of speech; cf. *H.* 1.1.1 *res populi Romani memorabantur pari
eloquentia ac libertate.* The tone of Roman high society had become
more courtly under the Empire. T. himself draws withering attention to this at *A.* 14.56.6 *Seneca, qui finis omnium cum dominante sermonum,
grates agit,* where Seneca, an older man and Nero's tutor, thanks
him for the interview in which he retired from public life. Men no
longer dealt with each other as social equals, because of course they
were not. The elaborate courtesies of Pliny's letters compared with
Cicero's demonstrate this. See J. Procopé, art. Höflichkeit, *RAC* xv
930–86, esp. 932 for changes to language.   ⟨a⟩ **qua:** the preposition is necessary, for only poets omit it with *degenero* (*TLL* v
1.382.34; cf. *G.* 45.6); cf. 6.6n. ⟨*in*⟩.

28–32 The 'second' speech of Messalla

He at last expounds the causes of decline, as he sees them. They
were much canvassed in the Rome of the early Principate, e.g. by
Seneca the Elder, *Con.* 1 pr. 6–11, and by his son, in *Ep.* 114; Quintilian had dealt with the issue in a monograph, now lost, entitled *De
causis corruptae eloquentiae* (cf. Brink (1989)). Of particular interest is
the extant beginning of Petronius' *Satyricon* (already perhaps mined
at 21.8); a discussion between a young declaimer, Encolpius, and
a rhetorician, Agamemnon, makes a number of the criticisms that
resurface here (see Bonner (1949) 76–7). It is hard, however, to be
sure that T. designedly recalls this debate, since its terms were very
much a commonplace at the time (see 35.5n. for instance, and
A. Collignon, *Etude sur Pétrone* (Paris 1892) 95–9). On the Greek
side there were treatises of the third-century Stoic philosopher,
Chrysippus, now lost (esp. his περὶ παίδων ἀγωγῆς, on the rearing
of children). (For modern treatments see Kennedy (1972) 515–26,
Williams (1978) 26–51, and Heldmann (1982) 255–86 and 294–9.)
What is remarkable here is the pessimistic tone; Messalla does not
foresee a possibility of reform. There may thus be a subtext, if T.
implies that Quintilian, whose activity was of course subsequent to
the dramatic date of the dialogue, had laboured in vain: the trend
was irreversible.

The layout of his speech follows a double pattern. One is chronological, taking the child from birth through the stages of its rearing and education. The other points up the contrast between former and better times and the present day. After a brief preamble (28.1–3) Messalla sets out the home life of the child of old (28.4–6), with which he contrasts contemporary practice (29.1–2). At 29.3–4 he redeems a promise made in his preamble (28.3) to speak of some defects peculiar to Roman youth. He then sets out his views on schooling, viz. idleness at both the primary and secondary stage (30.1) and excessive haste to reach the third, rhetorical stage (30.2), pointing out that it is in itself an unworthy successor to an older ideal. He thus reinstates his contrast between then and now, by describing the scheme of Cicero and its practical elaborations (30.3–32.2), all of which is nowadays neglected (32.3–4). He then concludes (32.5–7).

28.1 non reconditas ... requiris nec ... tibi ipsi ... ignotas: a reminiscence of the way in which Crassus opened his remarks on embellishment at Cic. *De orat.* 3.148: *peruolgatas res requiris ... et tibi non incognitas* (itself a reprise of 1.137).   **partes assignatis:** a theatrical metaphor, cf. Sen. *Ep.* 80.7 *mimus, qui partes quas male agamus assignat*, 16.1 above.   **quae omnes sentimus:** a formula of modesty that precedes the expression of one's own opinion (cf. 16.2 *meas cogitationes*), but *omnes* must include Aper, who everyone feels does not really believe in his own case.

28.2 Messalla's diagnosis of the causes of decline (and not just of oratory) centres, not for the first time, upon defective education (see Barwick (1929) 87).   **eloquentiam et ceteras artes:** cf. 30.5 *oratoris uis et facultas sicut ceterarum rerum*. Messalla sees a decline in general culture, not in oratory alone (cf. the complaint of Eumolpus the poet in Petr. *Sat.* 88 on decline in philosophy, sculpture, and painting). We might recall T.'s own sense of the degeneration of historical writing under the Principate, expressed at *H.* 1.1.1.   **desidia iuuentutis:** of course the young men of former days were always thoroughly committed, 30.2; cf. the complaint of Seneca the Elder, *Con.* 1 pr. 8 *torpent ecce ingenia desidiosae iuuentutis* (further examples in Bonner (1972) 98–9).   **neglegentia parentum:** cf. the criticism of the rhetorician Agamemnon at Petr. *Sat.* 4.1 *parentes obiurgatione digni sunt, qui nolunt liberos suos seuera lege proficere*. Messalla will develop this by describing the old training at §§4–6, in contrast with the new, 29.1–2.   **inscientia praecipientium:** this point is not developed in the event, though 29.4 is of a piece with the complaint that the teachers are themselves inadequate. Likewise 30.2 prepares for a blast against the professional rhetor. **obliuione moris antiqui:** this sums up all that has gone before (and it is appropriate that a Roman of Rome should say it). *moris antiqui* always confers approval in T.: *H.* 1.14.2 *uultu habituque moris antiqui* (Piso), 2.64.2 *Sextilia, antiqui moris,* and *A.* 16.5.1 *antiqui moris retinente Italia.*

28.3 quamquam 'to be sure' (*OLD* 3). **uestra uobis** suggests they are all provincial in origin, perhaps from Gaul (10.2n. *nostris*). **ego ... loquar:** Messalla speaks as one born in the City; he will get round to the topic at 29.3. **si:** 18.2n. **seueritate ac disciplina:** from §6 and 29.4, where the phrase is echoed, we see both that this is an important issue to Messalla (as it had been to Agamemnon, quoted in the previous section), and that the expression itself is a hendiadys. *disciplina maiorum* is itself a common phrase (*TLL* v 1.1323.55–7).

28.4 pridem contrasts with *nunc* at 29.1. **emptae:** the point is that, if a slave-girl had to be used at all, she should at least have been home-bred (*uerna*), so that her character for loyalty would be known to the parents; a bought slave (like the killer-nannies in the contemporary United States) was unpredictable (contrast *probatis ... moribus*). **gremio ac sinu matris educabatur:** cf. the Gracchi [*in*] *gremio* [of Cornelia] *educatos* (Cic. *Brut.* 211; the MS F omits *in*), and Agricola, *in huius* [Julia Procilla] *sinu indulgentiaque educatus* (*Agr.* 4.2). *in* need not be understood ἀπὸ κοινοῦ here, since *gremio ac sinu* can be simple local abl., cf. *TLL* vi 2.2321.39–40, where the passage from Cic. *Brut.* just referred to is cited. The synonymous doublet *gremio ac sinu* is not found elsewhere. The appropriate rearing of infants remains a much-debated issue among the prosperous, who can afford to pass on the chores to others. Tradition had consigned children to their mother; wealth, on the other hand, released her from the trammels of child-rearing. T. draws attention to the practice of the barbarous Germans: *G.* 20.1 *sua quemque mater uberibus alit, nec ancillis ac nutricibus delegantur.* Gellius records a long homily of Favorinus of Arles upon the virtues of a mother's care, *NA* 12.1 (for the general debate in antiquity see L. Holford-Strevens, *Aulus Gellius* (London 1988) 79, n. 38). Rousseau urged similar reform of French aristocratic habits in *Emile.* **autem** 'moreover' takes into account that the mother did not do everything; she had help, but carefully chosen on moral grounds.   **cuius ... committeretur:** final subjunc. in a relative clause.   **suboles:** Messalla deliberately uses an archaic and poetic word (so according to Cicero, *De orat.* 3.153) to stress the children's real value to the family. T. himself generally uses the word in the *Annales* of imperial offspring (even at 14.61.4!). **qua** refers to *suboles*, cf. the parallel phrase at 29.1 *coram infante domino*. **quod ... uideretur** 'anything that might be seen as', a generic relative clause.

28.5 remissiones 'relaxation'; the word is found with *cura* at *Agr.* 9.3.   **temperabat:** the subject seems now to be the mother again (cf. 8.4).   **Corneliam ... Aureliam ... Atiam:** Bonner (1977) 14–15 notes that all were young widows. For the famous Cornelia see Cic. *Brut.* 104, 211 (partially quoted at §4); Quint. *Inst.* 1.1.6. At Cic. *Brut.* 252 Atticus had ascribed part of Caesar's excellence as a speaker of Latin to *domestica consuetudo*.   **[matrem]** was deleted by Sauppe as a word intruded by one who did not see that the genitives of their son's names depend on *educationibus*. **principes:** take predicatively, 'to be in the front rank'.   **accepimus:** cf. 30.2: Messalla delights in the record of the past, and its exemplarity for the present.

28.6 disciplina ac seueritas: picked up from §3.   **sincera et integra:** a common synonymous pair (cf. Livy 40.11.3, *H.* 4.64.3, etc.).   **toto ... pectore:** 3.3n.   **artes honestas** 'respectable skills' (*A.* 14.15.3; cf. *TLL* VI 2.2909.77), like *ingenuae artis* at 30.4, and the *bonae artes* (29.3) ascribed to Messalla himself by T. at *H.* 3.9.3 (quoted in 14.1n.); these essential accomplishments – social skills – prepared a man for full participation in adult life (see T. E. J. Wiedemann, *Adults and children in the Roman empire* (London 1989) 157–9).   **siue ad rem militarem siue ad iuris scientiam siue ad eloquentiae studium:** these are the three classic careers and avenues to prestige in Rome; cf. Intro. 3–4 for a variety of sources. In practice, however, since the knowledge of the law, albeit commended by Cicero (*Orat.* 141), was deemed a specialism (cf. the debates in *De orat.* 1.165–84 and Quint. *Inst.* 12.3), there were chiefly two: *duae sunt artes quae possint locare homines in amplissimo gradu dignitatis, una imperatoris, altera oratoris boni* (Cic. *Mur.* 30). Messalla had himself

served in the army, cf. 14.1n.   **inclinasset:** the subjunc. is owed
to attraction to the mood of the verbs in the *ut*-clause (G–L §595 R2,
4; cf. *redderent* 1.3n.). The central idea was *si ... inclinabit, id solum aget*;
once the verb of the apodosis went into the subjunc. the mood of
the verb in the protasis necessarily changed, and its tense followed
sequence.

   29.1 At nunc contrasts with *pridem* 28.4; cf. 35.1.   **natus** 'at
birth'.   **delegatur:** cf. *G.* 20.1 quoted at 28.4n.   **Graeculae:**
3.4n.; the practice is noticed by Favorinus in the speech referred to
at 28.4n.   **unus aut alter** 'one or other' as a matter of indiffer-
ence; the usage of the expression at 9.4 is different; the present sense
is not noticed at *OLD unus* 1d. Messalla refers to the paedagogus,
whose duties were by now comprehensive (see Bonner (1977) 40–6).
His complaint was a common one, see Bonner (1977) 100–1 and
Mayor on Juv. 7.218 *custos*.   **cuiquam:** here adjectival and applied to a thing (*OLD quisquam* 6b says that it is more emphatic
than *ullus*).   **fabulis:** the danger of these had been stressed by
Plato, *Rep.* 2.377c–d.   **erroribus** 'delusions'.   **[et] uirides
[teneri] statim et rudes animi:** *teneri* is probably a gloss on the
metaphorical *uirides* (*OLD* 5); Cic. *Leg.* 1.47 *teneros et rudes* etc. shows
the stereotyped expression T. here avoids. Murgia (1979) 247–9 and
237 n.15 regards *et uirides* as a conflated doublet of *teneri*, but it is
hard to see a gloss in *uirides*.   **pensi habet** 'sets any store by'
(*OLD pendo* 7b); this gen. is now called by grammarians that of the
'rubric', a special type of defining gen. used of a general term (*NLS*
§72 (5.ii)).

   29.2 probitati ... modestiae: cf. 5.1.   **non** is the emendation of Baehrens, which resolves the confused record of the tradition, and reproduces a pattern found at 19.1 and 29.4.   **quae**
'which things'; for the neuter referring to feminine abstracts see G–L
§286.3, K–S 1 61–2.   **impudentia irrepit:** Plin. *Ep.* 3.20.8.
sui alienique contemptus 'utter disregard for themselves and for
anyone else'. For *sui contemptus* see Plin. *Ep.* 4.25.4 *se contemnit*, referring to a senator who wrote an obscenity on a ballot paper; somewhat similar, though less critical, is what T. himself says of the *dicta
factaque* of C. Petronius: they had about them a certain air of *sui
neglegentia* (*A.* 16.18.1), i.e. a kind of lack of self-consciousness. *suus*

and *alienus* are often combined in this sort of critique (see Woodman on Velleius 2.48.3, p. 79), but they then tend to refer to material possessions.

29.3 huius Vrbis: reverts to the promise at 28.3.   **histrionalis fauor:** cf. 26.2n. and *A.* 13.25.4 *fautores histrionum* (Nero encouraged them to riot), 13.28.1 (the praetor Vibullius tried to arrest them). A similar complaint, that enthusiasm for the stage is incompatible with the severe training of the true orator, is made by Agamemnon in Petr. *Sat.* 5.7–8 *neue plausor in scaenam sedeat redemptus histrionis ad rictus* (he refers to a 'claqueur'). The adj. *histrionalis* is used instead of an objective gen. (K–S I 212–13).   **gladiatorum equorumque studia:** the young have their favourites and study 'form'. Strictly speaking, it ought only to have been the *equorum studia* which Messalla had in mind as peculiar to Rome, for provincial towns had theatres, amphitheatres (for gladiatorial combats), and even races; but chariot racing on a grand scale took place only in Rome in the Circus Maximus (cf. Juv. 3.223 *si potes auelli circensibus*, and see J. H. Humphrey, *Roman circuses. Arenas for chariot racing* (London 1986) Chapter 10 'Other Italian circuses', esp. 576–8). Presumably too the best artistes among actors and gladiators preferred Rome.   **occupatus et obsessus animus** 'mental preoccupation and obsession'; the part. (usually perf. pass.) in agreement with a noun does the work of an abstract idea by a common idiom, see *NLS* §95. (T. becomes extremely fond of the construction and extends its forms in a variety of ways; see Nipperdey and Andresen on *A.* 3.9.3.) The participles are also paired at Cic. *Leg.* 3.19 and used metaphorically at Sen. *Ep.* 19.11.   **bonis artibus** 'cultural pursuits' (*OLD ars* 6).   **quotum quemque inuenies qui domi quicquam aliud loquatur?:** for the conversations of the élite centring on gladiators see T. E. J. Wiedemann, *Emperors and gladiators* (London, New York 1992) 23–4. For *quotum quemque* see 10.2n.   **auditoria:** the booths, or places in a colonnade where the schoolmaster set up his practice (see Bonner (1977) Chapter 10 'The problem of accommodation').

29.4 praeceptores: *grammatici*, teachers of literature, rather than *rhetores*, whose turn is coming up.   **fabulas:** 3.2n.   **seueritate disciplinae:** 28.3n.   **experimento** 'proof' (*OLD* 3).   **ambitione salutationum et illecebris adulationis:** teachers had to court the parents as well (cf. Lucian, *Merc. cond.* 10 for a suppliant Greek). By this means they might hope to secure continuing support and fresh pupils; Pliny, for instance, had to find a teacher (of rhetoric) for a friend's nephews, and knew that it would involve rejection of appeals for his 'patronage' (*Ep.* 2.18.5).

30.1 Transeo: see 23.1n. on *paraleipsis*. The sense of what follows was elucidated by Barwick (1929) 81–7, whose views are followed here.   **prima ... elementa:** primary education, learning to read, write, and reckon with the *grammatista*; see Bonner (1977) 165–88. (The charge that too little time is spent on the basics seems to lie behind what he says at 32.3 of failure to master colloquial speech.)   **nec ... insumitur:** this sentence, cast in the form of a tricolon crescendo, embraces the usual course of secondary education with the *grammaticus*, who helped students to read and understand the poets (*in auctoribus cognoscendis*) by explaining the use of language and metre. This was called *enarratio poetarum*, or *historice* (Quint. *Inst.* 1.8.13–17). At this time too students were to be acquainted with the customs and usages, forms and precedents of the past (*in euoluenda antiquitate*); this was also part of the duty of the *grammaticus*, what Quintilian called *enarratio historiarum* (*Inst.* 1.8.18–21; see Bonner (1977) 237–9).   **antiquitate:** see *OLD* 2b; Varro had written forty-one books on these topics entitled *Antiquitates* (*HRL* 598). Past events, what we call history, figure in the third element of the sentence: *in notitia uel rerum uel hominum uel temporum* (so Barwick (1929) 83). Cicero noted the distinction between antiquarian and historical study at *De orat.* 1.165 *de historia, de antiquitate* and 256 *historiam dico ... et antiquitatis memoriam.*

30.2 sed expetuntur quos rhetoras uocant: haste to get children into tertiary education is one of the flaws in contemporary schooling (the rhetorician Agamemnon seems to be making a similar charge in Petr. *Sat.* 4.1–2). A more general education in the *artes liberales* is necessary first.   **quando primum ... :** this is a topic in the extant work of T.'s contemporary, Suetonius, *De grammaticis et rhetoribus*, §25, itself only a portion of his larger *De uiris illustribus*. This was apparently the first work in Rome to give an account of their activities, and so shows that their status was sufficiently high to excite an interest in their biographies (see R. A. Kaster, *Suetonius, De grammaticis et rhetoribus* (Oxford 1995) xxviii–xxix). In fine, Messalla is

dealing with a serious rival.   **maiores:** 25.2n.   **statim dicturus, ⟨prius⟩** combines the emendation of the paradosis *de curiis*
by J. F. Gronovius and the supplement of Acidalius; cf. Quint. *Inst.*
8.3.41 *ceterum dicturus quibus ornetur oratio, prius ... attingam.* (This reading, printed by John and Peterson, is revived by J. Delz in *ŽRG* 114
(1997) 449, a reference owed to Professor M. D. Reeve.) Nevertheless
a problem remains, in that Messalla does not at once tell us when
rhetors first came to Rome; he fulfils his promise only at 35.1, after
he has concluded his remarks (32.7) and after Maternus has
prompted him to resume. The damage to the text may therefore not
yet have been healed.   **infinitus labor et cotidiana meditatio et in omni genere studiorum assiduae exercitationes:**
the subject words form a tricolon crescendo. *omni genere studiorum*
refers to the Greek 'general education', ἐγκύκλιος παιδεία. This
programme in its Greek context was a universal standard, not specifically a part of an orator's training. Yet it had been held up as the
ideal for the Roman orator in the *De oratore* by Cicero (and to it he
had added the Roman element of the *ius ciuile*), and his programme
had been resuscitated by Quintilian in the *Institutio oratoria*, composed in the 80s or early 90s, i.e. after the historical date of *D.* But it
should be stressed that Messalla, like any other *laudator temporis acti
se puero*, elevates the principles of a single remarkable individual,
Cicero, into a general practice (cf. Crook (1995) 145). It is clear from
the *De oratore* itself that there were some who did not believe that a
successful orator needed the elaborate education there encouraged
(cf. *De orat.* 1.5 for the opinions put in the mouth of Cicero's brother
Quintus).   **ipsorum ... libris:** this presumably refers to the
published speeches (and so §4; cf. 12.6n.) which the great orators of
the past left behind; these created the tradition against which men
like Messalla measured themselves and found the contemporary age
wanting.   **continentur:** the verb means that proof of their effort
is 'contained' in the books (*OLD* 11a, citing *A.* 1.11.4 *opes publicae
continebantur*).

   30.3 extrema parte: viz. *Brut.* 301–33 (the end of the text is
lost). For the significance of this dialogue to T. see Intro. 12–13.
uelut quandam: the apology (5.5n.) is due to the personification
of *eloquentiae*; only living beings are 'reared'.   **Q. Mucium:** Q.
Mucius Scaevola, called the Augur (*OCD* s.v. (1)), was a most emi-

nent jurist of Cicero's youth (*Brut.* 306), who appears in the first book of the *De oratore*. At 32.3 Messalla will deplore ignorance of the *ius ciuile* among the contemporary young, but barristers even in Cicero's day did not feel compelled to master it.   **Philonem Academicum ... Diodotum Stoicum:** Cicero sought a comprehensive philosophical education, hence his resorting to two schools for instruction (*Brut.* 306 and 309; see *OCD* s.vv. Philon (3) of Larissa and Diodotus (3)).   **omnes philosophiae partes:** traditionally three, as set out in *De orat.* 1.68, and listed in §4: dialectic, ethics, physics.   **neque iis doctoribus contentum** recalls, but in a different context, *Brut.* 316 *quibus non contentus Rhodum ueni.*   **copia** 'access' (*OLD* 8b).   **contigerat:** for the indicative see 17.4n. **Achaiam:** the Roman province of Greece, cf. 10.5n.   **peragrasse:** *Brut.* 314–15 describes his journeys abroad in the years 79–77 (and indeed this verb is taken from §315).   **omnem omnium:** the repetition is unusual, emphatic, and summary, expressing the completeness of Cicero's accomplishment; cf. Cic. *De orat.* 3.72 *omnem omnium rerum ... cognitionem.*

30.4–5 The sentence is discussed in the Intro. 45.

30.4 libris should refer to the published speeches (cf. §2), for Messalla's point ought to be that his oratory displays his knowledge. It goes without saying that it will be evident in the philosophical dialogues themselves.   **grammaticae:** this entailed, in addition to the *recte loquendi scientia*, a knowledge of the myths found in poems, of historical events, and of literary criticism, the *enarratio poetarum* (§1n.).   **ingenuae artis:** 28.6n.   **dialecticae subtilitatem** < Cic. *De orat.* 1.68 *disserendi subtilitatem.* The sentence refers to the three parts into which philosophy was divided (*omnes philosophiae partes* §3n.).

30.5 ex ... artibus et omnium rerum scientia exundat et exuberat ... eloquentia < Cic. *De orat.* 1.20 *orator ... erit omnium rerum magnarum atque artium scientiam consecutus: etenim ex rerum cognitione efflorescat et redundet oportet oratio.* It will be noted how Cicero's language is carefully reworked here and in what follows. A Ciceronian ideal needs his words for its expression.   **oratoris uis et facultas** < Cic. *De orat.* 1.142 without change; *uis* 'activity', *facultas* 'the range of his powers' (see Wilkins on Cic. *De orat.* 1.214; the word is especially common when used of an orator, see *TLL* VI 1.152–3).

angustis et breuibus: a common pair (Cic. *Part.* 75, *G.* 6.1 *frameas gerunt angusto et breui ferro*).   **terminis clauditur** forms a double cretic clausula.   **is est orator qui:** Messalla's definition is a conflation of a number offered by Cicero, chiefly *De orat.* 1.64 *is orator erit mea sententia hoc tam graui dignus nomine qui, quaecumque res inciderit quae sit dictione explicanda, prudenter et composite et ornate et memoriter dicet cum quadam actionis etiam dignitate, ibid.* 138 *ad persuadendum accommodate.*   **ad utilitatem temporum** 'as occasion requires'.

31.1 Messalla now observes that the older education was not purely verbal, but moral as well; the theory of morality was chiefly in the hands of philosophers, to whom the orator should go for instruction. Agamemnon at Petr. *Sat.* 4.3 *ut sapientiae praeceptis animos componerent* and 5.13 *Socratico plenus grege* had also noted the orator's need of a philosophical training, and later Quintilian concurred with Cicero that ethics was indispensable (*Inst.* 12.2).   **opus esse ... ut:** the construction with *ut* rather than the more normal inf. is found in comedy. This is the only example in T., and indeed it is the first example in any prose work, but since Pliny has *opus est ne ...* at *Ep.* 7.6.3 the usage is probably colloquial and suits the speaking voice (*OLD opus* 13b, H–S 645, K–S II 236). Presumably he chose the construction here to avoid using three dependent infinitives. **fictis ... controuersiis:** the complaint was a common one and it will be taken up with illustrations at 35.4. Again the thought is borrowed from Cicero, but with a twist. At *De orat.* 1.149 Crassus commends what we should call 'moots', pretend actions pleaded *quam maxime ad ueritatem accommodate*; but he does demur at those who *uocem modo ... exercent et linguae celeritatem incitant.* Thus Messalla has yet more to complain of, since modern moots are utterly unrealistic. **linguam** contrasts with the following *pectus*, as at Cic. *De orat.* 3.121.   **pectus implerent:** cf. 32.4, where again Messalla is concerned about the true orator's store of information.   **de bonis ac malis, de honesto et turpi, de iusto et iniusto:** the list hints at the basic themes of the three branches of oratory, which will be enumerated in 31.2: deliberative looks to good and bad, laudatory to honourable and disgraceful, forensic (the most important at this time) to justice. But it also suggests that the source of our knowledge of these categories is ethics. This becomes clear in 31.5–6. **subiecta ... materia** 'subject matter' < Cic. *De orat.* 1.201, 2.116,

3.54 *subiecta materies*. T.'s feel for the language did not allow him to borrow Cicero's form of the word, *materies*, for it probably seemed to him somewhat archaic (Brink on Hor. *AP* 131); he brings it into play only in his historical writings (Goodyear on *A.* 1.32.1).

31.2 nam explains more plainly the three *genera causarum*. These were distinguished by Aristotle, *Rhet.* 1.3.1, who was generally followed (D. A. G. Hinks offers an account in *CQ* 30 (1936) 170–6). ⟨**de utilitate, in laudationibus**⟩: the supplement of Ursinus, founded upon Cic. *De orat.* 1.141, is necessary to complete the trio of categories of oratory. **ita ⟨tamen⟩ ut:** the supplement of Acidalius is generally accepted by editors (cf. 16.5, 38.2), but it is not the case that *tamen* is invariably needed where a stipulation or restriction is made (K–S II 250–1). Quintilian agreed that the demarcation between the *genera* was often blurred (*Inst.* 3.4.16). **copiose et uarie et ornate:** found together also at Cic. *De orat.* 2.120, but often elsewhere variously combined. **nisi qui cognouit naturam humanam et uim:** a reworking of Cic. *De orat.* 1.53 *nisi qui naturas hominum uimque omnem humanitatis ... perspexerit.* **uim** 'meaning' (*OLD* 18). The objects of *cognouit* form a tricolon crescendo, and indeed the somewhat unnecessary *prauitatem* has been included to produce this structure. **intellectum** 'meaning' (*OLD* 5). **quae nec in uirtutibus nec in uitiis numerantur:** the morally 'indifferent' actions according to the Stoics. There is a similar expression in the description of the Stoic beliefs of Helvidius Priscus in *H.* 4.5.2 *potentiam nobilitatem ceteraque extra animum neque bonis neque malis adnumerant.* Crook (1995) 22 n. 58 observes that the reflections in this section anticipate the guiding principle of advocacy of the late twentieth-century *nouvelle rhétorique*, viz. that the advocate is seeking to persuade the judge to a proper, correct action in a given set of circumstances.

31.3 ut: explanatory of *illa*, 3.4n. Again the thought is a reworking of Cic. *De orat.* 1.53, where the orator's power to move the emotions of his audience is expounded. But Cicero's Antonius had objected at *De orat.* 1.220 that no true orator baulked at rousing the anger of a juryman for lack of a precise definition of anger; he questioned the practical value of a philosophical training. **quid ira:** the omission of the verb in the indirect question may be paralleled at 18.3 *nec quaero quis disertissimus*; but the addition of *sit* before *ira* by Lipsius is attractive, given the form of the succeeding indirect question.

31.4 apud infestos ... apud inuidentes: Aper had drawn attention to such jurymen at 5.5 *inuidis uero et inimicis.*   **cupidos** 'partial' (*OLD* 2).   **dicendum habuerit:** for the syntax see 8.2n., for the expression cf. 37.4.   **tenebit uenas animorum** < by recombination from Cic. *De orat.* 1.223 *teneat oportet uenas cuiusque generis ... et eorum mentis sensusque degustet.* Since Cicero did not apologize for the medical metaphor, T. does not either. Here *uenae* refers to the pulse of blood in the arteries, whose motion was used to diagnose the condition of the patient (*OLD* 2b).   **adhibebit manum:** again a medical expression, cf. Virg. *G.* 3.455 *medicas adhibere manus ad uolnera.*   **instrumento:** sustains the medical metaphor (cf. Isid. *Orig.* 4.11 tit.).

31.5 Messalla illustrates the need for differing approaches to different kinds of audience (e.g. the Princeps (who might prefer brevity, especially if he were a military man), or the Senate, or the centumviral court (where one could spread oneself)). Here he also has in mind the two chief functions of formal speech, to convince, *docere* or *probare* (*plus fidei meretur*) and to charm (*delectat*). His sentences are carefully constructed along parallel lines; he uses two tricola to describe the different characteristics of the philosophical styles. **astrictum:** 25.4n.; cf. Cic. *Brut.* 120 *Stoicorum astrictior est oratio,* and 309 *in dialectica exercebar, quae quasi contracta et astricta eloquentia putanda est* (he had just referred to his Stoic teacher, Diodotus). **collectum:** the metaphor in this unusual term seems to be drawn from clothing, gathered up so as not to impede movement (*TLL* III 1621.26–41).   **meretur:** the indicative after *sunt qui,* also found at *Agr.* 28.3, is rare in prose, though commoner in poetry. It indicates a specific group (K–S II 304–5).   **dedisse ... proficiet:** the perf. inf. with the future main verb looks to the time when the student first appears in public; cf. *Agr.* 3.3 *non tamen pigebit ... composuisse.* **dialecticae:** the Stoics gave special attention to this branch of philosophy, cf. Cic. *Brut.* 119.   **fusa** 'ample' (*OLD* 4).   **aequalis** 'uniform' (*OLD* 6d).   **communibus ducta sensibus oratio:** for the interlaced word-order see 12.2n. *communibus ... sensibus* 'feelings common to all' (*OLD communis* 7).   **locos:** the 'places' where an orator found the needed argument (*OLD* 24b; see Wilkins on Cic. *De orat.* 1.56 for the distinction from *loci communes*, for which see 19.3). Aristotle, the founder of the Peripatetic school, had divided topics into the formal (i.e. lines of argumentation) and the material (i.e. those that belong to a particular study like physics); he wrote a work entitled *Topica*, and his pupil Theophrastus also studied the theme (Kennedy (1963) 100–3, 273), as did Cicero (Kennedy (1972) 259). **iam** 'by now' (*OLD* 3).

31.6 The inspiration for this review of the literary style of the philosophers – to which Messalla unconsciously glides – may be found in Cic. *Brut.* 120–1, where the defects of the Stoic, Peripatetic, and Academic manners are set against the particular virtues of Plato, Aristotle and Theophrastus.   **Academici:** 15.2n.   **Plato altitudinem:** 21.3n. Plato was generally regarded as stylistically 'sublime', cf. Cic. *Brut.* 121 *Iouem sic aiunt philosophi, si Graece loquatur, loqui*; Plin. *Ep.* 1.10.5 *Platonicam illam sublimitatem*, Quint. *Inst.* 10.1.81 for his Delphic inspiration, Longin. *Subl.* 12.2–13.1 with Russell's n. **Xenophon iucunditatem:** Xenophon could be regarded either as an historian, or as a philosopher (so too Quint. *Inst.* 10.1.82, who also uses *iucunditas* of his style; cf. 10.4n.).   **ne Epicuri quidem et Metrodori honestas quasdam exclamationes:** 26.3n. Metrodorus was the pupil and friend of Epicurus (for both see the entries in *OCD*). *exclamationes* might refer to the pithy moral sentences collected under the title Κύριαι Δόξαι. There is a point to *honestas*, because many Epicurean doctrines were either misunderstood or vilified, particularly those relating to pleasure.   **alienum** 'out of place' (*OLD* 9).

31.7 Messalla corrects a possibly false impression.   **sapientem** 'a philosopher' (*OLD sapiens*[2] b).   **informamus** 'mould by instruction' (*OLD* 4), not 'sketch' (*OLD* 2 and *TLL* VII 1.1478.79, where this passage is cited).   **omnes libare** represents the Ciceronian ideal of the widely skilled orator (cf. Antonius' remarks at *De orat.* 1.218 *aliena libasse*).   **iuris ciuilis scientiam:** Messalla exaggerates: at *De orat.* 1.40 Scaevola had deplored the common ignorance among orators of the laws of the state (Crassus was an exception); cf. 28.6n.   **grammatica:** 30.4n.   **[et]** is transmitted by B, but editors follow Bekker in omitting it. If Messalla is aping Ciceronian style he was right to leave it out, for Cicero never joined the last two words of a trio in which none is linked by *et* (so Hofmann in *TLL* v 2.877.1).   **imbuebantur:** *imbutus* 2.2n.

31.8 incidunt enim ... : the gist of this awkward sentence seems to be as follows: 'in most, indeed in nearly all of our cases, legal knowledge is wanted (*desideratur*), but a number (*pleraeque autem*) crop up (*incidunt*) in which knowledge of those things too is essential (*requiritur*)'. This assumes first, a slight, and unusual zeugma, since the main verb suits only the second part of the subject, *pleraeque autem*; with the first subject we must supply the sense 'they occur as a rule'. Secondly, *pleraeque*, the emendation of Rhenanus, is here accepted instead of the paradosis, *plerumque*. ('totus locus suspectus' says Winterbottom in the apparatus of his Oxford edition; *pleraque* in his Loeb edition is presumably a misprint.)   **quibus** 'where', probably abl., as commonly in 'local' references to things spoken or written (K–S I 354–5); but dat. according to *TLL* v 1.708.79–83. **haec** = *harum rerum* (see 2.1n. *eo*), referring to the last named, criticism, music and measuring.

32.1 Nec ... respondeat: see 13.6n., *nec consulat ...*   **sufficere:** the impersonal use with a variety of constructions (here *ut*) develops during the second half of the first century (see *OLD* 7b). **ad tempus** 'for the occasion' (*OLD tempus* 10c) picks up the idea of irregular occurrence from *incidunt*.   **uniforme** 'of a single kind'; a very rare word in classical Latin.   **longeque** 'greatly' (*OLD* 7). **possideat ... an mutuetur:** the indirect alternative question is here not introduced by *utrum* (*OLD an*² 7).   **aliud agentes** 'focusing on something else' (*OLD alius*² B.6c), i.e. in a part of a speech which does not require a show of specialized knowledge. For the thought cf. Cic. *De orat.* 1.72 *si in dicendo non utimur, tamen apparet et exstat utrum simus earum* [sc. *artium*] *rudes an didicerimus*, and Quint. *Inst.* 1.10.7 *nos mirabimur, si oratio ... pluribus artibus egeat quae, etiam cum se non ostendunt in dicendo nec proferunt, uim tamen occultam suggerunt et tacite quoque suggeruntur.*

32.2 studuisse ... isse ... esse fateatur: supply *eum* as subject of the infinitives.   **numeros:** see 1.3n.   **oratorem:** cf. 15.1n.   **aliter ... nisi:** the expression involves a slight anacoluthon (change in the scheme of a sentence), for *alium* (conjectured in fact by Andresen) might have been expected instead of *aliter*. This way however the sentence preserves something of a spoken quality, as if Messalla decided to flesh out his idea on the spur of the moment.   **tamquam ... armatus:** a particularly common form of the usual military metaphor (see 5.5n., and Assfahl 93–4 cited there); for *tamquam in aciem ... in Forum* cf. Cic. *De orat.* 1.147 *ea quae agenda sunt in Foro tamquam in acie.* See Kraus on Livy 6.24.2 for the common pair *instructus, armatus.*

32.3 Messalla complains that modern pleaders display ignorance on a broad front, in respect of language, law, and philosophy (*sapientiae studium*).   **horum temporum disertis** recalls the opening of the dialogue, 1.1.   **huius quoque cotidiani sermonis foeda ac pudenda uitia deprehendantur:** this complaint is almost universally taken to mean that contemporary pleadings betray disgraceful faults associated with the use of everyday speech. So for instance Winterbottom's translation (1989): 'you may catch them in their cases with all the disgraceful and shaming faults of our everyday conversation'. (Similar are the renderings of Peterson in the Loeb, Grimal in the Pléiade translation (Paris 1990), and Bornecque in the Budé.) But colloquial language is not intrinsically faulty, at least when used by the well-educated, nor was there anything wrong with correct everyday usage in formal oratory: Quintilian had discussed its role at *Inst.* 12.10.40–2, and Cicero had said that in the narrative parts of a speech the orator did not want to use an historian's style: *narrationes credibiles nec historico sed prope cotidiano sermone explicatae dilucide* (*Orat.* 124; cf. *Brut.* 253 with Douglas's n., Quint. *Inst.* 4.2.37 and Aul. Gel. 10.3.6 for the conversational style of C. Gracchus). The jibe, and a much more withering one it is, seems rather to be that the modern *causidicus* is so ill-conditioned that he cannot 'even' (*OLD quoque* 4) use commonplace expressions correctly, but commits barbarisms and solecisms. (The translation of K. Büchner (ed. R. Häussler (Stuttgart 1985)), and the interpretation of Barwick (1929) 89 are along these lines.)   **teneant** 'grasp', 'understand' (*OLD* 23).   **senatus consulta** had from the late Republic on gradually acquired the force of law (Talbert (1984) 432–3); a large number of *senatus consulta* concerned inheritance (Talbert (1984) 459), so ignorance or neglect of them by those whose chief work lay in the centumviral court was especially reprehensible. **ius ciuitatis:** an expression hard to explain, if authentic. *ius ciuitatis*

usually referred to a person's civil status (*TLL* III 1239.70, VII
2.687.3), hardly an issue here. Some editors therefore supplement
the phrase, e.g. with *suae* or *huius*, or emend *ius*, e.g. to *instituta* (so
Heubner; but it is hard to imagine any Roman openly mocking the
national customs, and still expecting to succeed in public life). At
Cic. *Leg.* 1.14 *quid enim est tantum quantum ius ciuitatis* the expression
seems to be an elegant variant of *ius ciuile*, and that may be what T.
intended here. In the first book of Cicero's *De oratore* Antonius had
mockingly repudiated the need for an understanding of the Roman
legal science for a pleader (cf. *peruellit* at *De orat.* 1.265); many successful pleaders no doubt shared his view.

32.4 The ignorance of the moderns, who cannot for lack of information develop an idea, has therefore reduced the once splendid
figure of eloquence, here personified, to a drudge.   **sensus:**
20.4n.   **angustas sententias:** the epithet, which he had also
used disparagingly at 30.5, shows Messalla's distaste; for *sententia* see
20.2n.   **uelut expulsam regno suo ... omnium artium
domina:** Messalla has in mind the venerable personification of eloquence, or of persuasion, as a queen. It seems to derive ultimately
from Euripides, *Hec.* 816 Πειθὼ δὲ τὴν τύραννον ἀνθρώποις μόνην
'Persuasion, sole ruler of men', via Pacuvius in his *Hermione*, *o flex-
anima atque omnium regina rerum oratio* (fr. 177 R³); this line was admired
by Cicero, who quoted it at *De orat.* 2.187 (cf. *ND* 2.148 *domina rerum
... eloquendi uis*), and by Quintilian (*Inst.* 1.12.18).   **comitatu**
refers to the 'attendant' branches of a liberal education which
Messalla mentioned above (cf. *comites* at Cic. *De orat.* 1.75).   **pectora implebat:** 31.1n.   **circumcisa et amputata:** a doublet
and metaphor from vine-dressing common in Cicero (Wilkins on *De
orat.* 1.65).   **paene dixerim:** potential perf. subjunc.; for further
exx. *TLL* V 1.976.54–8.   **ingenuitate** 'breeding' (Winterbottom)
suggests that eloquence is now of servile status. The well-born
Roman male looked down on handicraft and money-making too,
so *sordidissimis artificiis* enhances the aristocratic Messalla's criticism.
una: the gender is owed to attraction to that of the more significant
subject word (K–S I 34).

32.5 Ergo hanc: part of the tradition offers *ego hanc*, but the
word order ought then to be *hanc ego*, since it is not the personal
pronoun that is here emphatic.   **cur ... recesserimus** answers

Maternus' question of 24.3.   **Demosthenen ... studiosissi-mum Platonis auditorem:** the expression neatly combines two passages from Cicero referring to Demosthenes: *De orat.* 1.89 *Platonis studiosus* and *Or.* 15 *Platonis auditor* (see Sandys's n. for this persistent but improbable notion).

32.6 et Cicero: Messalla uses a lively anacoluthon; after *potiores* and the reference to Demosthenes among the Greeks, we expect the sentence to run *et apud nos Ciceronem, qui ...* He refers to *Orat.* 12 *fateor me oratorem ... non ex rhetorum officinis* [whence the supplement in this text] *sed ex Academiae spatiis* ['walks'] *exstitisse* (a passage cited, less scrupulously, by Quintilian at *Inst.* 12.2.23 *nam M. Tullius non tantum se debere scholis rhetorum quantum Academiae spatiis frequenter ipse testatus est*; he had just referred to Demosthenes' interest in Plato).   **ut opinor:** cf. 21.1n. *ut puto.*

32.7 Having offered his first, and chief, ground for the inferiority of modern eloquence, Messalla is prepared to open the field to more general discussion.   **offendi:** Messalla, to indicate the close of his remarks, reiterates his initial warning at 27.2; he is prepared, unlike Aper (26.7), to give offence. *offendi* strikes a keynote of this work, that expression of one's opinion is likely to upset someone (2.1, 10.6nn.).   **si forte haec audierint:** cf. 14.3n.   **dum ... laudo:** the indic-ative is sometimes retained in a *dum*-clause in reported speech (*NLS* §221, n. iv, Kenney on Ov. *Her.* 20.204).   **ineptiis** 'silly pastimes', the self-disparaging connotation is common.

33–35 Interlude and completion of the speech

Messalla thought he had fulfilled his undertaking, to account for the causes of the contemporary decline in oratorical skill. Maternus disagrees and, pointing to a matter so far neglected, oratorical drill (*exercitationibus*), invites a yet deeper investigation (the strategy is not unlike that of Cicero at *De orat.* 2.124).

33.1 uelut ... quaedam: 5.5n. *uestigia ac liniamenta* are here used figuratively; for *uestigium* see *OLD* 5 'a track as indicating one's course or line of travel'.

33.2 ⟨artibus⟩ 'accomplishments' (*OLD* 4b), Schopen's sup-plement, based on §§4 and 5, is generally accepted by editors; it will have been omitted by homoeoteleuton.   **desidiae** picks up

Messalla's charge at 28.2.   **aduersus** 'compared with' (*OLD aduersus*[4] 12).

33.3 facultate et ⟨usu⟩: Maternus cannot be speaking here of an innate skill, but rather of one that is acquired (cf. 5) and enhanced by practice. The supplement of *usu* is owed to Tyrwhitt. **contineri** 'is dependent upon' (*OLD* 12b).

33.4 The resumption of Messalla's speech is formally indebted to Cic. *Brut.* 201 *uterque adsensus est; et ego tamquam de integro ordiens*, a passage laid under contribution at 9.1 too. T. characteristically offers synonyms for Cicero's expression, and omits a verb of speaking (Cicero goes on to add *inquam*).   **initia et semina:** cf. Cic. *Tusc.* 5.69 (with *tamquam* before *semina*), Quint. *Inst.* 4.2.54 (with an apologetic *quaedam*).   **ueteris:** 14.4n.   **institui erudirique:** paired also by Cicero, *De orat.* 3.35, *Verr.* II 3.161.

33.5 Messalla by the way comments on Maternus' point in 33.3, denying his implied opposition between the expert knowledge of the orator on the one hand and his drill on the other: acquiring the expert knowledge and the skills also involves practice, and their method is the same (cf. 2.2n. for the terms used here).   **quamquam:** 28.3n.   **inest** 'forms a part of' (*OLD* 2).   **tam uarias ac reconditas** is the word order proposed by Gudeman; it has the advantage, as Güngerich noted, of providing a double cretic clausula, *-conditas res potest*. The MSS present the epithets in reverse order (and with some other variations).   **nisi ut** 'except on condition that' (*OLD ut* 31). Messalla here uses the figure called *gradatio* (cf. Quint. *Inst.* 9.3.54) to link the various elements together.   **meditatio** 'reflection' (*OLD* 1).   **[eloquentiae]:** Sauppe's deletion should be accepted, since this is a general observation about the need for exercise.   **percipiendi quae proferas et proferendi quae perceperis:** the expression is structured according to the figure known as *commutatio* (*Rhet. Her.* 4.39 offers an example: 'eat to live, don't live to eat').

33.6 scientiam ab exercitatione separat: expert knowledge (*OLD scientia* 2) was something Cicero desiderated in his ideal orator, but his brother Quintus reckoned that practice sufficed (*De orat.* 1.5). The issue was much debated.   **longe:** 32.1n.   **uidentur** 'are deemed' (*OLD* 22). Its separation from **esse** seems deliberate to avoid the heroic clausula (cf. 23.1n.).

34.1 Ergo: resumptive, 'so, then' (*OLD* 5a). Messalla follows the line of the previous argument, contrasting former with present practice (35.1 *at nunc*). For the practice referred to see *assectabar* 2.1n. **foro:** here metaphorical, 'legal practice' (*OLD* 5), or possibly 'public life' more generally.   **propinquis** 'a relative' (one's father might be dead, amongst other possibilities: cf. *G.* 13.1). The Latin plural is equivalent to our use of a singular with the indefinite article; this is often found with words indicating relationship (cf. *A.* 14.1.2, where Poppaea is not, as some commentators believe, exaggerating when she refers to *triumphalis auos*; she means 'a grandfather who celebrated a triumph', viz. Poppaeus Sabinus; K–S I 87).

34.2 The sentence opens with an emphatic tricolon and anaphora. **contionibus:** public assemblies had been of great importance in the Republic (36.3n., 40.1), but lost ground under the Empire, though they seem to have been retained at municipal elections (cf. 41.4, and see Sherwin-White on Plin. *Ep.* 1.8.16, and *DNP* III 154, rather than *OCD* s.v. *contio*). Quintilian clearly believed that his readers might find themselves addressing a *contio*, though in Rome that was the prerogative of the Princeps alone (see *Inst.* 12.10.70, 11.1, and note *H.* 1.90.2 *uocata contione*). Still, a general had to address his troops, and might even find himself appealing to a civilian population, like Mucianus (see 37.2n. and cf. *H.* 2.80.2 for his crucial address to the citizens of Antioch, *satis decorus etiam Graeca facundia*: an exceptional speaker).   **altercationes** 'legal repartee' (*OLD* 1b, Quint. *Inst.* 6.4), as opposed to the uninterrupted speech.   **ut . . . sic dixerim:** frequent in T. (*OLD ut* 29b, *sic* 4; *TLL* v 1.976.38–45). The syntax and origin of the phrase, a replacement of the Ciceronian *ut ita dicam*, are variously explained: Woodcock on *A.* 14.53.3, p. 28, notes that the (potential) perf. subjunc. is 'aoristic' and refers to the future, and he further suggests that this expression arose from a conflation of an expression like *paene dixerim*, 'I might almost say' (32.4), with *ut sic dicam* (see O. Hey, *ALL* 15 (1908) 443–4, and Nipperdey on *A.* 14.53). The phrase apologizes for the following martial metaphor (Cic. *De orat.* 3.165, Quint. *Inst.* 8.3.7; cf. 5.5n.).

34.3 magnus . . . multum . . . plurimum: the trio builds to a climax.   **constantiae** 'self-possession' (*OLD* 3), important in a pleader (Quint. *Inst.* 1 pr. 27, 12.5.2).   **statim** 'from the outset' is emphatically repeated in the next sentence.   **in media luce**

contrasts with *studia ... in umbra educata* (Seneca's expression for his own training of Nero at *A.* 14.53.4).   **studentibus** carries a causal sense, 'because they were ...'   **ubi nemo ... aspernentur:** Quintilian makes the same point that in the lawcourts *nihil temere dictum perit, Inst.* 12.6.5.   **contrarie** 'inconsistently' (*OLD* 2). **quo minus** 'without' (*OLD* 2, subordinate to a negative in the main clause); the words, esp. in T., are virtually synonymous with *quin* (K–S II 269). The clauses form a tricolon crescendo.   **aduocati:** 1.1n.

34.4 incorrupta eloquentia: the expression is used at *A.* 13.42.3 (quoted at 5.5n.), where Suillius claims that Seneca envied the lively eloquence of real pleaders.   **causis et iudiciis:** the pair occur often in Cicero (to the list in *TLL* III 690.20–2 may be added *Diu. in Caec.* 1.1, *Brut.* 105, and Aul. Gel. 1.5.2). The terms are probably not synonymous here, and a distinction is intended between the trial (*OLD causa* 1) and the courts (*OLD iudicium* 3); see also Wilkins on Cic. *De orat.* 2.144, who refers to his note on 2.99. **deprehenderent:** consecutive subjunc.

34.5 deera(n)t is to be understood with the following subjects, *aduersarii et aemuli* and *auditorium* ('audience', *OLD* 2).   **faciem eloquentiae, non imaginem:** for the contrast cf. Quint. *Inst.* 10.2.11 *necesse est minus sit ... imago facie* and Apul. *Met.* 10.27 *fidei supprimens faciem, praetendens imaginem.* For *imago* 'semblance' see *OLD* 8 (to which these examples may be added).   **praestaret:** consecutive subjunc.   **ferro non rudibus:** the martial metaphor again (5.5n.), this time contrasting the reality of courtroom battles and the declamatory exercises; the phraseology seems to derive from Cic. *Opt. gen.* 6 *non enim in acie uersatur nec ferro, sed quasi rudibus eius* [Isocrates] *eludit oratio,* Sen. *Ep.* 117.25, Quint. *Inst.* 5.12.17 *declamationes, quibus ad pugnam forensem uelut praepilatis exerceri solebamus.* The *rudis* (*OLD rudis*² 2) was a wooden foil, or stick, used in practice fights by gladiators (?and soldiers). The reading is Lipsius' correction for the transmitted *sudibus* 'stakes', which really were used as weapons. **nouum:** because of the influx of *aduenae et peregrini* (7.4).   **ex:** 'indicating material or substance out of which anything is made or consists' *OLD* 16; the expression forms a third attribute for *auditorium.* For the *inuidi* cf. 31.4 *apud inuidentes.*   **dissimularentur** 'passed unremarked', 'were ignored' (*OLD* 3); T. rather affects this sense of the pass. (see Furneaux on *A.* 4.19.4).   **diuersis** 'of the opposing side' (*OLD* 7).   **fidelius** 'more lastingly' (*OLD* 3c). Messalla means that a pleader's true standing in the profession can be gauged from the sort of opposition he faces (cf. 37.8 *maiores aduersarios*); their respect, even their criticism, will confirm his position.

34.6 praeceptoribus ... discipulus ... auditor: Güngerich noted that each word is chosen to draw attention to the fact that the older form of training was not academic.   **eruditus ... alienis experimentis:** the same idea is found at *Agr.* 19.1 *doctus per aliena experimenta*. T. clearly saw that both the soldier and the orator learn by observing the practice of others in the field.   **noui** 'unfamiliar' (*OLD* 2).   **accusationem susceperat:** some speakers avoided prosecution so far as possible (Cicero for one), but it could sometimes be a duty, cf. Cic. *Off.* 2.49–50 *etsi laudabilior est defensio, tamen etiam accusatio probata persaepe est* (he offers instances).   **solus ... et unus:** the implication is that he needed neither a legal adviser (*pragmaticus*) nor an assistant prosecutor (*subscriptor*).   **statim** picks up §4; Messalla implicitly faults the prolonged rhetorical studies of the day. But the censors of 92 BC, whose edict is referred to at 35.1, had already complained that the then new schools of Latin rhetoric promoted *desidia*.

34.7 Messalla illustrates now the self-possession and precocity of the orators of old to which he has just referred. It was a well-established practice under the Republic for a promising young man to begin his career with a noteworthy prosecution. But they still began young in the early Empire, e.g. Crispinus, the son of Vettius Bolanus, praised by Statius, *Silu.* 5.2.98–110, for his defence at sixteen years of age of a friend charged with adultery; Pliny the Younger first spoke in the Forum at the age of nineteen (*Ep.* 5.8.8). Quintilian discussed the issue at *Inst.* 12.6.1, and drew up a list similar to this – Calvus, Caesar, and Pollio, but without the detail given here. (Cf. the reference to the early careers of the generals Pompey and Octavius at *A.* 13.6.3.) A number of the ages of the orators referred to here are erroneous, but some editors hesitate to alter the transmitted reading since the mistake may very well be T.'s own; cf. 17.3n.   **L. Crassus:** 18.2n.; he was actually twenty-one (so Cic. *De orat.* 3.74 *annos natus unum et uiginti*) when he prosecuted Carbo. **C. Carbonem:** C. Papirius Carbo, *cos.* 120, prosecuted on unspecified charges in 119, all too successfully: Carbo committed suicide by taking Spanish fly (Cic. *Fam.* 9.21.3).   **Caesar** was in fact twenty-two or twenty-three in 77 when he prosecuted Dolabella. **Dolabellam:** Cn. Cornelius Dolabella (*cos.* 81; *RE* IV 1297, Cornelius §134) was prosecuted for extortion in his province, Macedonia. Caesar's speech was famous (*nobilissima ... accusatio* says Velleius Paterculus, 2.43.3 – it was still known to Aulus Gellius, 4.16.8), and inaugurated his career as a leading public speaker, even though Dolabella was acquitted (Cic. *Brut.* 261, 371; Suet. *Iul.* 4.1, 55.1; Plut. *Caes.* 3.2).   **Asinius Pollio:** 12.6n.; in 54 at the age of eighteen he joined C. Licinius Calvus in prosecuting Cato.   **C. Catonem:** C. Porcius Cato (not Cato Uticensis), prosecuted in connection with the electoral disturbances of 56: Cicero mentions the trial(s) in *Att.* 4.16.5 and 4.15.4.   **Caluus Vatinium:** 21.2n.   **insecuti** 'pursue', 'harry' (as at 4.1); the verb is not used to mean 'prosecute'.

35.1 At nunc: similar contrast at 29.1. Messalla now dilates upon a topic announced at 30.2, the contemporary training provided by the professional rhetorician.   **qui rhetores uocantur:** cf. 30.2 for the scathing tone.   **paulo ante Ciceronis tempora:** Cicero's first trial was in 81.   **placuisse** seems to pick up the very word in the censors' edict, as transmitted by both Suetonius, *De gramm. et rhet.* 25.2 and Aulus Gellius, 15.11.2 (who may simply be following him): *haec noua ... neque placent neque recta uidentur ... nobis non placere.* Two points, however, should be noted. First, the censors concerned themselves only with Latin rhetoricians, whereas Messalla alleges a blanket condemnation, an exaggeration that suits his brief. Secondly, the edict, as quoted, did not go beyond an expression of disapproval (the possible grounds for that disapproval are discussed in Kaster's commentary on Suetonius, pp. 273–4); there was no official attempt at closure. Cicero however had Crassus refer to this edict at *De orat.* 3.93, and used the verb *sustuleram*, 'I had removed'; that perhaps led T. to assume that the schools were indeed closed. **censoribus:** in 92 BC; for Crassus see 18.2n. His colleague was Cn. Domitius (*OCD* s.v. Domitius Ahenobarbus (3)).   **ludum impudentiae:** taken from Crassus' words at Cic. *De orat.* 3.94; also referred to by Quint. *Inst.* 2.4.42.

35.2 Messalla roundly condemns the whole system of training: the place, the people, the syllabus; cf. Agamemnon's criticism at Petr. *Sat.* 4.4 *nunc pueri in scholis ludunt.*   **utrumne ... an ... an ...:**

COMMENTARY: 35.3-35.4   197

for this form of indirect qu. where the *-ne* is superfluous, see *OLD*
ne 5a, K–S ii 529, H–S 545; cf. 37.4. Each point mentioned will be
developed.

35.3 in loco nihil reuerentiae est 'the place commands no respect', because the teacher is as ignorant as the students. Messalla
also complains that lack of progress in school is due to the separation of younger from older boys. But mixing them together in class
notoriously led to physical or sexual abuse (cf. Juv. 7.239–41 with
Mayor's n. and addenda on p. 464), and so Quintilian had expressly
enjoined separation: *pueros adulescentibus permixtos sedere non placet mihi*
(*Inst.* 2.2.14–15).   **securitate** 'negligence', 'complacency' (*OLD* 2).
contrariae 'counter-productive' (*OLD* 4), cf. 39.3.

35.4 Attacks upon the declamatory exercises in rhetorical schools
were far from uncommon; so Cassius Severus *apud* Sen. *Con.* 3 pr.
12–15, and the salvo of Encolpius in Petr. *Sat.* 1–2 (there is a discussion of similarities in A. Collignon, *Etude sur Pétrone* (Paris 1892) 95–7;
see too Bonner (1949) 71–7). Quintilian was aware of the problem,
but defended the practice, *Inst.* 2.10.   **nempe enim:** not a common form of expression until the latter half of the first century, but
good usage (Quint. *Inst.* 2.13.9, Plin. *Ep.* 3.16.8; *TLL* v 2.589.8–
15).   **suasoriae:** the *suasoria*, a deliberative exercise, offered advice on a dilemma to an historical or mythological figure (cf. Juv.
1.15–16 *et nos | consilium dedimus Sullae*; Bonner (1949) 277–87); the
practice was indeed started early, right after exercises in composition, and so left even to a *grammaticus* (Quint. *Inst.* 2.1.2–3).   **controuersiae:** the *controuersia* was a judicial exercise for maturer students, and turned upon some nice point of legal interpretation
(usually fictitious) amid bewildering circumstances. For fuller discussion see Kennedy (1972) 316–18, and Crook (1995) 163–7.   **quidem tamquam:** this is the text of recent editions, but it entails the
suppression of a transmitted *etsi*, which Vahlen (1907) 146 defended,
supposing an ellipse in the thought, e.g. 'though the damage is less'.
But *quidem* itself can have concessive force (*OLD* 4), so the addition
of *etsi* seems otiose, indeed it might even have been a gloss upon
quidem. Shackleton Bailey in *CJ* 77 (1981–2) 256–7 proposed to keep
etsi and posited a lacuna after it, to be supplemented *exempli gratia*
thus: ⟨*consiliis magnis de rebus contineri solent*⟩. The only problem with
that addition is that the *suasoriae* quite often had trivial topics. For

tamquam see 2.1n.   **quales:** exclamatory and ironic, *OLD* 4.
per fidem: an exclamation (*OLD fides*[1] 1c).   **quam incredibiliter compositae:** the criticism strikes at both the subject matter
(*quales*) and the treatment.   **materiae abhorrenti a ueritate**
recalls the same charge at 31.1.   **declamatio** is here assumed to
refer to a declamatory manner of delivery (*OLD* 2).

35.5 Messalla lists some outlandish themes for declamation
(Bonner (1949) 75, 77). They could be defended, however, for appealing to the youthful imagination more than realistic situations (so
Quint. *Inst.* 2.10.5, but he too deplored the degeneration of the exercise at 2.10.1–12). A recent interpretation, that declamatory themes
constructed 'a fictional world of "traditional tales" for negotiating,
and re-negotiating, the fundamental rules of Roman society' (so
M. Beard, 'Dumézil, declamation and the problem of definition'
in F. Graf, ed., *Mythos in mythenloser Gesellschaft: das Paradigma Roms*
(Colloquium Rauricum 3; Stuttgart and Leipzig, 1993), 56), would
presumably have bewildered Messalla.   **tyrannicidarum praemia:** wittily pilloried by Juvenal, 7.151 *cum perimit saeuos classis
numerosa tyrannos* (see Mayor *ad loc.*).   **uitiatarum electiones:**
the commonest form of the 'rape-law' upon which the declamation
depended offered the victim one of two options: *rapta raptoris aut mor-
tem aut indotatas nuptias optet* (Sen. *Con.* 1.5; Bonner (1949) 89–91).
pestilentiae remedia: this theme is also sarcastically referred to
by Encolpius at Petr. *Sat.* 1.3 *responsa in pestilentiam data, ut uirgines tres
aut plures immolentur.*   **incesta matrum:** Quintilian records one
such *controuersia* from the elder Seneca's collection at *Inst.* 9.2.42.
quidquid: normally *quidquid aliud* (5.9, 19.13), but for *aliud* omitted
cf. *Agr.* 40.1, *H.* 1.89.2, 2.6.2, 3.52.1.   **prosequantur** 'describe'
(*OLD* 8b).

There is at this point a lacuna, the length of which is discussed
in the Intro. 49–50. We can reconstruct at least the kind of end this
sentence would have had from Sen. *Con.* 9 pr. 2 *cum uentum est in
Forum ... aut deficiunt aut labant* and Petr. *Sat.* 1.2 *cum in Forum uenerint,
putent se in alium orbem terrarum delatos.*

36–41 The speech of Maternus

That Maternus is now speaking is clear from 42.1 (Barwick (1929)
90–102 demonstrated that the speaker cannot be Secundus). His

theme to this point was clearly oratory in Greece, with which he is now going to compare that in Rome (hence *eadem ratio in nostra quoque ciuitate*; cf. 40.4 *nostra quoque ciuitas*). That the effect of oratory in both communities was damaging rather than salutary was a commonplace in attacks upon it (cf. Quint. *Decl.* 268.19). Maternus sees true *eloquentia* as the product of a free, albeit hectic, community; Cicero had been of the same mind, and so for instance never used *eloquens* of contemporary non-Romans (see 1.1n. *diserti*). An apparently similar political analysis of the cause of the sorry state of contemporary Greek literature is offered by an unnamed 'philosopher' in Longinus' treatise *De sublimitate* 44 (that work, apart from the question of its authorship, is also difficult to date, and the generally accepted view that it was written sometime in the first century has been shaken by M. Heath, 'Longinus, *On sublimity*', *PCPS* 45 (1999) 43–74). Longinus' 'philosopher' friend regards the political account for the decline of oratory as hackneyed (44.2 ἐκείνωι τῶι θρυλουμένωι), but it is not clear whether he is referring to the transition from Republic to Principate in Rome, or to the subjection of Greek cities to Roman rule (see Heath's careful discussion, 53–4): he may even be referring to both. Either way, Longinus himself repudiates this explanation, preferring the sort of moral account of decline favoured by the elder Seneca and by Messalla above (see also D. Russell's commentary on Longinus (Oxford 1964) 185–7, and Kennedy (1972) 450–2).

36.1 nihil humile, nihil abiectum: a Ciceronian doublet: *Orat.* 192 *humilem et abiectam orationem*, *Fin.* 5.57 *nihil abiectum, nihil humile cogitant.*   **magna eloquentia:** the expression is picked up at 40.2. **flamma:** Cicero uses this term metaphorically of the orator's impassioned delivery at *Brut.* 94; but he does not make this sort of extended comparison, preferring to use the verb *inflammare* (*TLL* VII 1.1455.24). At 40.1 the sinister import of this simile is brought out by *ardorem* and *faces.*   **motibus** has also a political sense 'disturbances' (*OLD* 9).

36.2 etsi ... tamen illa: Maternus will harp upon just this phraseology, cf. §4n. and 38.1.   **composita ... publica:** the emphasis upon contemporary peace prepares for the redefinition of oratory at 40.2.   **licentia:** a common word in political contexts to describe unrestrained freedom; it too will be picked up at 40.2. Its condemnation goes back to Cicero's translation at *Rep.* 1.66 of Plato, *Rep.* 8.562d (so A. Michel, *REL* 47 *bis* (= *Mélanges Marcel Durry*) (1969)

251 n. 1.).   **sibi** is to be taken with *assequi*.   **uidebantur** 'are seen to have ...' (so at §4 as well); the subject must be understood from *horum quoque temporum oratores* to be 'orators of past ages' (cf. 38.1 for a similar case).   **moderatore uno:** this allusion to the fundamental alteration in the Roman constitution will recur at 41.4. **erranti** is picked up by 40.4 *errauit*.   **persuaderi poterat** 'persuasion could be brought to bear upon ...'; alliteration emphasizes the notion. Some editors favour Heumann's alteration to *persuadere*. But it is hard to see why, if this were original, anyone would want to turn it into the passive. The run of the sentence seems to be similar to *A.* 15.68.1 *breuiter respondens non aliter tot flagitiis eius subueniri potuisse.*

36.3 leges assiduae: at *A.* 3.26–8 T. inserts a digression upon the steady multiplication of laws under the later Republic, a symptom of its disordered constitution (cf. esp. *A.* 3.27.5 *corruptissima re publica plurimae leges*).   **populare nomen** 'a reputation for supporting the people's interests' (*OLD populapris* 4).   **hinc contiones magistratuum paene pernoctantium in rostris:** the phraseology recalls Cic. *Brut.* 305 *hi quidem habitabant in rostris*. The importance of the rostra and the speeches to the people from its platform (*contiones*) are discussed by F. Millar, 'Political power in mid-Republican Rome: curia or comitium?', *JRS* 79 (1989) 138–50, and in *The crowd in Rome in the late Republic* (Ann Arbor 1998). **accusationes ... reorum:** for the phraseology cf. *A.* 11.5.1 *accusandis reis*, and Suet. *Cal.* 53.2 *magnorum ... reorum accusationes*. **assignatae** suggests quasi-legal provision by inheritance. An example: Mark Antony wanted to warn P. Claudius, son of Cicero's enemy, against maintaining bad blood between their households, *non esse tradendas posteris inimicitias*, *Att.* 14.13A.3.   **assidua:** the repetition from the beginning of the sentence seems unintentional.

36.4 exercebant tamen illorum ... eloquentiam: the phraseology is repeated at 38.1 *eloquentiam tamen illud ... exercebat*, thus reinforcing Maternus' point about the change of conditions. **magnis ... praemiis:** these had been referred to by Cicero as well (*De orat.* 1.15, *Brut.* 182): 'in the criminal law of the Republican period, under the régime of the *quaestiones perpetuae*, there were rewards, laid down in the statute constituting each *quaestio* (hence called *legum praemia* 'statutory rewards') for ... securing a verdict of guilty ... The rewards were not financial: they might include such elements as ..., for citizens, praetorian or even consular *sententiae locus* (position in the speaking order [in the Senate]), ... transfer to a *tribus* of higher social standing, or exemption from the call-up' (Crook (1995) 160). Seneca the Elder reckoned that the loss of these rewards had led to decline in enthusiasm for oratory in the young (*Con.* 1 pr. 7).   **tanto ... :** each member of a tricolon crescendo is introduced by this word; the last member is subdivided into a further tricolon, of which each element is introduced by *plus*.   **honores** 'public office', as usual in the plural (*OLD* 5).   **notitiae ac nominis:** 11.2.

36.5 hi: quintuple anaphora articulates the sentence and emphasizes their importance.   **clientelis:** the 'clientship of administration' of Republican non-military *patroni* is described by E. Badian, *Foreign clientelae* (Oxford 1958) 158–9 nn.1 and 2. Cicero as patron of the Sicilians against Verres is a classic example of what Maternus has in mind.   **ituri in prouincias magistratus reuerebantur ... reuersi colebant:** their purpose was to ensure support in case of prosecution for restoration of property (*res repetundae*) on their return from abroad.   **consilio et auctoritate** form a common pair (numerous examples in *TLL* II 1219–21).

36.6 eminentem locum forms a double cretic clausula.

36.7 Maternus gives four reasons (all introduced by *cum*) for the need to hold one's own as a public speaker in former times. Collectively, they cover the two fundamental spheres of oratory, deliberative (either before the people or the Senate), or forensic (either in self-defence or as witness for someone else).   **producerentur:** a magistrate or tribune could summon anyone, even a consul, to give an account of himself at a *contio* (see *OLD* 2, and Nisbet on Cic. *Pis.* 14 *productus*).   **parum esset ... nisi quis** 'it wasn't enough to ... no, one had to ...' The construction whereby *nisi* is virtually an adversative seems illogical, but is highly idiomatic and colloquial (cf. Vahlen (1907) 66–7, H–S 668–9, *OLD* 5); Latin here subordinates what English presents as a co-ordinate adversative idea.   **ingenio et eloquentia** < Cic. *Brut.* 318 (*TLL* VII 1.1527.49–55 has further instances of this and related phrases, e.g. 37.3).   **inuidiam aut crimen:** a Ciceronian collocation (*Verr.* II 2.73, 5.133 *te in crimen et in inuidiam uocari*), also found at *H.* 3.75.3.   **respondendum haberent:** for the construction see 8.2n.   **testimonia ... per**

tabellam: the practice was called *testatio* 'deposition', but it is not clear that it was by now commoner in civil cases (see M. Kaser, *Das römische Zivilprozessrecht* (= *Handbuch der Altertumswissenschaft* x 3.4, edn 2 by K. Hackl, Munich 1996) 368; J. A. Crook provides a contemporary example of such written evidence in *Law and life of Rome* (London 1967) 49). The point is that a witness who spoke in person had not only to be convincing, but to endure cross-examination, a further test of his *ingenium* and *eloquentia*. For *per* see 24.1n. **coram et praesentes** 'present and in person', a well-established synonymous doublet (*TLL* iv 943.24–6).

36.8 The sentence forms an asymmetrically balanced, but elegant, chiasmus: *disertum haberi* corresponds to *mutum et elinguem uideri*, *pulchrum et gloriosum* to *deforme*.   **mutum et elinguem:** a common pair (*TLL* v 2.391.29–30).

37.1 The sentence, forming the conclusion of a part of Maternus' argument, is composed as a tricolon crescendo of negative purpose clauses; as usual the third member is subdivided.   **clientulorum:** the diminutive is contemptuous as at *A.* 12.36.3.   **traditae a maioribus necessitudines:** in Republican Rome friendships and clients were inherited (cf. e.g. Plut. *Marius* 5; *RE* iv 35).   **impetrarent aut impetratos:** a part., usually perf., at the head of its clause which repeats the previous finite verb formed a figure called *epiploce* (ἐπιπλοκή): H–S 812.

37.2 Maternus now offers specific examples to bolster his general reflections. Asyndeton marks the transition.   **antiqu⟨ari⟩orum:** cf. 21.4n.   **cum maxime:** 16.7n.   **Muciano:** Gaius Licinius Mucianus (*OCD* s.v.) had been instrumental in securing Vespasian's elevation to the purple (34.2n); he also wrote voluminously, and was frequently cited by the elder Pliny. He seems to have published interesting excerpts about historical figures, rather than whole works (we note the historian's eye for a source of recondite information). These *Acta* 'Records' are not of course the official *diurna urbis acta* (discussed by B. Baldwin, *Chiron* 9 (1979) 189–203), or the *acta senatus*. **ut opinor:** cf. *ut puto* 21.1, 32.6nn.

37.3 Cn. Pompeium et M. Crassum: Cn. Pompeius Magnus and M. Licinius Crassus, the triumvir, were chiefly known in their military or political capacities. Cicero refers to their adequate oratory in his *Brutus*, esp. §§233 (Crassus) and 239 (Pompey) (Kennedy

(1972) 282).   **Lentulos ...:** for the generalizing plurals see 21.7n. All of these statesmen too had figured in Cicero's *Brutus*: for the Lentuli see §234, for the Metelli, §247, for the Luculli, §222, and for the Curiones, §210.   **operae curaeque:** a very common synonymous pair (*TLL* IV 1453.75–7, IX 2.661.75–6).   **potentiam:** cf. 5.5n.   **aliqua** 'some degree of' (*OLD aliqui*[1] 2). Maternus is aware that they relied for their positions chiefly on wealth, prestige, and connections; hence his qualification of the role of oratory in their careers.

37.4 Maternus turns to a new topic, but one still relating to the superiority of the past. Humdrum legal issues depress talent, while cases of wider interest excite it.   **splendor reorum et magnitudo causarum:** Pliny has a similar expression, in a similar context, at *Ep.* 2.14.1 (quoted at 38.2).   **quae ... ipsa:** it is common for the neuter plural to refer to a number of non-personal antecedents (K–S I 57–8).   **et** 'as well' (*OLD* 5).   **utrumne ... an:** see 35.2n. What falls within the *utrumne*-clause concerns civil actions, within the *an*-clause criminal trials.   **formula:** 20.1n.   **interdicto** 'injunction' (*OLD* 2).   **dicendum habeas:** for the construction see 8.2n., for the expression 31.4.   **ambitu comitiorum** 'bribery at elections' (*OLD ambitus* 6, with defining gen.). Many of the great trials of the late Republic were indeed about electoral bribery (e.g. Cicero's *Pro Murena* and *Pro Plancio*), the plundering of provinces (e.g. his *In Verrem, Pro Fonteio, Pro Flacco, Pro Scauro, Pro Rabirio Postumo*), or the 'slaughter' of a Roman citizen (we might recall the crucifixion of Gavius by Verres). Some of his murder trials, e.g. the *Pro Rabirio* and *Pro Milone*, had a strong political angle too.   **de expilatis sociis et ciuibus trucidatis:** for the idiom see 29.3n. The chiastic order is desirable in itself, but also helps to produce a welcome clausula (cretic + spondee).

37.5 sicut here has concessive force, 'though' (*OLD* 1c).   **ciuitatis status** 'constitution'.   **crescit ... inuenit:** a related notion is found at *A.* 4.32, where the historian deplores that his predecessors had exciting affairs at home and abroad to relate, whilst his imperial annals are by comparison dreary and limited. **claram et illustrem:** the synonymous doublet is common.

37.6 Demosthenen orationes ... aduersus tutores: see Plut. *Dem.* 6, Aesch. *Ctes.* 173; he spoke against Aphobus and

Demophon in 363 BC when he was twenty. These speeches launched his career as a judicial orator. 'Demosthenes' earliest speech, his prosecution of his guardian Aphobus, is a remarkable product, as much a piece of accounting as of rhetoric ... The second speech against Aphobus ... is less successful, less thought out ... The speech is not a poor one ... The third speech against Aphobus ... has great versatility not only in argument but also in style' (Kennedy (1963) 209–10).   **P. Quinctius defensus aut Licinius Archias** 'the defence of Q. or of A.'; for the idiom see 29.3n. *defensus* must be taken with *Archias* ἀπὸ κοινοῦ. The speech in defence of Quinctius, delivered in 81 BC, is now our first extant one by Cicero; the case may have been a poor one and the defendant convicted. That on behalf of the Greek poet Archias, who was charged with passing himself off as a Roman citizen, was delivered in 62 BC. It is referred to here just because it was much esteemed as an example of oratorical skill, in spite of the comparative insignificance of the case. Quintilian quotes from it on a number of occasions (indeed, once from the exordia of both speeches together, 11.1.19).   **Catilina et Milo et Verres et Antonius:** adversative asyndeton (10.6n.) introduces the significant figures. Cicero composed four orations in 63 BC, the year of his consulate, against the insurgent L. Sergius Catilina (*OCD* s.v. Sergius Catilina), he defended T. Annius Milo (*OCD* s.v. Annius Milo) in 52 BC on the charge of murdering Clodius, and he prosecuted C. Verres (*OCD* s.v.) in 70 BC on behalf of the Sicilians – he thus wrested oratorical primacy from Hortensius. He launched the fourteen so-called Philippic orations against M. Antonius in the last years of his life. Thanks to Cicero's oratory Catiline, Verres and Milo entered the literary tradition as *exempla* (cf. Juv. 2.26–7). Of the speeches against Antony Velleius Paterculus says *continuis actionibus aeternas Antonii memoriae inussit notas* (2.64.3), and Juvenal called the second Philippic *conspicuae diuina Philippica famae* (10.125).   **non quia tanti fuerit rei publicae malos ferre ciues ut ...** 'I don't say this because it was worth the state's while to produce bad citizens just in order that orators should have ...' The sense of *non quia* is here somewhat elliptical (*OLD quia* 3b). In classical Latin *non quia* + subjunc. repudiates a suggested reason, which is also denied as a fact, hence *fuerit* has been accepted generally by editors here (but there are exx. with the verb in the indic. (e.g. *A.* 15.60.2 with

Miller's n.), and so *fuit*, the reading of the MSS, might stand: K–S ii 386–7). The construction of *tanti est ut* ... developed two distinct usages. Here the subject of *tanti fuerit*, the inf. phrase *ferre* + acc., expresses 'the price to be paid', while the *ut*-clause (in essence here final) expresses 'the prize to be gained'. At 40.4, on the other hand, the construction is exactly reversed: there the subject of *tanti fuit*, *eloquentia*, expresses 'the prize to be gained', while the *ut*-clause, *ut pateretur et leges* (in essence there consecutive), expresses 'the price to be paid'. The difference is carefully elucidated by Duff in a fine note on Juv. 3.54–6 *tanti ... non sit ... harena Tagi ... ut somno careas*.   **subinde admoneo:** e.g. at 36.2 (and finally at 40.2). Since we lack the opening of Maternus' speech, we cannot be sure that he did not define at the outset what his theme or point at issue (*quaestio*) was to be.   **meminerimus sciamusque:** jussive subjunctives. **turbidis et inquietis:** contrast with 36.2 *composita et quieta*. **exstitit**, the reading of the MS tradition, is defensible, and need not be altered to the pres.; the perf. established a fact for all time (H–S 318).

37.8 The argument takes a decisive turn. The common metaphor of strife or battle has been constantly applied to forensic oratory by all speakers in the dialogue (see *armatus* 5.5n.; *tamquam in acie* recalls 32.2). Here Maternus redeploys the metaphor, along with the personification of eloquence, in a form more elaborated than any previous one so as to sap the claims of all its manifestations. Where there is peace and concord, there can be no call for it. The first part of the sentence in 37.8 forms a tricolon crescendo, articulated by the anaphoric *quo*.   **altior et excelsior** 'more sublime' (*OLD* 2b): the synonymous pairing is common; for *altior* cf. 18.2n.   **nobilitata:** the combination of the positive with the comparatives *altior* and *excelsior* after *tanto* is not irregular, cf. *A.* 2.5.2 and 3.43.1 (Furneaux Ch. 5 §64(2)). In all three cases the words in the positive degree had no comparative form; it may therefore be that they borrow a comparative colour from their neighbours.   **in ore hominum agit** 'appears before men' seems to be the sense here, as at Sall. *Hist.* 1.51 *in ore gentibus agens*, 2.47.4 *in ore uestro ... egi*, and at *H.* 3.36.1 *non in ore uulgi agere* (cf. *TLL* ix 1987.12–15). But many take the sense here to be 'is generally spoken of' (so even *TLL* ix 1980.33), which is undeniably appropriate. The text of this sentence from *maiores* on has been successfully restored by many hands, and meets with editorial consensus. From *ut secura uelint* on there is plainly a lacuna, but no agreement about how to fill it. The idea seems clear enough: men admire what is difficult and dangerous for others so long as it puts them at no risk.

38.1 Maternus opens a new topic, judicial practice; its current forms are inimical to old-fashioned oratory.   **ueterum:** 14.4n. **quae ... nunc:** *quae* refers only to *forma et consuetudo*; *nunc* obviously cancels out *ueterum*. For this common, loose use of the relative see Courtney on Juv. 5.44–5 *quas*, and compare the use of the subject *oratores* at 36.2 (*uidebantur* n.).   **ueritati** 'integrity' is the emendation of Agricola for the transmitted *ita erit*; for this sense, common in a forensic context cf. *A.* 1.75.2 *dum ueritati consulitur, libertas corrumpebatur*.   **eloquentiam tamen illud ... exercebat:** see 36.4n. **perorare** 'get through his speech'.   **comperendinationes** 'compulsory adjournments'. These became part of the procedure of the *quaestiones repetundarum* (and possibly other classes of trial) in the late Republic (Jones (1972) 71); when the trial was resumed, the case had more or less to be put to the jurors afresh, an *actio secunda* which gave scope for new evidence or new argument (for advice on the exordia appropriate to such occasions see Quint. *Inst.* 4.1.4). **modum dicendo sibi quisque sumebat:** this contrasts with what Aper says at 19.5 about judges who impose limits upon pleaders; in days of old they took as much time as they needed.   **numerus ... patronorum:** Asconius noted that before the civil wars the number of *patroni* had risen to as many as twelve, but that a *lex Iulia* reduced the number (*In Scaur.* 18). Reasons for the rising number of advocates are discussed by Crook (1995) 127–9, esp. 128; he draws attention to two: political prestige and the need for specialist pleaders to deal with particular aspects of the case.

38.2 Cn. Pompeius: in his third consulship of 52 BC by provisions of the *lex Pompeia de ui et ambitu* two hours were allotted to the prosecution and three to the defence (both on the same day), a maximum of four days was fixed for trial, and the number of *patroni* was restricted (Asconius, *In Milon.* 31, 34 and Dio Cass. 40.52.2 list the provisions; Kennedy (1972) 16). In fact, time for pleading, the *legitimae horae*, had already been determined, and later laws, e.g. Augustus' *lex iudiciaria*, corroborated the regulations (see Sherwin-

White on Plin. *Ep.* 2.11.14, and cf. *Ep.* 4.9.9). But this applied only to criminal jurisdiction; in civil suits the parties might agree with the judge on the length of speeches (Sherwin-White on Plin. *Ep.* 6.2.5). **ueluti** apologizes for the metaphor in *frenos*, alongside the personification of eloquence. A like simile comes at 39.2.   **legibus:** 19.5n. **negotia:** 9.3n.   **causae centumuirales:** 7.1n.   **liber:** 12.6n. The books published by the ancients presumably included some speeches delivered before this court, which was not in itself insignificant (cf. Cic. *Brut.* 144, 194–8), but they were not the most important in the pleaders' careers. (It is remarkable that Quintilian commonly draws upon Cicero's great criminal trials for examples in his educational treatise, even though he is chiefly preparing men for the centumviral court.) Even under the Principate the comparative insignificance of the speeches delivered there is to some extent confirmed by Pliny: *sunt enim paruae et exiles; raro incidit uel personarum claritate uel negotii magnitudine insignis* (*Ep.* 2.14.1). In the Republic there was a greater chance to show off one's oratory in criminal trials, which often had political overtones that gave the published speeches an enhanced interest.   **exceptis orationibus Asini:** this case was often referred to by Quintilian (*Inst.* 7.2.26; Kennedy (1972) 306). The reference serves another purpose, for it helps to pinpoint the onset of decline.   **postquam ...:** the clause is composed of a tetracolon. All four elements are similarly formed: adjective + gen. + subject word. But there is an ascent through the ranks of Roman society: *populus, senatus, princeps.*   **principis disciplina:** cf. Plin. *Pan.* 46.5 *principum disciplinam* (*OLD* 4b). The emperor maintained public 'order' as no republican authority had managed to do. **omnia:** *alia* is added in part of the tradition, but it is unnecessary since *omnia* alone can imply 'all other things', see *TLL* IX 2.615.9–37 on such *breuiloquentia* (Cic. *Att.* 11.25.3).   **depacauerat:** for imperial peace and good order see also *H.* 1.1.1, *A.* 1.9.5, 3.28.3. The unique form of the verb is offered only by B, and so rejected by most editors. Syme (1958) 724, among others (e.g. F. M. Fröhlke in *MH* 36 (1979) 116–20), favoured it, comparing the unusual (but not unique) use of *deiungo* by Maternus at 11.3. The verb, if authentic, is perhaps a witty nonce-formation, the opposite of its possible model, *debellare*, where the prefix implies thoroughness or completeness, an idea entirely appropriate to Maternus' argument here.

39.1 Maternus adds, asyndetically, two further aspects of contemporary procedure (our only evidence for them) which enhance the insignificance and diminish the power of modern pleading. The two questions introduced by *quantum* + gen. are carefully balanced in construction, especially *putamus = credimus*, and *eloquentiae = orationi*, whilst *attulisse* contrasts with *detraxisse*.   **uel:** 26.1n.   **paenulas:** a heavy travelling-cloak. This is mentioned nowhere else as worn by pleaders during a trial; *istas* (belittling) seems to imply that they were commonly so worn. Pleaders in the Forum still had to wear the toga (exhaustive references are provided by Mayor on Juv. 16.45–6 *iam facundo ponente lacernas | Caedicio*), but perhaps in the basilicas the dress-code was somewhat more relaxed, and the 'overcoat' (*lacerna* or *paenula*) was kept on. Maternus' point seems to be that the *paenula*, unlike the toga, restricted body movements, which contributed to the orator's impact on his audience (for the importance of *gestus* see 20.3n.). Mähly conjectured *pergulas*, defended by Gudeman (1914) and accepted by Crook (1995) 136 n. 110; but 'loggias' provides no metaphor to apologize for in saying that 'we' are *inclusi* in them). **fabulamur:** 23.3n.   **auditoria et tabularia:** i.e. the speakers are not in the Forum, with all that its publicity entailed.   **iam:** 31.5n.   **fere plurimae:** Persson (1927) 49–50 regarded this as a pleonasm of a common sort, and compared Ter. *Phorm.* 89–90 *hic solebamus fere | plerumque eam opperiri*.

39.2 Maternus develops in a simile the metaphor prompted by *frenos*, 38.2. He apologizes for its boldness with *aliquis* (*OLD aliqui*[1] 1b). **cursus et spatia** 'roomy track': hendiadys.   **liberi et soluti ... debilitatur ac frangitur:** both form common, synonymous pairs (*TLL* VII 2.1286.80–1, 1287.26–7, 1288.2–3; V 111.17–20, 112.62–4).

39.3 curam et diligentis stili anxietatem: Maternus clearly held with Quintilian (*Inst.* 12.9.16) that the conscientious pleader ought (when possible) to write out carefully what he was to memorize for delivery (speeches were not read) (cf. *commentarius* 23.2n.), but all his care could be spoiled by the president of the court.   **contrariam:** 35.3n.   ⟨**ante**⟩**quam:** part of the tradition reads *quando*, which produces sense of a sort ('when do you intend to get under way?'), and is the vulgate, but ζ offers *quam* (a variant found elsewhere in the tradition too). That makes no sense, but is prob-

ably a faithful transmission of what was in the exemplar. *quando* is
thus arguably a conjecture produced to make sense of the passage.
Güngerich's supplement of *ante* before *quam* more neatly restores
the context: the pleader had prepared his speech, but before he
could start the judge put an unexpected question, and it is 'from' or
'upon' (*OLD ex* 10) that question that the speaker must now begin.
[patronus] is clearly not wanted, for the subject is still the *iudex*; no
subject word seems necessary, even after the interruption of *incipiendum est* (but it should be noted that Ritter did not simply delete
patronus; like many others he tried to emend it). It is perhaps a gloss
to explain more precisely *unus ... aut alter.*   **assistit:** 19.5n.
uelut in solitudine: Maternus seems to be slyly picking up the
point made by Aper at 9.6, to the effect that the woods sought out
by poets were a 'desert'; so too is the modern courtroom. The next
sentence provides a contrasting image, *uelut quodam theatro* (with the
usual apology, 5.5n.).

39.4 Maternus observes that the classic orators of old had the sort
of atmosphere to inspire high eloquence. The orator's need for a
large audience is stressed by Cicero, *De orat.* 2.338 *orator sine multi-
tudine audiente eloquens esse non possit* and by Quintilian, *Inst.* 10.7.16
actio auditorum frequentia ... excitatur. Maternus develops his idea in a
grand tricolon sentence articulated by repetition of *cum.* The first
two *cum*-clauses form a polar expression: Rome's notable citizens on
the one hand, and her humbler ones on the other. The latter notion
is carefully subdivided into two groups (joined by *et*): those who
dwell in the City (two subgroups joined by *ac*) and those from outside
the City (again two subgroups joined by *ac*); the parallelism is further
enhanced, since *quoque* is matched by *etiam.* The third *cum*-clause
recombines the previous two with the dignified expression *populus
Romanus.* The fondness of Roman crowds for speeches in the republican period is amply attested (Kraus on Livy 6.27.7).   **clamore
plausuque** form a common pair (e.g. *H.* 3.83.1; *TLL* III 1255.73–4).
The orator indeed expected this sort of noisy approbation (see *RAC*
s.v. Beifall II 96).   **uelut quodam theatro:** for *uelut quodam* see
5.5n. That the lawcourt was a kind of stage is noticed by Cicero
too, in the context mentioned above, *De orat.* 2.338 *maxima quasi
oratoris scaena,* and *Brut.* 6 *Forum ... quod fuisset quasi theatrum illius*
[Hortensius'] *ingeni.*

39.5 C. Cornelium et M. Scaurum et T. Milonem et L. Bestiam et P. Vatinium: Maternus refers to famous cases of Cicero's. The two successful speeches for Cornelius, who was charged *de maiestate* in 65 BC, are lost, though substantial fragments are preserved by Asconius (see J. W. Crawford, *M. Tullius Cicero: the fragmentary speeches* (Atlanta 1994) 65–144); Quintilian records that the Roman people expressed its approval of one of these speeches with shouts and applause (*Inst.* 8.3.3; cf. §4). Likewise fragmentary is Cicero's defence of Scaurus on a charge of extortion in 54 BC. For the defence of Milo see 37.6. No fragments remain of the defence of L. Calpurnius Bestia, accused *de ambitu* in 56 BC; for his identity and for an account of the case see J. W. Crawford, *M. Tullius Cicero: the lost and unpublished orations* (Göttingen 1984) 143–9. For Vatinius see 21.2n.; the reference here may also be to the admired speeches of Calvus.   **ipsa certantis populi studia:** Maternus has been urging that an orator needs enthusiastic popular response if he is to excel, and so far this response has been set in a flattering light. But here his tone changes, and popular support is seen as a manifestation of civic disorder; he is preparing the way for his definition at 40.2.   **frigidissimos** 'torpid' emotionally (*OLD* 8); the metaphor is matched by *incendere*.   **quoque:** 6.5n.   **itaque ... censeantur:** a sentence of much-debated meaning: 'and this is why, surely, these speeches are extant, and are so fine that their authors need cite no other evidence to be put in their true class' (Winterbottom (1989)). This translation accords with the view of John and Peterson that *eius modi* is a predicate. The only difficulty is that it does not account for *ipsi quoque*, which appears to be in contrast with the *libri*.   **libri:** 12.6n.   **egerunt** 'delivered' (*OLD ago* 43). **censeantur** 'have their reputation based on' (*OLD* 8b).

40.1 cont⟨ent⟩iones 'disputes'. The supplement of W. Richter is here accepted, since there seems no particular point in this forensic context in referring to addresses to the people (*contiones*, cf. 36.3n.); the same error, where the shorter word has ejected the longer, is found in Cic. *Fam.* 10.31.5.   **P. quidem Scipione aut Sulla aut Cn. Pompeio:** all were men of the highest position in the Republic, and all were subjected to attack in the courts, though what trials particularly Maternus might have had in mind is uncertain. There were, for instance, the so-called 'trials of the Scipios', for which see

John Briscoe's art. in *OCD* 398b, s.v. Cornelius Scipio Africanus (the
Elder), Publius. Sulla had been prosecuted in 92, but the case was
abandoned. Valerius Maximus records some attacks on Pompey in
court at 6.2.4–8.   **natura inuidiae:** it was a proverbial notion
that envy battens on the prominent, *principes uiros* (Otto §871).
†populi quoque et histriones auribus uterentur†: the passage
seems hopelessly corrupt, and emendation is stymied by uncertainty
about the very gist at this point.   **quantum ardorem ingeniis,
quas oratoribus faces:** chiasmus emphasizes the notions of
warmth and fire (cf. *incendere* 39.5). Maternus reverts to his image of
36.1, but *faces* might suggest the incendiary torches of the mob; he is
ready now for his redefinition of great oratory.

40.2 The sentence begins asyndetically, to draw attention to the
urgency of Maternus' summation. The style is elaborately varied.
Eloquence is now personified, and given six broad characteristics:
first come three substantive terms (*alumna, comes, incitamentum*); there
follows a pair of asyndetically repeated prepositional phrases, and
an asyndetic trio of adjectives; a relative clause concludes the sentence. At bottom, Maternus has in mind and parodies the language
of Cicero at *Brut.* 45 *pacis est comes otique socia et iam bene constitutae
ciuitatis quasi alumna quaedam eloquentia.* (Remarkably, the apologetic
terms surrounding the metaphorical *alumna* are dropped.) It is worth
noting however that on a strict analysis the view of Cicero – one he
consistently held to (cf. *De orat.* 1.14, 30, 2.33, *Orat.* 141 *urbanis pacatis
rebus,* and *Phil.* 8.11) – is not controverted, since he was speaking of
the absence of foreign wars (rather than of civil discord), and of
a state whose constitution was mature rather than unformed (see
Douglas's n. *ad loc.*).   **otiosa et quieta:** contrast 36.2 (*composita
et quieta ... re publica*) and 38.2 (*quies, otium, tranquillitas*), where
Maternus made it plain that the ordered calm of contemporary
Rome rendered impossible the sort of oratorical excellence once
achieved.   **probitate et modestia:** cf. the pair of adjectives at
5.1.   **gaudeat:** Maternus' use of this verb with a non-personal
subject (though *eloquentia* is personified here) is the mark of the poet
(cf. *OLD gaudeo* 2). With the last three syllables of the preceding word
it forms moreover a double cretic clausula.   **licentiae, quam
stulti libertatem uocant:** the phraseology designedly recalls the
expression of Scipio in Cic. *Rep.* 1.68 *ex hac nimia licentia, quam illi*

solam libertatem putant (cf. 36.2n.).   **effrenati populi incitamentum:** Maternus again subverts Cicero, an encomium of the
orator in *De orat.* 2. 35 *et languentis populi incitatio et effrenati moderatio.*
obsequio 'rational/deliberate compliance', cf. 41.3, a word much
used approvingly, e.g. to describe Agricola's restrained behaviour
(Syme (1958) 28 with n. 2, 58, 227 with n. 4, and (1970) 127 n. 2).

40.3 To prove his point about well-regulated states, Maternus refers to two whose constitutions were much admired (by some) for
their soundness. (For the appeal to historical exempla see Barwick
(1929) 100–2; Rome's experience is thus shown to be part of an historical process.)   **Lacedaemonium:** Cicero's *Brutus* is still in
play, and still being subverted: *Lacedaemonium* [sc. *oratorem*] *uero usque
ad hoc tempus audiui fuisse neminem* (§50); in its original context the point
of this remark of Cicero's was to praise Athens for having developed
the art of oratory (cf. §49). Authoritarian Sparta was a byword for
opposition to artistic speech, hence 'laconic'. Crete is added because
their constitutions were reckoned similar, indeed related (so Arist.
Pol. 2.10 and cf. *A.* 3.26.3).   **contenta** 'satisfied with'; despite the
view of some commentators (most recently Güngerich) and trans-
lators, this word ought not to mean 'restrained' (i.e. as being the
perf. part. pass. of *contineo*), but have its usual sense. If T. had
wanted to indicate 'restraint', he had less ambiguous words to hand.
seuerissima ... seuerissimae: the repetition of the word (which
recalls *sine seueritate* above) will become a feature of the heightened
style of Maternus' peroration (41.3 *minimum*, 41.4 *tam*, 41.5 *magnam*).
Rhodii quidam: for the oratorical renown of Rhodes see Douglas
on Cic. *Brut.* 51, where Cicero drew attention to it. The classic orators Aeschines and Hyperides were associated with the island, and
Cicero had gone there to study under Molon.   **omnia populus:**
the democratic constitutions of these states support Maternus' point
that oratory flourishes only amid disorder. The emphatic anaphora
of *omnia*, and the tricolon crescendo enhance the urgency of his
claim.   **imperiti:** strictly speaking this was true, but critics
omitted to point out that it was by design that the Athenians repudiated specialists in their courts and government.   **omnia ...
omnes poterant:** a proverbial expression (Otto §1288).   **ut sic
dixerim:** 34.2n.

40.4 nostra quoque ciuitas: the same progression from Greece to Rome was presumably found at 36.1 *in nostra quoque ciuitate*. The *donec*-clauses, which describe the late Republic, form a tricolon crescendo, of which the third is subdivided into isocola by the emphatic anaphora of *nullus*. For *donec* see 8.3n. Maternus elaborates his sentence with a simile, and draws upon historical exempla to close. **errauit** picks up 36.2 *erranti*.   **nullus magistratuum modus:** a lack of self-restraint on the part of elected officials themselves obviously sets a bad example; Maternus has given an instance of it at 36.3. (Interpretations of this phrase are remarkably various, and the paraphrase offered here is only one possibility.)   **indomitus ager habet quasdam herbas laetiores:** the agricultural simile is perhaps intended to recall Aper's at 6.6. Maternus goes on to assert that supreme oratory is secured at too high a price for both the state and the speaker.   **tanti ... fuit ut:** for the construction see 37.6n.   **Gracchorum eloquentia:** Gaius was the more renowned, and some of his speeches were preserved (18.2n.), but Tiberius did not lack praise (Cic. *Brut.* 103–4).   **et** 'as well'. **leges:** their controversial *leges agrariae*, for which see *OCD* s.vv. agrarian laws and policy, Sempronius Gracchus (3), Tiberius, and Sempronius Gracchus, Gaius.   **famam eloquentiae Cicero tali exitu:** Cicero's *Philippic* orations against Antony got him proscribed, and he paid for them with decapitation; this became a declamatory theme (see Courtney on Juv. 10.118–26).

41.1 Sic quoque 'even as things stand' (*OLD sic* 9b), a reference to the *donec* clauses in the previous sentence.   **quod superest [antiquis oratoribus] forum** 'the survival of a forum, i.e. lawcourt'; the substantival clause is the subject of *argumentum est* (cf. *TLL* II 545.44–7). The transmitted text is unsatisfactory, but no consensus has been reached among editors. The sense of what Maternus means to say is fairly clear: the need for lawcourts demonstrates that Rome is not yet ideally regulated, though he acknowledges some improvement in civil condition since the time of the Gracchi and Cicero. Murgia (1978) 176–7 removed *antiquis oratoribus* and explained it as a wandering phrase (cf. 39.4), not uncommon in MS traditions.   **ad uotum** 'as much as could be wished' (*OLD ad* 34b, *uotum* 3). **compositae:** cf. 36.2.

41.2 Maternus illustrates his point by listing the various clients and their reasons for needing a pleader's services. His list moves in

ascending order of importance (individual, township, province), the
rhetorical figure *gradatio*, and each opening term is carefully varied
in gender or case (*quis, quod, quam*), the figure *polyptoton*.   **quod
municipium ...:** T. provides an example of this sort of case at *A.*
14.17: the citizens of Nuceria and of Pompeii got into a brawl at
a gladiatorial show, and their dispute had to be settled at Rome by
the Senate and consuls.   **quam prouinciam ...** recalls Aper's
point at 5.4 (and T. himself may have had in mind the trial of
Priscus).   **spoliatam uexatamque:** the words are commonly
paired by Cicero. This is the only sentence in the work to end with
-*que*, an ending which appears with unusual frequency in the historical works (for a discussion of the phenomenon see C. S. Kraus,
HSCP 94 (1992) 321–9, esp. 324 n. 10).   **atqui** raises an objec-
tion to the state of affairs just outlined, similar to that at 37.4 *quae
mala ...*   **melius fuisset:** Romans generally expressed notions
of power, possibility, duty, and convenience as facts in the indicative; but like us they also perceived that such expressions referring to
the past might imply a failure to realize, in which case the subjunc.
was often employed (G–L §254 R1, K–S I 174, H–S 327).

41.3 superuacuus esset inter innocentes orator: Cicero
had made a similar point about the Islands of the Blest in the
Hortensius (fr. 50 Mueller, fr. 110 Grilli): *quid opus esset eloquentia, cum
iudicia nulla fierent.*   **tamen**, if correct, implies an ellipse in the
train of Maternus' thought: [though we do not have an ideal state, in
which pleaders would be unnecessary], our civil condition nowadays
is 'none the less' such that their position is of reduced importance
and so they are less well thought of.   **medentis:** for this part. as
a noun cf. *H.* 5.6.1 *umor in usu medentium est, A.* 11.6.2 (it is first found
at Lucr. 1.936). It is used here to avoid repeating *medicus* from the
previous sentence.   **obscurior[que]:** ζ's omission of *que* is approved by Murgia (1977) 341.   **inter bonos mores** contrasts
with 12.2 *ex malis moribus natus* (of modern eloquence).   **obsequium:** cf. 40.2n. *sine obsequio*. The use of the plain objective gen.
regentis 'towards the ruler' is exceptional; usually we find *erga* or *in.*

41.4 Maternus now asks how the traditional forms of oratory can
survive. He divides his argument into four sentences, of which the
first two describe deliberative oratory, before Senate and people respectively; the second two describe forensic oratory in terms of pros-

ecution and defence.   **longis in senatu sententiis:** Maternus
glances ironically at Messalla's point (36.7) that senators of the day
are content with too brief an expression of their view (cf. Syme
(1986) 454).   **imperiti et multi:** the unusual word-order contrasts with *sapientissimus et unus*; for *imperiti* cf. 40.3.   **sapientissimus** picks up a fundamental characteristic of Cicero's ideal
ruler in *Rep.* 2.43 (*unius sapientia*).   **unus:** cf. 36.2 *moderatore uno*,
H. 1.1.1 *omnem potentiam ad unum conferri pacis interfuit*, *A.* 4.33.2 *neque
alia rerum salute quam si unus imperitet*; cf. Quint. *Inst.* 6.1.35 *omnia curae
tutelaeque unius innixa*, and Plin. *Ep.* 3.20.12 quoted in the Intro. 4
n. 12.   **uoluntariis accusationibus:** the scrupulous were re-
luctant to initiate a prosecution (see 5.5n.). It was better to have
it assigned by the Senate at the request of the injured party.
inuidiosis: the advocate sometimes tries to produce a loathing of
the prosecution in the jury, even by transgressing the limits of pro-
priety. Cicero's treatment of Clodia and her brother – he hints
at their incest – in his defence of Caelius illustrates the last point.
cognoscentis: 19.5n.

41.5 Maternus now puts the cap on his argument by stressing that
time has wrought changes in Rome's civil condition.   **optimi
et ... disertissimi:** Maternus combines the forms of appeal
used by Aper at 23.5 (*disertissimi*) and by Messalla at 30.5 (*optimi*) (so
Dienel).   **in quantum opus est:** urbane qualification (cf. 2.2)
is crucial to Maternus' position: great eloquence is nowadays
unnecessary.   **prioribus saeculis** recalls *priora saecula* of the
opening sentence, in which the question was posed by Fabius Justus which the dialogue sets out to answer; an instance of ring-
composition on the grand scale.   **deus aliquis:** for the common
notion of divine intervention to perform a miracle, cf. Hor. *Serm.*
1.1.15–19 with Lejay's note.   **modus et temperamentum:** the
pair reappear in the speech of Otho in *H.* 1.83.2. Maternus uses an
argument found also in Horace, who maintained that if the somewhat uncouth satirical poet Lucilius were translated into Horace's
own day (*Serm.* 1.10.68 *hoc nostrum fato delapsus in aeuum*), he would find
himself conforming to contemporary artistic practices.   **nunc** 'as
it is' (26.7n.).   **quietem** 'abstention from public affairs', 'discre-
tion', 'lack of ambition' (see Woodman's commentary on Velleius
Paterculus II 239–40), used by Nerva to describe his previous way of

life (Plin. *Ep.* 10.58), and found in T. generally (Syme (1958) 27 noted that *quies* was once the mark of the Roman knight, but had become a virtue in an imperial senator). For the resigned, nostalgic note at the close see Syme (1958) 220, Winterbottom (1964) 97 n. 29.   **citra:** 27.2n. Aper had run down the past, Messalla contemporary education; Maternus urges an historical point of view, founded upon the fact of constitutional change.

42 Conclusion

42.1 dies esset exactus: reference to the end of the day is a closural device in dialogues, as in poems; e.g. Cic. *N.D.* 3.94 *quoniam aduesperascit* (with Pease's n.), Min. Fel. *Oct.* 40.2 *quod iam sol occasui decliuis est.*   **conferemus** 'discuss' (*OLD* 13, and cf. 12). There is a similar conclusion to Cic. *Fin.* 4.80, where a rematch is suggested.

42.2 An embrace and laughter ensure that good will has not been forfeited by frank discussion.   **poetis:** for his remarks in 9–10. **antiquariis:** 21.4n.; for his remarks in 11–13.   **criminabimur** returns us to the notion of a mock trial with which the dialogue got under way. The plural, especially in T., is quite regular (H–S 434), as is the adversative asyndeton (restored by Puteolanus).   **rhetoribus et scholasticis:** Messalla had identified Aper with this faction at 14.4.   **arrisissent:** the urbanity of the closing note is a peculiarity of Roman treatises; other dialogues ending with laughter or expressions of good humour are Cicero's *Ac.* 2.148 *ridens, De orat.* 1.265 *arridens, Fin.* 2.119 *arridens,* 5.96 *iocans,* Min. Fel. *Oct.* 40.4 *laeti hilaresque discessimus.* But Tacitus, silent to the last, did not even join in the laughter.   **discessimus:** cf. *intrauimus* 3.1n.; it is also the last word of Cic. *Fin.* 3.80.

WORKS CITED BY AUTHOR AND DATE

Standard commentaries referred to by the name of the commentator (e.g. 'Austin on Quint. *Inst.* 12.1.25') are not included in this list.

1 Bibliographical studies

Benario, H. W. (1995–6). *CW* 89: 120–2 for the years 1984–93.

Borzsák, E. (1968). Art. P. Cornelius Tacitus in *RE* Suppl.-Band xi 428–42.

Hanslik, R. (1974). 'Tacitus 1939–72', *Lustrum* 16: 143–304, esp. 256–74.

Merklin, H. (1991). *Aufstieg und Niedergang der Römischen Welt* ii Principat 33.3, 2276–7 (Forschungsberichte), 2277–80 (Editions, Commentaries, Translations), 2280–2 (Transmission, Reception, MSS, Authenticity), 2282–3 (The Lacuna).

2 Editions, commentaries, and translations

Andresen, G. (1918). *P. Cornelius Tacitus, Dialogus de oratoribus, für den Schulgebrauch erklärt.* 4th edn. Leipzig and Berlin.

Bennett, C. E. (1902). *Tacitus, Dialogus de oratoribus.* Boston.

Bo, D. (1974). *C. Taciti Dialogus de oratoribus.* Turin.

Dienel, R. (1908). *Cornelius Tacitus, Dialogus de oratoribus, Der rednerdialog des Tacitus.* Leipzig.

Goelzer, H. (1910). *Œuvres de Tacite: Dialogue des orateurs.* 2nd edn. Paris.

(1960). *Tacite: Dialogue des orateurs* (Budé). 4th edn. Paris.

Gudeman, A. (1894). *P. Cornelii Taciti Dialogus de oratoribus.* Boston.

(1898). *Tacitus, Dialogus de oratoribus.* Boston.

(1914). *P. Cornelii Taciti Dialogus de oratoribus.* 2nd edn. Leipzig and Berlin.

Güngerich, R. (1980). *Kommentar zum Dialogus des Tacitus*, ed. H. Heubner. Göttingen.

Halm, C. and Andresen, G. (1914). *P. Cornelius Tacitus, Dialogus de oratoribus.* 5th edn. Leipzig and Berlin.

Heubner, H. (1983). *P. Cornelius Tacitus, Dialogus de oratoribus.* Stuttgart.

John, C. (1899). *P. Cornelius Tacitus, Dialogus de oratoribus.* Berlin.

Köstermann, E. (1970). *P. Cornelii Taciti Dialogus de oratoribus.* 3rd edn. Leipzig.

Lenaz, L. (1993). *Tacito, Dialogo sull'oratoria.* Milan.

Michel, A. (1962). *P. Cornelii Taciti Dialogus de oratoribus* (Collection Erasme). Paris.

Orelli, J. C. and Andresen, G. (1877). *Cornelii Taciti Dialogus de oratoribus.* 2nd edn. Berlin.

Peter, C. (1877). *Cornelii Taciti Dialogus de oratoribus.* Jena.

Peterson, W. (1893). *Cornelii Taciti Dialogus de oratoribus.* Oxford.

(1914). *The Dialogus of Publius Cornelius Tacitus* (Loeb edn). London and New York.

Ritter, F. (1848). *Cornelii Taciti Libri Minores.* Cologne and Leipzig.

(1859). *Cornelii Taciti Dialogus de oratoribus.* 2nd edn. Bonn.

Winterbottom, M. (1970). Revision of Peterson (1914).

(1975). *Cornelii Taciti Opera Minora.* Oxford.

(1989). *Classical literary criticism,* eds. D. A. Russell and M. Winterbottom. Oxford.

3 Other works

Barnes, T. D. (1986). 'The significance of Tacitus' *Dialogus de Oratoribus*', *HSCP* 90: 225–44.

Barwick, K. (1929). 'Zur Erklärung und Komposition des Rednerdialogs des Tacitus', in *Festschrift Walther Judeich* 81–108. Weimar.

Bonner, S. F. (1949). *Roman declamation.* Liverpool.

(1977). *Education in ancient Rome. From the elder Cato to the younger Pliny.* London.

Brink, C. (1989). 'Quintilian's *De Causis Corruptae Eloquentiae* and Tacitus' *Dialogus De Oratoribus*', *CQ* 39: 472–503.

(1994). 'Can Tacitus' *Dialogus* be dated? Evidence and historical conclusions', *HSCP* 96: 251–80.

Brunt, P. A. (1990). *Roman imperial themes.* Oxford.

Crook, J. A. (1995). *Legal advocacy in the Roman world*. London.

D'Alton, J. F. (1931). *Roman literary theory and criticism. A study in tendencies*. London.

Delz, J. (1970). 'Der Namensatz und weitere korrupte Stellen in den kleinen Schriften des Tacitus', *MH* 27: 224–41.

Draeger, A. A. (1882). *Über Syntax und Stil des Tacitus*. 3rd edn. Leipzig.

Fantham, E. (1978). 'Imitation and decline: rhetorical theory and practice in the first century after Christ', *CP* 73: 102–16.

—— (1996). *Roman literary culture from Cicero to Apuleius*. Baltimore.

Furneaux, H. (1896). *The Annals of Tacitus*. Vol. i: *Books 1–6*. 2nd edn. Oxford.

Gugel, H. (1969). *Untersuchungen zum Stil und Aufbau des Rednerdialogs des Tacitus* (Commentationes Aenipontanae 20). Innsbruck.

Heldmann, K. (1982). *Antike Theorien über Entwicklung und Verfall der Redekunst* (Zetemata 77). Munich.

Jones, A. H. M. (1972). *The criminal courts of the Roman Republic and Principate*. Oxford.

Kappelmacher, A. (1932). 'Die Abfassungszeit von Tacitus' *Dialogus de oratoribus*', *WS* 50: 121–9.

Kaster, R. A. (1992). *Studies on the text of Suetonius 'De grammaticis et rhetoribus'* (American Classical Studies 28). Atlanta.

Kennedy, G. (1963). *The art of persuasion in Greece*. Princeton.

—— (1972). *The art of rhetoric in the Roman world 300 BC–AD 300*. Princeton.

Leo, F. (1960). *Ausgewählte kleine Schriften*, ed. E. Fraenkel. 2 vols. Rome.

Levick, B. (1999). *Vespasian*. London and New York.

Lier, H. (1996). 'Rede und Redekunst im Diskurs. Tacitus' Dialogus de oratoribus als Schullekture', *AU* 39.1: 52–64.

Luce, T. J. (1993). 'Reading and response in the *Dialogus*' in (eds.) T. J. Luce and A. J. Woodman, *Tacitus and the Tacitean tradition*. Princeton.

Martin, R. H. (1981). *Tacitus*. London.

Millar, F. (1977). *The emperor in the Roman world*. London.

Murgia, C. (1977). 'The minor works of Tacitus: a study in textual criticism', *CP* 72: 323–43.

—— (1978). 'Loci conclamati in the minor works of Tacitus', *CSCA* 11: 159–78.

(1979). 'Notes on the *Dialogus* of Tacitus', *CP* 74: 245–9.

(1980). 'The date of Tacitus' *Dialogus*', *HSCP* 84: 99–125.

(1985). 'Pliny's letters and the *Dialogus*', *HSCP* 89: 171–206.

von Nägelsbach, K. F. (1905) *Lateinische Stylistik*. 9th edn. Nuremberg.

Norden, E. (1909). *Die Antike Kunstprosa vom vi. Jahrhundert v. Chr. bis in die Zeit der Renaissance*. 2 vols., 2nd edn. Leipzig and Berlin.

Persson, P. (1927). *Kritisch-exegetisch Bemerkungen zu den kleinen Schriften des Tacitus* (Skrifter utg. av. K. Humanistiska Vetenskaps-Samfundet i Uppsala, 24.4, 3–52). Uppsala.

Reitzenstein, R. (1915). 'Bemerkungen zu den kleinen Schriften des Tacitus', *Nachrichten von der Gesellschaft d. Wiss. zu Göttingen* 1914: 173–276 (= *Aufsätze zu Tacitus*, Darmstadt 1967, 17–120).

Reynolds, L. D. (ed.) (1986). *Texts and transmission*. Oxford.

Richardson, L. (1992). *A new topographical dictionary of ancient Rome*. Baltimore and London.

Römer, F. (1991). 'Zur Überlieferung der Taciteischen Schriften', in *Aufstieg und Niedergang der Römischen Welt* ii Principat 33.3, 2322–33, with a chronological bibliography (1901–86) specifically on the *opera minora* at 2336–8.

Sabbadini, R. (1967). *Le scoperte dei codici latini e greci ne' secoli xiv e xv*. Revised edn. Florence.

Sherwin-White, A. N. (1966, corr. 1968). *The letters of Pliny. A historical and social commentary*. Oxford.

Summers, W. C. (1910, often reprinted). *Select letters of Seneca*. London.

Syme, R. (1958). *Tacitus*. 2 vols. Oxford.

(1970). *Ten studies in Tacitus*. Oxford.

(1979). *Roman papers*, ed. E. Badian. 2 vols. Oxford.

(1986). *The Augustan aristocracy*. Oxford.

(1991). *Roman papers*, vol. vii, ed. A. R. Birley. Oxford.

Talbert, R. J. A. (1984). *The Senate of imperial Rome*. Princeton.

Vahlen, I. (1907, repr. 1967). *Opuscula academica*. 2 vols. Leipzig.

Wackernagel, J. (1926, repr. 1981). *Vorlesungen über Syntax*. 2 vols. Basle.

Wagenvoort, H. (1926). 'De Reguli in Taciti Dialogo partibus', *Mnemosyne*[2] 54: 416–39.

Wilkinson, L. P. (1963). *Golden Latin artistry*. Cambridge.

Williams, G. W. (1978). *Change and decline. Roman literature in the early empire* (Sather Classical Lectures 45). Berkeley, etc.

Winterbottom, M. (1964). 'Quintilian and the *Vir Bonus*', *JRS* 54: 90–7.

(1986). 'Tacitus: minor works', in Reynolds (1986) 410–11.

Zwierlein, O. (1997). 'Die chronische Unpässlichkeit des Messalla Corvinus', *Hermes* 125: 89–91.

INDEXES

References are to pages of the Introduction and to lemmata in the Commentary.

1 Latin words

assistere (different senses), 6.4, 19.5, 20.3, 39.3

breuitas, 23.6

commentarius, 23.2
compositio (different senses), 21.4, 22.5

dissimulo, 34.5

et epexegetic, 20.4, 33.2

genius, 9.5

habeo + gerund(ive), 8.2, 19.5, 31.4, 37.4, 36.7

imbutus, 2.2
in ore . . . agere, 37.8
in proximo (and similar expressions), 16.6, 25.2, 27.1

liber 'a published speech', 12.6, 21.1, 21.6, 25.4, 26.4, 30.4, 38.2, 39.5
liuere, 25.6
locus (different senses), 19.3, 31.5

manifestus + infin., 16.3

nam elliptical, 9.1
non quia elliptical, 37.6; with indic., 9.3; with subjunc., 37.6

obnoxium + infin., 10.5
opus esse + *ut*, 31.1

prior, 1.1

que epexegetic, 22.2
quominus, 3.4, 21.2, 21.9, 25.2, 34.3

salutatio (metonymy), 11.3
sensus (different senses), 20.4, 21.4, 22.3
sententia (different senses), 20.2, 21.2
si virtually temporal in expression of diffidence, 18.2, 28.3
sunt qui + indic., 31.5

tamquam, 2.1
tanti est ut, 37.6, 40.4

uetus, 14.4, 38.1
unus, 29.1
ut epexegetic, 3.4, 5.1, 26.3, 31.3

2 General

ablative
  absolute, with clause for subject, 3.2 (*sublatis*)
  locative, 13.6, 28.4, 31.8
  of measure, 16.5

Academy, 15.2, 31.6
Accius, 20.5, 21.7
accusative, Greek forms preferred in Greek names, 3.4, 16.5